What was history?
The art of history in early modern Europe

From the late fifteenth century onwards, scholars across Europe began to write books about how to read and evaluate histories. These pioneering works – which often take surprisingly modern-sounding positions – grew from complex early modern debates about law, religion, and classical scholarship. In this book, based on the Trevelyan Lectures of 2005, Anthony Grafton explains why so many of these works were written, why they attained so much insight – and why, in the centuries that followed, most scholars gradually forgot that they had existed. Elegant and accessible, *What was history?* is a deliberate evocation of E. H. Carr's celebrated and icononclastic Trevelyan Lectures on *What is history?*, and will appeal to a broad readership of students, scholars, and historical enthusiasts. Anthony Grafton is one of the most celebrated historians writing in English today, and *What was history?* is a powerful and imaginative exploration of some central themes in the history of European ideas.

ANTHONY GRAFTON is Henry Putnam University Professor of History at Princeton University. His many previous publications include *The footnote* (Harvard University Press, 1997), *Leon Battista Alberti* (Harvard University Press and Penguin, 2000), and (with Megan Williams) *Christianity and the transformation of the book* (Harvard University Press, 2006).

WHAT WAS HISTORY?

The art of history in early modern Europe

ANTHONY GRAFTON

Princeton University

CAMBRIDGE
UNIVERSITY PRESS

CAMBRIDGE UNIVERSITY PRESS
Cambridge, New York, Melbourne, Madrid, Cape Town, Singapore, São Paulo

Cambridge University Press
The Edinburgh Building, Cambridge CB2 8RU, UK

www.cambridge.org
Information on this title: www.cambridge.org/9780521697149

First published 2007

Printed in the United Kingdom at the University Press, Cambridge

A catalogue record for this publication is available from the British Library

ISBN 978-0-521-87435-9 hardback
ISBN 978-0-521-69714-9 paperback

CONTENTS

v

Illustration acknowledgements: cover image, illustrations 1, 2, 3, 4, 5, 6, and 7, courtesy of the Department of Rare Books and Manuscripts, Princeton University Library; illustration 11, courtesy of the Herzog August Bibliothek, Wolfenbüttel; illustrations 8, 9, 10, and 12 from the author's own collection.

PREFACE

This book is a revised and enlarged version of the four George Macaulay Trevelyan Lectures that I had the honor of delivering at Cambridge University in January and February 2005. My heartfelt thanks go to the Faculty of History at Cambridge for the invitation to address them, and in particular to David Abulafia, John Morrill, and Quentin Skinner, who presided over my visit with great kindness and warm hospitality. My thanks, too, to the many Cambridge friends, old and new, whose comments and questions led me to rethink my arguments: above all Simon Goldhill, Lauren Kassell, Scott Mandelbrote, Joan-Pau Rubiés, Ulinka Rublack, and Richard Serjeantson.

My teachers at the University of Chicago, Hanna Gray and Eric Cochrane, introduced me to the *artes historicae* in the late 1960s, and since then I have had the pleasure of discussing these complex and provocative texts with many friends and colleagues. I owe debts of long standing to Carlotta Dionisotti, Donald Kelley, Jill Kraye, Joseph Levine, and Zachary Schiffman; to Lisa Jardine, with whom I had the good fortune to collaborate in studying that preeminent artist of history, Gabriel Harvey; to Ingrid Rowland, Wilhelm Schmidt-Biggemann, and Walter Stephens, who have done so much to illuminate the achievements of the Renaissance's most exuberant outlaw historian, Giovanni Nanni; to Paola Molino, for letting me read her forthcoming work on Hugo Blotius and Theodor Zwinger; to Nancy Siraisi and Gianna Pomata, who invited me to devote the summer of 2003 to a collaborative study of early modern *Historia* in all its forms, based at the Max Planck Institute for History of Science at Berlin, and who offered invaluable criticism and advice, as well as to the other participants in the research group that they formed, especially Ann Blair, Ian Maclean, Peter Miller, Martin Mulsow, and Brian Ogilvie; and to Lorraine Daston, who supported our work and posed us many valuable, difficult questions. The invitation to deliver the Camp Lectures at Stanford University in January 2006 enabled me to test revised versions of my arguments on a new public. My thanks to the irrepressible John Bender, Matthew Tiews, and Julie Cheng, who made my stay at the Stanford Humanities Center so memorable, and to Keith Baker, Giovanna Ceserani, Dan Edelstein, and Paula Findlen, whose objections and suggestions have proved immensely helpful as I put the book through its last revisions.

A number of former and present students – Kate Elliott van Liere, Carol Quillen, Tamara Griggs, Greg Lyon, Jacob Soll, and Nick Popper – have taught me far more than I ever taught them about Jean Bodin and his colleagues and readers. So did the wonderful group of graduate students from many Princeton departments who responded to versions of the arguments put forth here in my spring 2006 seminar on visions of the past in Renaissance Europe.

My research was chiefly carried out in the Firestone Library of Princeton University, where Stephen Ferguson has shown endless generosity and resourcefulness in acquiring works of early modern erudition and Don Skemer has provided endless help in the exploration of manuscripts, and at the Herzog August Bibliothek, Wolfenbüttel; the Biblioteca

Apostolica Vaticana; the Bibliothèque Nationale de France; the Bodleian Library; the British Library; and the Cambridge University Library. An earlier version of chapter 1 appeared as "The Identities of History in Early Modern Europe: Prelude to a Study of the *Artes historicae*," in *Historia: Empiricism and Erudition in Early Modern Europe*, ed. Gianna Pomata and Nancy Siraisi (Cambridge, Mass. and London: MIT Press, 2005), 41–74. A semester's leave from Princeton University in 2004 and a Residency at the American Academy of Rome provided time for both research and contemplation.

Arnaldo Momigliano took only a modest interest in most of the traditions of historical thought discussed here. Nonetheless, this little book reflects, imperfectly, the model of his scholarship and the impact of his teaching, and I hope that it contributes something to the international discussion of the historical tradition that he helped bring into being more than half a century ago.

Princeton, New Jersey
21 May 2006

1

Historical criticism in early modern Europe

Part I: Quintus Curtius and the Gordian Knot of tradition

In the years around 1700, a roomy but fragile imaginary mansion housed the citizens of the Republic of Letters. Scattered geographically from Edinburgh to Naples, they were connected intellectually by their shared passion for the central issues of the day: Newton's physics, Locke's politics, the chronology of ancient Egypt, and the mythology of ancient Greece. Touchy, alert, and fascinated by learned gossip, they scanned the new review journals for every reference to their own work or that of their friends and enemies. Public arguments repeatedly flared up. Many of those who dwelled in this ample new house of learning feared that it was in danger of going up in flames.[1] And no one tried more systematically to resolve these conflicts than Jacob Perizonius, professor of ancient history at Franeker and Leiden. Perizonius dedicated himself to putting out fires in the Republic of Letters – or at least in its philological and historical wing. In detailed essays, couched in the serpentine Latin of late humanism and larded with quotations from sources in many languages, he did his best

---

[1] For some recent perspectives see Bots and Waquet (eds.) 1994; Bots and Waquet 1997; Goldgar 1995; Miller 2000; Grafton 2001; Malcolm 2002; Malcolm 2004.

to show that a sensible historian could rescue the early histories of Egypt, Babylon, and Rome from the attacks of historical skeptics, without making dogmatic assertions of the reliability of ancient writers.[2] He tried to save as much as he could of the Greek and Latin writers' *fides historica*, even as a new set of writers sharpened a new set of weapons and prepared to mount a merciless attack on the scholarly and rhetorical traditions he held dearest.[3]

No one agitated Perizonius more than those self-appointed avatars of modernity, the captious critics who despised the ancients. And no herald of the new banged his drum more loudly as he invaded Perizonius's favorite intellectual space than Jean Le Clerc, journal editor and prolific writer on the themes of the day.[4] In 1697, Le Clerc issued what he defined as a manual for a new kind of critical thinking and reading – the *Ars critica*, a massive introduction to philology and history. Le Clerc spoke a contemporary language when he claimed that he would teach the reader to test texts and traditions against the eternal principles of "right reason," insofar as these affected philology and hermeneutics. In practice, as when Le Clerc told the critic who had to choose between two readings to assume that authorial intent more probably lay in the *difficilior lectio* – the harder reading of the two, which a scribe might have tried

---

[2] Perizonius 1685; Perizonius 1740a; Perizonius 1740b. See Erasmus 1962; Meijer 1971; and Borghero 1983.

[3] Manuel 1959; Manuel 1963; Grell 1983; Sartori 1982; Sartori 1985; Raskolnikova 1992; Grell 1993; Grell 1995; Grell and Volpilhac-Auger (eds.) 1994. For the wider context see also Borghero 1983; Völkel 1987; Miller 2005; Mulsow 2005.

[4] Barnes 1938; Pitassi 1987.

to emend or soften, producing the easier one – he borrowed liberally from earlier humanists like Erasmus.[5] But he cast his arguments in the period dialect of iconoclasm and innovation. Le Clerc took a special pleasure in choosing a classical, rather than a medieval or a modern, text as his exemplary evidence that any text, however venerable, could reveal fatal flaws when subjected to the right sort of scrutiny.

Forty-five years ago, E. H. Carr, the wartime "Red Professor of Printing-House Square," devoted his Trevelyan lectures to the question *What is History?* Carr lived, like the actors in my story, at a moment when massive and muscular rival philosophies of history clashed, like monsters, across the world. In 1961, as in 1691, some of Europe's most brilliant intellectuals espoused radically different views on the past and knew how to marshall dazzling arguments in their favor, and Carr's intervention in their debates helped to make clear how significant the moment was for the development of historical thought and practice. Even before Carr wrote, however, Herbert Butterfield and Arnaldo Momigliano had shown that the new history of the post-war period represented the culmination of two centuries of debates about historical method and changes in historical practice. The point of this short book is to argue that the battles over history of the years around 1700 rivalled those of the 1950s and 1960s in seriousness as well as in sheer, wild eccentricity – and that they too were the culmination of long decades of challenge and debate.

In Part III of the *Ars critica*, Le Clerc trained the harshly brilliant lamp of his critical principles on the Roman historian

---

[5] Bentley 1978.

Quintus Curtius Rufus – a writer of the earlier Imperial period who adapted Greek sources to tell the story of Alexander the Great.[6] His work, though incomplete, had won great popularity in the Renaissance, when illustrated versions of it in Italian made popular reading for princes.[7] Alfonso of Aragon, a connoisseur of history, staged "hours of the book" at his court in Naples. At these intellectual precursors of modern all-in wrestling, humanists like Bartolomeo Facio and Lorenzo Valla savaged one another as they debated passages in the text of Livy.[8] Alfonso himself read Curtius while ill and out of sorts, and recovered at once. He declared the work as effective and pleasant a remedy as anything in Hippocrates or Galen.[9] Numerous manuscripts and, after around 1470, many

---

[6] For recent perspectives see Bosworth and Baynham (eds.) 2000, and especially Bosworth 2000 and Atkinson 2000. On the earlier popularity of the text, in diversely interpolated and adapted forms, see Cary 1956 and Ross 1988.

[7] For a fascinating account of the way in which ancient historians were reconfigured to meet the tastes of courtly audiences in the Middle Ages and the Renaissance, see Dionisotti 1997 (for Curtius see especially 540–41).

[8] The richest – though not always the fairest – source for what went on at the *ore del libro* is Valla 1981.

[9] See François Baudouin's account, Baudouin 1561a, 160; Wolf (ed.) 1579, 1, 706: "Denique cum Aeneas Sylvius ex Germania misisset Arrianum de Alexandri rebus gestis, non tam Latinum factum, quam ad Sigismundi Imperatoris captum vix Latine balbutientem, Alphonsus ne eum quidem neglexit. Adeo nihil eorum praetermittebat, quibus haec studia historiarum adiuvari eo seculo posse putaret. Denique cum aeger aliquando decumberet, et legendo Curtium, qui eam Latine scripsit historiam, quam Graece Arrianus, ita se oblectasset, ut animi et corporis languentis vires collapsas etiam recreasset, exclamavit, non esse in Hippocrate vel Galeno saniorem medicinam suavioremque curationem."

printed editions made the text accessible.[10] Erasmus considered Curtius ideal reading for those who wished "to maintain their rhetoric in a state of high polish." He even prepared an edition with marginal notes that called attention to some "novel turns of phrase" that could enrich the standard Latin lexicon.[11]

The humanists who formulated influential protocols for reading ancient history in the later decades of the sixteenth century – Justus Lipsius and his allies – preferred Tacitus and Polybius to the historians that Alfonso and his contemporaries had loved most, especially Livy.[12] Yet they shared their predecessors' love of Curtius. Lipsius spared no adjectives when he praised this "Historian who is, in my opinion, as honorable and worthy of respect as any other. The felicity of his language and the charm of his way of telling stories are marvelous. He manages to be both concise and fluent, subtle and clear, precise and unpedantic. His judgements are accurate, his morals are shrewd, and his speeches show an indescribable eloquence." Scholars as distant from one another in space – if not in

The same story appears, with further corroborating examples, in Jean Bodin's proem to his *Methodus*, in Wolf (ed.) 1579, I, 5: "quid autem suavius quam in historia velut in proposita subjectaque tabula res intueri maiorum? quid iucundius quam eorum opes, copias, ipsasque acies inter se concurrentes cernere? quae certe voluptas est eiusmodi, ut omnibus interdum corporis et animi morbis sola medeatur. testes sunt, ut alios omittam, Alphonsus ac Ferdinandus Hispaniae et Siciliae reges, quorum alter a T. Livio, alter a Q. Curtio valetudinem amissam, quam a medicis non poterant, recuperarunt."

[10] Winterbottom 1983.

[11] Allen *et al.* (eds.) 1906–58 ep. 704, III, 129–31.

[12] The fullest study is now Jan Waszink's introduction to Lipsius 2004.

their tastes – as Christopher Colerus, who went from teaching history at Altdorf to serving as a master of ceremonies at the Imperial court, the Rostock professor and historian David Chytraeus, and the first Camden praelector on ancient history at Oxford, Degory Wheare, who quoted all three of them on Curtius, agreed with Lipsius.[13] In particular, the speeches in Curtius compelled admiration, as models of rhetoric well applied to history. Nicodemus Frischlin put Curtius first among the five authors from whom he drew an anthology of Latin speeches for the use of his students in Braunschweig.[14] In his lectures he analyzed in detail the ways in which the Roman historian made Darius narrate events, devise arguments, and

---

[13] See Wheare 1684, 46: "Q. etiam *Curtius Rufus*, Scriptor valde bonus et argutus, sed ἀκέφαλος, vel hominum vel temporum vel utrorumque iniquitate factus. *Arrianus et Quintus Curtius, floridus uterque* (inquit *Colerus) sed nitidior Curtius, et quovis melle dulcior. Lectorem citius defatigatum, quam satiatum dimittat. Sententiae passim directae et obliquae, quibus mire illustretur vita humana.* Idem de *Curtio J. Lipsii* judicium. *Historicus* (inquit), *me judice, probus legitimusque, si quisquam fuit. Mira in sermone eius felicitas, in narrationibus lepos. Astrictus idem et profluens: subtilis et clarus: sine cura ulla accuratus. Verus in iudiciis, argutus in sententiis, in orationibus supra quam dixerim facundus.*" This passage begins with a sentence rewritten from David Chytraeus, who had remarked: "Inter Latinos Q. Curtius extat, argutus, elegans et nervosus scriptor, sed ἀκέφαλος": Wolf (ed.) 1579, II, 480. The former of the two italicized quotations comes from Colerus's letter of 31 October 1601 *De ordinando studio politico*, in Grotius *et al.* 1645, 171–98, at 188; the latter from from Lipsius's notes to his *Politica*, 1.9, in Lipsius 2004, 734. Note that Wheare omits Lipsius's final qualification: "Quod si varium magis argumentum habuisset; fallor, aut variae Prudentiae eximium magis specimen praebuisset. Sed Alexander, quid nisi bella?" Both Colerus's text and Lipsius's constitute brief *artes historicae.*
[14] Frischlin (ed.) 1588, 1–21.

6

create a feeling of loyalty and pathos among his soldiers. Frischlin made clear that he attributed these feats of rhetoric not to the Persian emperor, but to the Roman historian – especially when he noted that Hannibal used one of the same arguments that Darius did "in book 21 of Livy."[15]

Le Clerc admitted that he had long shared the traditional admiration for this master of classical rhetoric. At last, though, he tested Curtius against two eternal touchstones at once: the particular rules of the art that he professed, history, and the general rules of right reason, "which hold for all human beings, whatever nation and whatever age we may live in."[16] Close and repeated scrutiny revealed errors so grave that they undermined Curtius's standing as a historian. Reason demanded that the historian learn to use geography and

[15] Notes on Frischlin's lecture on Darius's speech in Curtius 4.14.9–26 appear in a copy of Frischlin (ed.) 1588, which in turn forms part of a Sammelbändchen in the Herzog August Bibliothek, Wolfenbüttel (A: 108.3 Rhet. [3]). The quotation appears ibid., 4: "Annibal lib. 21 apud Livium eodem argumento utitur."

[16] Le Clerc 1712a, Pars iii, 395–512, esp. 396: "Omnium Scriptorum libri expendi possunt et debent ad regulas Artis, quam privatim profitentur, legesque rectae Rationis, quibus homines omnes, sine ullo gentium ac saeculorum, quibus vivimus, discrimine tenemur. Qui utrasque per omnia observarunt, sunt per omnia laudandi, at perpauci sunt: alii omnes, quatenus tantum observarunt. Quae recta sunt laudari, sine malignitate, debent: quae minus, sine superbia, reprehendenda. Nos ergo *Curtii* opus ad Leges Historiae, quandoquidem se Historicum professus est, et ad rectam Rationem, cuius scitis ac decretis aeque ac nos tenebatur, exigemus." This is Le Clerc's definitive formulation, revised after Perizonius responded to his work. Originally he described his plan more briefly, but in substantively similar, terms, as "ut quidquid habet exigerem ad severas Historiae leges et veri immutabilem normam" (Le Clerc 1697, ii, 538).

chronology, the two eyes of history. Curtius had mastered neither discipline. He thought that the Black Sea was directly connected to the Caspian, and he did not mention the years, or the seasons, when the events in his account took place.[17] Reason demanded accuracy, but Curtius's account swarmed with obvious errors. When he described the scythed chariots of the Persians, he imagined that their blades projected through the spokes of their wheels, a manifest impossibility, rather than from their hubs.[18] Reason, finally, demanded independence from popular follies. Curtius supinely followed Greek writers when he portrayed the Persians and Indians as worshipping Greek divinities, rather than "barbarous" gods of their own, with their own names and cults. From ancient texts and contemporary travel accounts, Le Clerc wove a compelling case against the *interpretatio Graeca*, the "Greek rendering," of foreign gods.[19]

Le Clerc traced most of Curtius's errors to a single source: the fact that he was a rhetorician rather than a historian. Historians followed the sources they thought most accurate. Rhetoricians spread their stylistic wings without regard to whether the stories they told were credible:

> Those who have composed histories from ancient sources
> fall into two categories ... Some try to work out the truth,
> so far as that is possible, and examine everything diligently
> so that, when it is impossible to produce a certain account,
> they follow the more plausible narrative. Others take little
> interest in the truth, and choose instead to report the
> greatest possible marvels, since these are more susceptible

[17] Le Clerc 1712a, 402–21, 457–75.   [18] Le Clerc 1712a, 430–36.
[19] Le Clerc 1712a, 448–57.

of rhetorical adornment, and supply the matter for exercises in the high style.[20]

Evidently, Curtius belonged in the second category.[21] That explained why he claimed that over one hundred thousand Persians and only a few score Greeks had died at the Battle of the Issus. "For this to have happened," Le Clerc commented with contemptuous clarity, "the Persians would have to have had wooden swords."[22]

Curtius revealed the professional deformations of the rhetorician most vividly when he stuffed his narrative with supposedly eloquent speeches. No serious historian, Le Clerc argued, should include speeches in his narrative, either in direct form or even in oblique summary.[23] He knew, of course, that Curtius had followed normal ancient practice. But doing so

---

[20] Le Clerc 1712a, 422: "Sunt autem duo genera hominum, qui ex antiquis monumentis Historias contexere ... Alii, quantum licet, veritatem expiscari conantur, et diligenter omnia expendunt, ut verisimillimam sequantur narrationem, cum non licet res exploratas proferre. Alii vero de veritate non multum laborantes ea eligunt, quae maxime mirabilia videntur: quia facilius exornari possunt, et grandiori orationi materiam suppeditant." (Le Clerc here rather resembles the contemporary theologians and natural historians who tried to extirpate marvels from other sectors of the encyclopedia in which they had traditionally played central roles.)

[21] Le Clerc 1712a, 423: "In posteriorum numero fuisse *Q. Curtium* res ipsa ostendit."

[22] Le Clerc 1712a, 423: "Ut hoc esset, oportuisset gladios Persarum fuisse ligneos, nec ulla tela cuspidibus ferreis praefixa ... "

[23] Le Clerc 1712a, 488: "Ut nunc ad orationes veniamus, quas directas plurimas habet Curtius, ut vix totidem alibi occurrere in tam parvo volumine existimem; ante omnia, profiteri necesse habeo me esse in eorum sententia, qui in Historia gravi orationes omnes et directas et

9

violated the historian's primary responsibility to tell the truth. Inventing a speech that the actor in question had not made was a lie, every bit as much as inventing an action that he had not carried out.

Curtius's practices, moreover, were especially ludicrous, for his speeches lacked all verisimilitude. His wildly varied cast of characters all spoke exactly the same fluid, cultivated Latin: "All the characters in Curtius declaim, and in a way that reflects the author's wit, not their own. Darius declaims, Alexander declaims, his solders declaim. Even the Scyths, completely ignorant of letters, make their appearance duly singed by the rhetorical curling iron. This reminds of me of the family, all of whose members sang."[24] Traditionally, historians had made their characters say the things appropriate to the situations in which they spoke. But doing this without regard to local customs and cultures was absurd: "What more ridiculous invention could there be, than to make ignorant men or barbarians speak as eloquently as if they had spent many years studying rhetoric?"[25]

The voice of modernity resounds, harsh and self-confident, through Le Clerc's denunciation of Curtius. Cutting

obliquas omittendas censent; nisi exstent, aut earum sententia certissime sciri possit."

[24] Le Clerc 1712a, 490: "Apud *Curtium* omnes sunt declamatores, qui Scriptoris ingenio sapiunt, non suo. Darius declamat, Alexander declamat, milites eius declamant: Scythae ipsi, omnium litterarum rudes, rhetorico calamistro inusti in medium prodeunt. Hoc in memoriam mihi revocat familiam illam quae tota cantabat."

[25] Le Clerc 1712a, 489: "Nam quid absurdius fingi potest, quam idiotas aut barbaros inducere loquentes aeque eleganter et diserte, ac si per multos annos Rhetoricae operam dedissent?"

himself off from a tradition that had lasted for a millennium and a half, he set out to show that history must no longer form a part of the classical art of rhetoric – the art to which the greatest ancient authorities, above all Thucydides and Cicero, had assigned it, and to which most writers still attached it. The formal study of history, according to this tradition, was a matter of production rather than consumption: of defining the devices which enabled the historian to instruct, and at the same time to touch, the reader. Good history narrated past events, in an accurate, prudent, and eloquent way. Readers studied it in the hope of understanding the political calculations of ancient leaders, as expressed in speeches, and of sharpening their grasp of moral precepts and their applications, as embodied in crisp, specific historical examples. They read in the same intense, reverential, dedicated way in which young Romans had once gazed at the wax death masks of their ancestors while hearing descriptions of their deeds.[26]

Le Clerc, by contrast, saw the historian's task as centrally concerned with critical thinking and the intelligent weighing of evidence. The historian must examine his sources, take from them only what was demonstrably credible, and reproduce it, in plain prose. He must introduce nothing of his own. Even if he had good reasons for ascribing particular plans or arguments to a given individual, he should simply lay these out in his own normal indirect speech, not let them expand to fill pages in the gaseous, fictional form of a spurious oration.[27]

---

[26] For eloquent explications of this exemplar regime, see Nadel 1964 and Landfester 1972.
[27] Le Clerc 1712a: 488–89: "Si credibile sit eos, quorum vitae aut res gestae litteris mandantur, rationibus quibusdam usos, aut permotos fuisse,

The fact that Curtius had written under the Roman emperors did not confirm his classical standing: it underlined his obsolescence as a model, just as other errors proved his uselessness as a source. In the age of the New Philosophy, Le Clerc called for nothing less than a New History – a genre as rigorous, critical, and devoid of traditional, meretricious appeal as Cartesian philosophy.

This radical attack on the humanist tradition brought Perizonius hurrying into action. And no wonder. For it represented the sharp end of a larger and more general attack on both the ancients and their students, an assault that Le Clerc mounted in more than one language and genre. The witty *Parrhasiana* of 1699, supposedly pseudonymous but transparently the work of Le Clerc and written in accessible French, denounced humanist scholars as mere pedants who bit every back that was turned on them: "ils mordent tout le monde, ils se querellent entre eux pour des bagatelles."[28] In the same work, Le Clerc made clear that he wanted to see a new, non-classical kind of history take shape. He denied that "one must be an orator in order to be a historian, as Cicero claimed."[29] Drawing a radical implication from this renunciation of rhetoric, he urged writers of history to consider adding full citations of sources to their works, even though the ancients had not done so. Indeed, he made the willingness to depart from ancient models a criterion of good sense and "right reason":

> quas Historici commenticiis illis orationibus intexunt; eas proferat ipse Historicus suo nomine, moneatque Lectores se existimare has aut similes fuisse rationes, quibus ii, de quibus scribit, adducti fuerint ad ea gerenda, quae fecerunt."

[28] Le Clerc 1699–1701, I, 249.   [29] Le Clerc 1699–1701, I, 175.

If the thing is bad in itself, the example of the ancients does not make it any better, and nothing must prevent us from improving on them. The Republic of Letters has finally become a country of reason and light, and not of authority and blind faith, as it was for so long. Numbers prove nothing, and cabals have no place here. No law, divine or human, forbids us to perfect the art of writing history, as men have tried to perfect the other arts and sciences.[30]

Like earlier humanists, Le Clerc adopted a universal standard when he set out to criticize ancient texts. But where they had applied the methods of rhetoric in order to explain why certain devices worked and others did not, he applied the rule of right reason in order to show that ancient authority and its votaries had passed their sell-by date.

Le Clerc's public dissection of a reputable author appalled Perizonius. Perhaps he took it as a personal attack – especially when Le Clerc sent him a copy of the *Ars critica*, accompanied by a letter in which he apologized for not having cited and praised Perizonius more often in the work, "since I had decided to abstain, so far as possible, from citing recent

---

[30] Le Clerc 1699–1701, I, 145: "En effet, si la chose est mauvaise en soi, l'exemple des Anciens ne la rend pas meilleure, et rien ne nous doit empêcher de faire mieux qu'eux. La République des Lettres est enfin devenue un païs de raison et de lumière, et non d'autorité et de foi aveugle, comme elle ne l'a été que trop longtemps. La multitude n'y prouve plus rien, et les cabales n'y ont plus de lieu. Il n'y a aucune Loi divine ni humaine, qui nous défende de perfectionner l'Art d'écrire l'Histoire; comme on a tâché de perfectionner les autres Arts et les autres Sciences."

examples."[31] Certainly, Perizonius took the third part of the *Ars critica* as just the sort of captious, excessive criticism that had recently begun to flourish in all too many fields of scholarship. He replied to Le Clerc, briefly, in his 1702 edition of Aelian, arguing that no author could stand up to the sort of examination to which Le Clerc had subjected Curtius.[32] And in 1703 he published a lucid, careful essay, in which he did his best to show that Le Clerc's critique had missed its mark. A vigorous defender of tradition, Perizonius dismantled the pretensions of avant-garde critics as passionately as Le Clerc had denounced the pedantry of old-fashioned grammarians. The critics claimed that they had devised standards of taste and decorum far superior to those of the ancients. But they lacked both manners and judgment, which explained why some of them had even attacked one another physically, using books as weapons, at a sitting of the French Academy in 1683.[33] More seriously, many of them did not understand the texts or the content of the classical authors they attacked: "the greatest error is committed by those who take pleasure in denouncing

---

[31] Le Clerc 1991: 256–57. Cf. Le Clerc's sharp comment in 1712a, I, 247: "Dein duo loca *Aeliani* profert [sc. Casaubonus], quorum alter exstat Var. Hist. Lib. II. c. 13. de quo tamen loco nihil dixit *Jac. Perizonius*, homo loquax, quem *socordiae*, quam aliis obiectat, merito hic ut alibi accuses." This is noted on the flyleaf of a copy of Perizonius, *Dissertationes septem*, Leiden, 1740 in the Herzog August Bibliothek, Wolfenbüttel, Ll 6937:2.

[32] Aelian 1731: 678–79, 783–84. Le Clerc replied in 1702. See Le Clerc 1715: [*8 vo] – ** 2 ro, and Meijer 1971: 152–55.

[33] Perizonius 1703: 28–30. For the French Academy see the Swiftian description at 30: "... in ipsa Lupara et Regio conclavi, a conviciis res devenit ad tela Codicum ingentium, quos alter alteri in os et caput impegit."

the ancients, in ignorance of their language, and also of events and histories, without knowledge of which they cannot be understood."[34] This form of textual violence, Perizonius pointed out, formed a specialty of the French – presumably a reference to Charles Perrault, whose *Parallèle des anciens et des modernes en ce qui regarde les arts et les sciences* had appeared in 1692–7. They seemed bizarrely bent on ridding the world of the "elegance, wit, style, and skill" of ancient writers. Perizonius set out to repel this attack on the canon. He meant to defend both the ancients and his fellow grammarians – who, he insisted, did not "reach senility still obsessed with grammatical trivialities," as Le Clerc maintained.

Perizonius insisted that he himself was no uncritical admirer of the ancients.[35] From the start, he admitted that Curtius "had delighted in rhetorical descriptions of events, and perhaps more so than is appropriate to a serious historian."[36] So he defended his author against Le Clerc's accusations by

---

[34] Perizonius 1703, 52: "Maxime tamen peccatur ab illis, qui Veteres ita lubenter vellicant et carpunt, imperitia Linguae, tum rerum et Historiarum, de quibus agunt Scriptores, et sine quarum cognitione intelligi non possunt."

[35] Perizonius 1703, 37: "Sed nemini minus, quam mihi, opponi debebat nimia illa Antiquitatis admiratio, per quam fiat, ut vitia Auctorum Veterum neque ipse agnoscam, neque ab aliis commonstrari velim"; 191: "Nullus apud me tantae auctoritatis est Scriptor, si ab Sacris discessero, quem in iis, quae scripsit, nullum humanae imbecillitatis monumentum reliquisse putem, sive ille sit ex Antiquis, sive ex Recentibus."

[36] Perizonius 1703, 3: "Sed et Rhetoricis rerum descriptionibus delectatum censeo, et magis forsan, quam gravem deceat Historicum: immo et Rhetorem fuisse, et hanc potissimum ex antiquis selegisse autumo Historiam, quam Latino exsequeretur sermone, quia sublimi stylo et oratoriis narrationibus videbatur maxime opportuna."

invoking a standard radically different from the eternal "right reason" that Le Clerc had inscribed on his critical pennant. Perizonius appealed Curtius's conviction to the high court of history itself. Criticism, he pointed out, was always hard, even when one dealt with those who wrote in one's own language. Anachronistically harsh criticism – criticism that took no account of a writer's context – was also wrong-headed. "Nothing could be more ridiculous," Perizonius pointed out, "than to reject an author's judgement because he is following the received customs of his age and his people."[37] Admittedly, Curtius gave wrong geographical information. But he did so because he faithfully followed Greek writers of the time of Alexander, and they, like all the other Greeks and Romans, had had a far more limited and inaccurate knowledge of geography than modern Europeans. His errors derived from the cultural situation in which he wrote, not from a failure to meet those supposedly eternal standards of which Curtius – like everyone else in his time – had necessarily been unaware.[38]

[37] Perizonius 1703, 51: "Nihil itaque absurdius, quam Auctoris judicium explodere, quia sequitur receptos sui temporis et populi mores, aut quia pro virtutibus aut vitiis eadem, quae pariter tum reliqui omnes, etiam ipse habet."

[38] Perizonius 1703, 148–49: "Sed et nulla in re Veteres in universum magis sunt nobis inferiores, quam in eo, quod situm terrarum et regionum minus recte cognoverint tradiderintque: quum Graeci et Romani vix navigaverint extra Mare Mediterraneum, cuius littora ideo satis habebant explorata, at interiora regionum ultra, quam armis suis pervenerant, vix norant aut nosse poterant: quippe quae demum coeperunt ultimis hisce tribus saeculis, post factam in Indiam et Asiae Africaeque extremae littora navigationem, et sic commercia inter diversissimos populos constituta, atque inde coeptas tutius ac ideo frequentius fieri nostrorum hominum peregrinationes, Europeis innotescere."

Curtius's use of speeches could be defended on exactly the same grounds. A history should, after all, be stylistically unified, and to that extent Curtius's homogeneous orations lay within the main borders of the humanist tradition.[39] But Perizonius's central line of defense lay elsewhere. To condemn Curtius for composing speeches, when virtually every other ancient historian had done so, meant holding an ancient writer up to a modern standard. And this procedure, Perizonius insisted, made no sense. Every nation and every period had its own ways of thinking and writing: "They pass judgement on ancient matters from the standpoint of their own time and its customs. This is completely idiotic. Each people, and each period in the history of a given people, has its own customs."[40] Here Perizonius seems as rigorously modern as Le Clerc, though he casts his

---

[39] Perizonius 1703, 92: "quum historici munus sit, omnia in unum Historiae corpus redigere, et ita omnia uno etiam exprimere stylo, ne corpus illud evadat monstrosum aut inaequalitate sua deforme."

[40] Perizonius 1703, 49–50: "Si ita se res habet etiam vernaculis in Linguis, quanto major, necesse est, oboriatur hominibus censendi recte difficultas in Lingua extraria, immo Vetusta, et tantum in Libris nunc superstite: ut adeo eius Linguae Auctores non ita temere damnare deberent, ii certe, qui nec sermonis ipsius satis sunt periti, nec satis cognoscunt mores, ritus, Historias vetusti temporis, neque vero satis attente ipsos legerunt Auctores, nec priora cum posterioribus contulerunt, ut nexum et vim disputationis perciperent. Cui vel unum deest illorum, ille vero ad judicandum de Antiquis illis Auctoribus est ineptissimus. Et tamen qui legerunt cursim quosdam ex iis, nec satis vel res vel verba intellexerunt, illi non suo, sed Auctoris, id vitio tribuentes, eum igitur inscitiae continuo et stultitiae insimulare non verentur.

Judicant etiam de rebus priscis ex sui temporis moribus, quo nihil est insulsius, quum singulae Gentes, singula etiam earundem Gentium saecula, proprios habeant mores, eosque prae extrariis aut antiquis et desitis singuli tunc homines sequi debeant, plane ut mutatam

critical arguments in a different vein. Where Le Clerc found his standard for judging literary texts in the clear and distinct reason of Descartes, Perizonius found his in the historicism, the contextual reading and thinking most notoriously represented, in his world, by Spinoza. Spinoza had argued that the Bible was written for a primitive people, not for sophisticated moderns, and could claim no authority in matters of history or metaphysics or natural philosophy, or even general morality: "Though those five books contain detailed discussions of moral questions as well as descriptions of ceremonies, these are not contained there as moral teachings that apply to all human beings, but as commands fitted to the intellect of the Hebrew race alone."[41] Perizonius used the same form of argument to save the coherence and interest of ancient texts. If these could be judged only by setting them into the contexts in which they had originally taken shape, then the modern critic who disclosed their faults by applying a universal standard was making a category error. The Dutch critic adumbrated the historicist rejoinder to the claims of universal reason that would prove so powerful in eighteenth- and nineteenth-century Germany.

This debate was not simply one skirmish among many in the Battle of the Ancients and the Moderns, one more scuffle between a traditional scholar clad in a shabby frock-coat who

subinde vestium formam, licet aliquando improbemus, recipimus tamen et ipsi, volentes, nolentes."

[41] Spinoza 1670, 56: "Et quamvis quinque illi libri, praeter ceremonias, multa moralia contineant, haec tamen in iis non continentur, tanquam documenta moralia omnibus hominibus universalia, sed tanquam mandata ad captum et ingenium solius Hebraeae nationis maxime accommodata, et quae adeo etiam solius imperii utilitatem spectant."

responded to all innovations with a chorus of "Whatever it is, I'm against it" and a savvy, up-to-date journal editor who tried at all costs to create buzz. Both Le Clerc and Perizonius argued for forms of critical history that lay outside the boundaries of the older rhetorical tradition. Le Clerc appreciated, as he noted in his inaugural lecture of 1712 on ancient history, that

> the ancients must be read in a particular spirit, in order to learn what they thought and how they behaved, as if they had nothing to do with us – not what, in our opinion, they should have thought or done. Before we may judge them, we must ask how learned they were and how holy their customs were. Only when one knows these things properly, not before, will it be safe to judge them. If judgement precedes knowledge, we will think we have found in them whatever we like, not what is really there. And we will twist everything they said or did so that we may contemplate, in their history and books, an image conceived ahead of time in our minds.[42]

He too could deploy the rhetoric of tolerant historicism.

---

[42] Le Clerc 1712b: 23–24: "Ante omnia, si Historiam Apostolicam Novi Testamenti seposuerimus, eo tantum animo legendi sunt Veteres, ut quid senserint et quibus moribus fuerint, quasi ad nos nihil pertinerent, cognoscamus: non quid, ex nostra ipsorum sententia, sentire aut facere debuerint. Antequam iudicium de iis feramus, quae fuerit eorum eruditio, quae morum sanctitas inquirere debemus. His demum probe cognitis, non prius, tuto de hominibus judicare licebit. Sin vero cognitionem antecedat judicium, quidquid libitum fuerit, non quod in iis revera est, invenisse nobis videbimur: omniaque quae dixerunt aut fecerunt, torquebimus; ut prius animo temere conceptam imaginem, in eorum Historia et Libris, contemplari possimus."

Le Clerc and Perizonius both seem appropriate col-
leagues for such proverbially critical contemporaries as Richard
Bentley, who demolished the epistles of Phalaris, and Jean
Hardouin, who did the same to all of ancient literature except the works of Cicero, Virgil's *Georgics*, Horace's *Satires* and
Epistles, and his favorite ancient work, Pliny's *Natural History*.
Both of them had evidently read *What is History?* Certainly
Le Clerc and Perizonius did not need Carr to explain to them
the principles, seen as rather shocking by most critics when he
formulated them forty-five years ago, that "you cannot fully
understand or appreciate the work of the historian unless you
have first grasped the standpoint from which he himself ap-
proached it," and that "that standpoint is itself rooted in a social
and historical background." They would also have agreed with
his demand that critical readers "study the historian before you
begin to study the facts."[43]

For all the divergence of their methods and results,
both the firebrand and the fireman seem to be characteristically modern thinkers – figures that naturally belong in the vast
fresco of *Radical Enlightenment* recently painted, with magnificent energy and erudition, by Jonathan Israel, as they did long
ago in that sly black-and-white masterpiece filmed in the 1930s
by Paul Hazard, *La Crise de la conscience européenne*.[44] Yet Le
Clerc admitted, at least once, that he was not the first to wield
some of the edged tools that he applied to dissecting Curtius.
Gerardus Joannes Vossius, seventeenth-century polyhistor and
author of a treatise entitled *Ars historica*, had devoted two chapters of his work to the question whether historians should

[43] Carr 1962, 48, 26.   [44] Israel 2001; Hazard 1935.

20

include speeches in their work, and Le Clerc cited Vossius's work in one of his rare footnotes.[45] By doing so, moreover, he raised a question of central importance for our purposes.

Vossius's work – as he himself made clear – was one of a number of scattered recent entries in a vast bibliography of early modern works on the reading and writing of history. The genre of the *Artes historicae* grew from deep roots in ancient and fifteenth-century thought, took a clear shape in the middle of the sixteenth century, and assumed canonical form in the years from 1576 to 1579, when the jurist Johannes Wolf published his influential anthology, the *Artis historicae penus.*[46] It would flourish more or less until the late eighteenth century.

The earliest of these works – like the Neapolitan humanist Giovanni Gioviano Pontano's dialogue *Actius* – treated history chiefly from the standpoint of production. Humanists were professional rhetoricians, and many of them worked as chancellors or secretaries. They wove histories out of older chronicles and contemporary diplomatic dispatches in order to make plain the views and policies of their republican or despotic bosses. Their first elaborate discussions of history concentrated on issues of style and presentation: how, for example, to describe the topography of a battle scene or to narrate simultaneous events without confusing the reader.

By the middle of the sixteenth century, however, artists of history began to compose their works in a new key. From the fourteenth century, as we will see in the next chapter, humanists had discussed the credibility of historical sources. Gary

---

[45] Vossius 1699, 31–35; Le Clerc 1712a, 488 and n. See also Le Clerc 1699–1701, I, 182, with a characteristic barb in the tail.

[46] On Wolf and his enterprise see chapter 3 below.

Ianziti and Robert Black have made clear that practising historians like Leonardo Bruni reflected on their use of sources and that of their ancient predecessors. The debates of Pontano and others made a number of influential historians – Black cites Bartolomeo Scala, Giorgio Merula, Tristano Calco, and Francesco Guicciardini – show a new energy in research and a new discrimination in the use of sources.[47] Even some of the good and the great – for example, Tommaso Parentucelli, the Tuscan cleric who became a great patron of historical learning as Pope Nicholas V – learned from the humanists they supported that Livy, for example, had drawn his material partly from the earlier Greek history of Polybius and partly from the lost Latin one of Valerius Antias.[48] Early-sixteenth-century controversies over humanism in the universities and the Reformation in the streets and churches made the interpretation of all texts seem newly difficult. Machiavelli's pragmatic and chilling vision of political history in ancient Rome and modern Italy, which had excited and provoked individual readers since the 1510s, reached print in the 1532 first edition of his *Discourses on Livy*. Though Machiavelli's readers found lessons of many kinds in his work, the soldier and statesman Lazarus Schwendi used the *Discourses* in 1548 to guide him in thinking about problems in ancient history that ranged from the character of Romulus to the Melian Dialogue in Thucydides. Schwendi's prescient marginalia showed how to learn from Machiavelli a pragmatic way of reading classical and modern historians –

[47] Ianziti 1998; Black 1987.
[48] See Albanese 2003, 87–88, 107–08. Niccolò Perotti, whose Latin translation of Polybius 1–5 Nicholas read with enthusiasm, discussed Livy's dependence on Polybius at length in his prefatory letter (ibid., 273).

one that also reflected the cold humanism of Thucydides himself.[49] The rivers of new information suddenly available in print that flowed into European libraries in the fifteenth and sixteenth centuries also called for new forms of bibliographical and interpretive control.[50]

In the Italian sixteenth century, the greatest age of capital-T theory before our own proud epoch, numerous scholars began to follow Pontano's example and compose full-scale treatises on history. The first to do so, Francesco Robortello, was a philologist and commentator on texts. He had a serious interest in the sources of knowledge about the past, and took the task of rationalizing history quite seriously. A few years later he would write the first systematic treatise on textual criticism, in which he boasted of having been the first who set out to reduce history, satire, elegy, and epigrams, as well as textual criticism, to arts with their own systematic rules.[51] Robortello devoted most of the *Disputatio* on history that he published in

---

[49] Baillet 1986; for the larger context see Anglo 2005.

[50] Zedelmaier 1992; see also Grafton, Siraisi, and Shelford 1992 and Blair 2003.

[51] Robortello 1662, 98: "Ars haec corrigendi veteres autores a nullo ante tradita fuit: sed nunc primum a me excogitata, nec temere tamen, verum bene, et ratione (ut res ipsa demonstrabit) confecta. Multa enim adhuc restant, quae ad certam rationem et artem redigi possunt. Atque utinam ego is essem, qui possem hoc praestare. In eo enim multum operae ponerem. Sed efficiam quod potero. Nec patiar, ulla in re meam a bonis et cupidis discendi adolescentibus operam desiderari. Effeci hoc ante et saepe. Nam de historica facultate, de satyra, de elegia, de epigrammate, quum nullus apte disseruisset: in iis ego artem constituere conatus sum, ut facilius percipi possent. Itidem de imitatione, de ratione vertendi, de aliis multis rebus, quum fuit in hoc ipso loco disputandum; nihil perturbate, nihil confuse, est a me unquam dictum. Ut iam perspicere

1548 to showing that history was a branch of rhetoric, meant to offer attractive political and moral education. But he also noted that the historian who dealt with events that happened long before his own time must emulate the best ancient historians and master a whole range of disciplines, mostly antiquarian:

> If the historian must take into account this whole long sweep of years, it is clear that he must be knowledgeable about all of antiquity, so far as it pertains to customs, to ways of life, to the building of cities, to the movements of peoples. Let Thucydides serve as our example. In book six he offers a very thorough and precise account of the antiquity of the cities and peoples of Sicily. And since the remains of old buildings and the inscriptions cut into marbles, gold, brass, and silver can help us greatly when we try to gain knowledge of ancient times, he must also master them. In book six Thucydides – for why do we need to depart from the authority of this outstanding historian? – uses a marble inscription that was placed on the citadel as a monument for posterity to prove that Hippias was the tyrant of Athens and had five children, which many others recorded differently

– a clear effort, well buttressed by classical example, to show that history required skill in inquiry as well as eloquence in expression.[52] Robortello also noted that a competent historian must know geography, military science, and much more.

---

quivis possit, non magnarum tantum rerum, sed et harum, quae ad sermonem spectant, artem tradi posse."

[52] Robortello 1548 in Kessler (ed.) 1971, 25–26: "Si seriem hanc annorum quam longissime debet respicere historicus, patet totius antiquitatis, quae ad mores, ad victum antiquorum, ad urbium exaedificationes, ad

Christophe Milieu, a French writer whose *ars historica* appeared in Florence just after Robortello's, went much further. Following Erasmus's friend Juan Luis Vives, he offered a program – as the publisher of the 1551 edition of his work, Joannes Oporinus, put it in a blurb on the title-page – for a history of nature and the arts as well as states, forms of learning, and scholars: a comprehensive effort to draw up a full history of culture in a form that came to be known, in the next few decades, as "Historia litteraria" – "the history of letters".[53] In doing so he connected the *ars historica* to a wide range of contemporary projects – for example, the wide-ranging efforts of Georg Joachim Rheticus, Petrus Ramus, and others to draw up histories of the sciences that would explain why they had flourished in antiquity and suggest ways of reviving them in modern times.[54] Through the middle decades of the sixteenth century,

populorum commigrationes spectant, bene peritum esse debere. Thucydides nobis exemplo sit, qui libro sexto omnem antiquitatem urbium ac populorum totius Siciliae diligentissime ac verissime explicat. Et quoniam ad hanc antiquitatem cognoscendum multum nos iuvant vetustorum aedificiorum reliquiae, atque aut marmoribus, aut auro, aere, et argento incisae literae haec quoque teneat oportet. Idem Thucydides (quid enim opus est ab huius tam praeclari historici authoritate discedere?) ex inscriptione marmoris, quod in arce fuerat positum, ut posteris esset monimentum, probat, quod multi aliter recensebant, Hippiam Atheniensium fuisse tyrannum, et liberos quinque suscepisse [Thucydides 6.55.1–2]."

[53] Milieu 1551, title page: "LECTORI S. Quae sit huius naturalis, historici et continentis rerum omnium ordinis sententia, Naturae, Artium, Reipub. Principatuum, Doctrinarumque atque Literatorum hominum ab ipsis primordiis ad nostra usque tempora perbrevem enumerationem comprehendens, ex Epistola, Prooemio et Partitionibus protinus intelliges." See Schmidt-Biggemann 1983 and Kelley 1999.

[54] See Grafton 1997b and Goulding 2006a and 2006b.

moreover, scholars made multiple efforts to formalize inquiry into the past. In 1545 Conrad Gesner's *Bibliotheca universalis* offered an efficient first response to the crisis in information management and assessment; in 1567 Flacius Illyricus produced the first formal modern treatises on hermeneutics.[55]

By 1560, both in Italy and in the north, a new *ars historica* had taken shape – an art cast as a guide not to writing, but to reading history, and one that offered an Ariadne thread through the frightening, demon-haunted labyrinths of historical writing, ancient and modern, trustworthy and falsified, that every learned man must explore. The new genre found plenty of contributors and readers. By 1600 everyone agreed with Tommaso Campanella, who found a characteristically striking way to advertise his own addition to the literature: anyone who refused to study the past, he warned, and to trust the sense-evidence reported by historians and other witnesses, "like a worm in cheese, would know nothing, except the parts of the cheese that touch him." In this sense, "every narrator is a historian."[56]

Some of the authors who offered guidance to history conceived strikingly radical intellectual projects – projects that might astonish modern scholars who see humanists as modest, sheeplike creatures placidly grazing on their classical texts. Sheep, as Monty Python taught us long ago, can be ambitious,

---

[55] Gesner 1545; Flacius Illyricus 1968; cf. Zedelmaier 1992.

[56] Campanella 1954, 1228: "Sensus quidem proprius unicuique de praesentibus hic et nunc contestatur; praeterita autem et absentia ab historicis petimus aliisque testibus: sicuti enim propriis sensibus fidem adhibet mens, ita et alienis. Alioquin, sicut vermis in caseo, nil sciret, nisi quae ipsum casei partes tangunt. Omnis narrator, sive per epistolam, sive ore tenus, sive motibus, historicus est; proprie tamen qui de pluribus contestatur in scriptura secundum artem."

and ambitious sheep can be dangerous. The most ambitious of these writers, such as Jean Bodin, used the term "history" in its full ancient sense, which they knew very well: a systematic inquiry that moved from particulars, natural, human, or other, rather than first principles.[57] Their hopes and aspirations for its study were as immense as the world itself. Bodin envisioned parallel histories of nature, man, and God, Milieu called for a history of literature and the arts, and Bartholomäus Keckermann sketched a history of logic as well as a logic of history. Campanella showed his flair for picking the unexpected instance to support a widely accepted principle when he described Galileo's *Starry Messenger* as "historical, since it does not say why four planets move around Jupiter, or two around Saturn, but says that it was found to be so."[58] Many others struck equally plangent, thrilling notes in their comments on history in the narrower sense.

Before we declare either Le Clerc or Perizonius a victor, proudly waving the scalp of a fallen humanist tradition, it will be prudent to examine the treatises on the *ars historica* that lined library shelves accessible to both of them. Certain questions arise at once. What critical approaches did the authors of these *artes* devise and apply as they examined ancient historians? Did they adumbrate or formulate any of the shiny new

---

[57] For a nice instance, see the letter in which Ramus asked Rheticus if it would be possible to erect an astronomy, without hypotheses, valid for the future as for the past, "ex historia temporum, quam tu notissimam tenes"; Ramus and Talon 1599 (1969), 216. And see more generally the brilliant account given by Pomata 2005.

[58] Campanella 1954, 1244: "Galilei *Nuncius* de novo coelo stellisque historicus est: neque enim cur circa Iovem quattuor spatientur planetae, duoque circa Saturnam dicit, sed quia sic inventum est."

CTITICALCRIT

methods and questions that gleamed like brand-new tungsten steel drill bits in the toolboxes of Le Clerc and Perizonius? Or did they remain – as Le Clerc and Perizonius evidently did not – within traditional boundaries, treating history, in the words of Felix Gilbert, as "a branch of rhetorics" even as they transformed it into an art of interpretation?[59]

The *ars historica* formed an organic part of a massive early modern effort to capture and use the whole world of particulars, and it did so in more than name only.[60] True, Jean Bodin argued, influentially, that one should distinguish *historia humana* from *historia naturalis* and *historia divina*. But as Bodin's astute critic Bartholomäus Keckermann pointed out, he could hardly maintain this separation in practice, since human history unrolled within nature. In practice, Bodin himself agreed, since he treated climate as a determining factor in the development of each nation's *genius*.[61] Writers on the *ars historica* emphasized the resemblance between civil history and other forms of empirical knowledge – for example, when they stressed that history had a strong visual component, best mastered by studying chronological tables, which revealed the course of history at a glimpse, and maps, which made it possible to know "the sites and distances of the kingdoms and places in which events are said to have taken place."[62] They highlighted the vital elements of knowledge about nature that could be derived only from reading history – for example, when they noted the value of the detailed description of the plague given by Thucydides, and the explanations for it offered by Diodorus Siculus.[63] And they did their best, at times, to tie the creation of new forms of human history to the devising of equally original narratives in other fields. Campanella strongly emphasized the identity of all forms of *historia*, divine, natural, or human, as narratives that provided just the facts without offering causal explanations. He praised not only Galileo's *Starry Messenger* but also Baronio's history of the church as modern models of true history. With characteristic exuberance, he called both for someone to correct natural history by adding the many secrets of nature that had been discovered since Pliny, and for someone else to play the role of a "Baronius . . . mundi," weaving the traditions of all nations, the Chinese, the Japanese, the Tartars, and the inhabitants of the New World, into a single universal history of man.[64] The pathos and the power of *historia* were blazoned across these treatises.

Yet the authors of the *artes* took highly individual positions on many issues – positions not always predictable from their professions or their other interests. Francesco Patrizi, for example, enlarged the scope of history to include the new forms of research and writing widely practised in his time by travel writers and antiquarians.[65] Patrizi was himself a skilled antiquarian. He did pioneer work on the military affairs of the Greeks and the Romans long before Justus Lipsius made the subject fashionable, and it seems tempting to connect his novel view of history as a set of genres to his own historical practices.[66]

[63] Franckenberger 1586, 142–43.
[64] Campanella 1954, 1244, 1252–54; cf. Spini 1948; Spini 1970.
[65] Miller 2005; Mulsow 2005; Pomata 2005.
[66] Patrizi 1583; Patrizi 1594.

As we will see, a number of contemporaries, especially in northern Europe, concurred. But Patrizi's teacher, Francesco Robortello, also did elaborate antiquarian work, as did the Ferrarese scholar Alessandro Sardi. Yet both wrote *artes historicae* that stayed more firmly within the rails of the rhetorical tradition.[67] Reiner Reineck, historian and teacher of history at Wittenberg, Frankfurt an der Oder, and Helmstedt, produced a substantial *Methodus legendi cognoscendique historiam tam sacram quam profanam* in 1583. A member of the most sophisticated circle of antiquaries in the Holy Roman Empire, Reineck exchanged coins, medals, and site reports with expert collectors and learned travellers like Georg Fabricius, Joannes Sambucus, Joannes Crato von Kraftheim, and Obertus Giphanius.[68] Yet these ventures into the study of material objects, which shaped Reineck's massive compilations on ancient chronology and genealogy, had, as we will see, a substantial but limited impact on his work as a theorist.

Doing justice to this vast range of texts and writers is not simple. Great historians of historiography like my own teachers Arnaldo Momigliano and Eric Cochrane have more or less bracketed the *artes historicae*, finding few connections between them and such innovations in scholarly practice as the new history of Perizonius or Le Clerc. Others, like Julian Franklin, George Huppert, Donald Kelley, and John Salmon have shed a flood of light on the treatises and traced parts of the complex web of connections that links these early theorists to contemporary historical practice. George Nadel, finally, in a

---

[67] For Robortello see Roberti 1691–2, I, 593–686; for Sardi see Sardi 1577: [*8 vo].

[68] Reineck 1583 documents these sophisticated circles in detail.

great article published in the same year as Carr's lectures, called attention to a central and supremely puzzling fact. The authors of these works were gripped by a strange repetition compulsion – one that crossed political and confessional lines and lasted, apparently, for centuries. Bodin, Vossius, and Bolingbroke, the three representatives he chose to examine, repeated the same commonplaces about *historia magistra vitae* century after century, like children of very different generations, trying on the same grand Ciceronian garments, as they played in an attic that became dustier with time. What does this strange continuity tell us about the genre it characterized?

Some historians of the *ars historica* have argued that all of these treatises show essential resemblances. Both Italian and northern scholars, they point out, dealt with the reading, as well as the writing, of history: Jacopo Aconcio was as conscious as Bodin or Baudouin of the need to read history systematically and critically, and like them he offered elaborate practical instructions to printers and readers. Aconcio, not Bodin, was the first to treat the study of history in material terms, as a problem in how to make useful notes – a practice that northern writers like Keckermann and Wheare would examine, in vastly greater detail, a century later.[69] More important, both northern and Italian scholars continued, throughout the sixteenth and seventeenth centuries, to see history as above all a form of rhetoric and a source of exempla – moral and prudential precepts worked out in the concrete form of speeches, trials, and battles. Thus George Nadel, Reinhart Koselleck, and

---

[69] Aconcio 1944: 305–13, repr. in Kessler (ed.) 1971; cf. Blair 1992, 1996, 1997, 2000a, 2000b, 2003, 2004a, 2004b, and 2005.

Eckhard Kessler, while recognizing the individual differences between certain texts, cogently argue that the rise of the *ars historica* generally reinforced, rather than challenged, the rhetorical model of history. And Ulrich Muhlack has suggested that this outcome was only natural, since all humanists, however sophisticated their historical methods, applied them to attain the traditional ends of *historia magistra vitae* rather than to recreate an alien past *wie es eigentlich gewesen.*[70]

Still others – notably John Lackey Brown in the 1930s, and some of the pioneering German and American scholars who revived the study of the *artes historicae* in the 1960s – have highlighted the differences between the smooth, humanistic Italian treatises and the "crabbed," erudite northern ones. Both Baudouin and Bodin, after all, argued for a study of history that would be catholic, rather than confined to the traditional territory of learning, Greece and Rome. Both urged scholars to consider the histories of the New World, Asia, and Africa as significant as those of Europe. Both emphasized the need to read and write history in a critical manner, with an eye always on the credibility of sources and the proper ways to combine and reconcile their testimony. Both explained the excellence of the most prestigious ancient and modern historians – like Polybius and Guicciardini – in part from their ability to draw on official documents and other reliable sources. Most important, both treated the *ars historica* as a hermeneutical discipline, a set of rules for critical readers, as well as (or, in Bodin's case, instead of) a set of canons for effective writers. To that extent,

---

[70] See respectively Nadel 1964; Koselleck 1984; Kessler (ed.) 1971: 7–47; Kessler 1982; Muhlack 1991.

both began to treat history in a new way – as a comprehensive discipline that ranged across space and time, and as a critical discipline based on the distinction between primary and secondary sources.[71]

But Baudouin and Bodin were not the only ones to make these crucial distinctions. Melchior Cano, as Albano Biondi has shown, did much the same, though he came from a very different theological and cultural world.[72] So, as we shall see, did Patrizi. The Lutheran *artes historicae* of Chytraeus and others, for their part, show a concern for identifying the "scopus," or central point, of both ancient texts and the actors they described, that links them to the new Protestant hermeneutics of Flacius Illyricus.[73] The scholars who have emphasized these traits have put their collective finger on vital features of the sixteenth-century *artes*. Yet they rarely try to explain what became of these new forms of source-criticism in the seventeenth and eighteenth centuries. This short book will set out some of the ways in which tradition and innovation fused and interacted in the *artes historicae*, Italian and northern. It will trace the larger contours of the *ars historica* and its fate from the sixteenth to the eighteenth century. And it will work out, in detail, some of the ways in which the *artes historicae* shaped, and the ways in which they reflected, the practices of contemporary readers and writers of history.

---

[71] See especially Brown 1939; Klempt 1960; Franklin 1963; Huppert 1970; and Couzinet 1996.

[72] See especially Albano Biondi's introduction in Cano 1973, and cf. Grafton 1991, 78, 96–97.

[73] Chytraeus in Wolf (ed.) 1579, II, 460.

Part II: The historian's speeches: rhetorical decorum as a hermeneutical tool

Following the fortunes of Quintus Curtius will not enable us to decide these open questions. But it can give us the chance to pull one thread from the variegated tapestry of the *artes historicae* and subject it to an examination – and the quarrel from which we began suggests the thread we should choose. As Le Clerc pointed out, Vossius, in his seventeenth-century *ars historica*, had already discussed the larger question of whether historians should compose speeches for their characters. And Vossius, in turn, noted that a number of scholars had raised the issue before him.[74] Let us begin by asking what arguments about historical speeches feature in the *ars historica* tradition.[75]

One matrix within which systematic discussion of history grew was literary, and it gave shelter to those who liked historians' speeches. As early as the fifteenth century, humanists

---

[74] See in general Wickenden 1993.

[75] On the *ars historica* see in general the full bibliography of primary sources given in Witschi-Bernz 1972a. Contemporary lists include Keckermann 1614, II: 1309–88, with commentary, and Draud 1625, 1125–26. The development of the genre has been traced by von Bezold 1918; Moreau-Reibel 1933; Strauss 1936; ch. 6; Brown 1939; Spini 1948; Spini 1970; Reynolds 1953; Pocock 1957; Klempt 1960; Franklin 1963; Kelley 1964; Nadel 1964; Cotroneo 1966; Huppert 1970; Kelley 1970; Cotroneo 1971; Kessler (ed.) 1971; Landfester 1972; Witschi-Bernz 1972b; Cano 1973; Seifert 1976; Dubois 1977; Hassinger 1978; Kessler 1982; Schmidt-Biggemann 1983; Muhlack 1991; Grafton 1991: 76–103; Wickenden 1993; Couzinet 1996; Salmon 1997; Kelley 1999; Couzinet 2000; Bellini 2002; Lyon 2003. Two anthologies, Wolf (ed.) 1579 and Kessler (ed.) 1971, contain the most influential *artes historicae*, and serve as the chief foundation for the exposition that follows.

in Naples and elsewhere began to discuss the nature and value of history. Most of them remained within the relatively narrow comfort of the rhetorical tradition, endlessly quoting Cicero's definition of history from *De oratore* 2.36 and looking in the texts for evidence that history really was "opus . . . oratorium maxime" (*De legibus* 1.5).[76] But from the start, stimuli from outside the historical tradition abounded, starting with Lucian's essay on the writing of history, which Guarino of Verona adapted in a formal letter on the subject.[77] One outsider spoke with special authority. Aristotle argued in the *Poetics* that poetry offered profound and general truths, while history could tell only what a given person did or suffered.[78]

As early as the 1440s, Lorenzo Valla set out to counter this view in the prologue to his *Gesta Ferdinandi Regis*

[76] Cicero *De oratore* 2.36: "Historia vero testis temporum, lux veritatis, vita memoriae, magistra vitae, nuntia vetustatis, qua voce alia nisi oratoris immortalitati commendatur?" *De legibus* 1.2.5: "**Atticus:** Postulatur a te iam diu uel flagitatur potius historia. Sic enim putant, te illam tractante effici posse, ut in hoc etiam genere Graeciae nihil cedamus. Atque ut audias quid ego ipse sentiam, non solum mihi videris eorum studiis qui [tuis] litteris delectantur, sed etiam patriae debere hoc munus, ut ea quae salva per te est, per te eundem sit ornata. Abest enim historia litteris nostris, ut et ipse intellego et ex te persaepe audio. Potes autem tu profecto satis facere in ea, quippe cum sit opus, ut tibi quidem uideri solet, unum hoc oratorium maxime."

[77] For Guarino and Lucian see Regoliosi 1991, providing a new text of the letter (28–37). For further evidence of diversity in Quattrocento discussions of history, see Regoliosi 1995a and Grafton 1999, and note the remark in Giovanni Lamola's copy of Aulus Gellius, Vat. lat. 3453, 46 ro, perhaps reflecting Ferrarese thought about the discussion of history in 5.18: "Cicero tamen ita diffinit: Historia est res gesta sed ab aetatis nostrae memoria remota."

[78] Aristotle *Poetics* 1451b 5–11.

Aragonum, and in doing so he gave speeches a new theoretical justfication. Historians, Valla pointed out, did not record speeches word for word, but composed them, artistically, to teach the same sort of general lessons that the poets embodied in the actions of their mythical heroes: "Does anyone actually believe that those admirable speeches that we find in histories are genuine, and not rather fitted, by a wise and eloquent writer, to the person, the time, and the situation, as their way of teaching us both eloquence and wisdom?"[79] But he took the artificiality of these texts as a source of strength. Valla himself devised splendid examples of imaginary historical speeches to serve as cases in point. In his *Declamatiuncula against the Donation of Constantine,* he notoriously cited the anachronistic usage and medieval syntax of that document to show that it could not have been written in the fourth century. But in the same text, Valla also composed speeches in which the Roman senators, Constantine's sons and the pope himself argued that the emperor should not give away the western empire. These were, of course, not historical documents. Rather, they represented Valla's versions of the speeches that these gentlemen should have held, at that time, in that place, in the light of their status and their circumstances. The rhetorical doctrine of decorum, which showed how to work out the ways of acting and speaking that were appropriate in a particular situation and to particular actors, provided Valla with his basic tools. He used these techniques first to think himself into his protagonists'

---

[79] Valla 1973, 5: "An est quisquam qui credat admirabiles illas in historiis orationes utique veras fuisse, et non ab eloquenti ac sapienti opifice personis, temporibus, rebus accommodatas, quibus nos eloqui et sapere docerent?"

situation, and then to write what they should have said, the utterances that fit their identities, stations, and circumstances.[80] Decorum, in fact, was a technical and conceptual crossroads – the point where the protocols of rhetoric, which taught one how to compose speeches appropriate to a particular situation, met those of moral philosophy and political prudence. By inhabiting it, the historian could make his work as general as that of the poet. In the end, Valla argued, "so far as I can judge, the historians show more gravity, prudence and civil wisdom in their speeches, than any of the philosophers manage to in their precepts."[81]

The first formal theorists of history, like Pontano, agreed with Valla. But they generally ignored the philosophical stimulus to which he had responded, and argued that the historian should introduce not only historical speeches, but also compositions that had verisimilitude, as often as he possibly could.[82] Pontano voiced the conventional wisdom: "Speeches

[80] Cf. esp. Most 1984 and Kablitz 2001.

[81] Valla 1973, 6: "Etenim quantum ego quidem iudicare possum, plus gravitatis, plus prudentie, plus civilis sapientie in orationibus historici exhibent, quam in preceptis ulli philosophi."

[82] Pontano, *Actius*, in Wolf (ed.) 1579, I, 575–76: "Iam vero cum sit homini data a natura oratio, magna cum excellentia animalium caeterorum, ipsorumque hominum inter ipsos: sitque orationis propria vis movere animos, et quo velit flectere, nuncque pro re ac loco a metu trahat ad fiduciam, a dolore ad laetitiam, ab ocio ac mollitie ad laborem: eademque fugientes retineat, irruentes impellat, dubitantes confirmet: huius esse memor rerum gestarum scriptor cum primis debet. Itaque quoties res tulerit, imperatores ipsos inducet nunc confirmantes suos in periculis, nunc excitantes illos ad ea obeunda, alias exhortanteis, alias obiurganteis, et modo praemia proponenteis, modo admonenteis infamiae, turpitudinis, servitutis, mortis. Videntur enim eiusmodi

greatly adorn a history – especially those cast in direct speech, where rulers are introduced speaking and acting in their own persons, so that one seems to be watching the event take place. But they must be fitted to their place and time, and decorum must be retained in every case."[83] Sebastian Fox Morcillo was only one of the numerous later writers who agreed that speeches could work splendidly so long as the historian observed decorum and made them appropriate to the actors in question: "but these speeches are to be made, when the context demands, in such a way as to maintain above all the decorum of the person speaking."[84] The speech served two dialectically related central purposes. Writing it forced the historian to think his way formally into the situation in which his actors had had to make and explain their choices. And reading it enhanced the reader's prudence by enabling him to do the same.

allocutiones, quae nunc ad multos, nunc ad singulos habentur, decorare historiam, et quasi animare eam. In quibus quoties res ipsa tulerit, nervos orationis atque ingenii sui ostendet rerum scriptor. Nec solum quae dicta fuisse referuntur ab imperatoribus, verum etiam ea afferet, quae verisimilia, quaeque dicenda tempus, periculum, reique ipsius natura postulare videatur. Vteturque in increpando acrimonia, in excitando vehementia, in sedando lenitate, in impellendo contentione, in extollendis rebus propriis, adversarii deprimendis magnitudine ac linguae suae acie, rerum ipsarum qualitates, ac ducum maxime personas secutus."

[83] Pontano, *Actius*, in Wolf (ed.) 1579, I, 576: "Magnificant autem historiam conciones potissimum rectae illae quidem, ubi imperatores ipsi et loqui et agere introducuntur, ut quasi geri res videatur. Adhiberi tamen debent suo et loco et tempore, suumque ubique decorum retinendum."

[84] Sebastian Fox Morcillo, *De historiae institutione liber*, in Wolf (ed.) 1579, I, 794: "Ea vero cum locus fieri postulet, ita dicenda sunt, ut decorum personae loquentis maxime observetur."

In the mid-century age of hermeneutics, however, less decorous voices joined the discussion. At least one ancient historian – the Augustan world historian Pompeius Trogus, whose work survived only in a later epitome – had already argued that historians should not normally compose speeches simply to show off their rhetorical skill.[85] And a modern, the ever-independent Paduan professor Francesco Patrizi, really put the methodological cat among the rhetorical pigeons. In his brilliant, ferocious work of 1560, *Della historia diece dialoghi*, he concentrated on epistemological and methodological issues. The first law of history, as Cicero had pointed out, was to tell the truth. But fear, prejudice, and the opacity of high politics in a world of courts made this impossible. And the traditional, rhetorical form of historiography also led its practitioners to violate their own laws. For by including fictional speeches in their works, they introduced deliberate lies: "So I answered: 'Didn't you say that making speeches is the work of the orator?' 'Yes, I did.' 'And doesn't the orator use words to make that which is less seem greater?' 'Yes.' 'Well, that is how the work of the orator goes against the truth of the historian.'"[86] Even

---

[85] Justin *Epitome* 38.3.11: "Pompeius Trogus . . . in Livio et in Sallustio reprehendit quod conciones directas pro sua oratione operi suo inserendo historiae suae modum excesserint." Perotti wrote approvingly of this passage in his preface to Polybius; see Albanese 2003, 273.

[86] Patrizi 1560, in Kessler (ed.) 1971, 58 vo: "Cosi risposi io: Non diceste voi, che il far oratione era cosa dell'oratore? Si dissi. Et l'oratore, soggiunsi io, non fa con parole di meno, piu? Si. Eccovi adunque come sono l'oratorie cose oltre il vero dell'historico"; Wolf (ed.) 1579, 1, 533: "Non dicebas tu prius orationes oratorum opus esse? Dicebam. Eosque verbis ex eo quod minus est, maius efficere? Ita. En tibi igitur, quomodo orationes veritati, quae debet historico proposita esse repugnent."

the defense that historians followed "the decorum of persons," Patrizi showed, could not hold. With manifest inconsistency, moderns represented ancient Romans, and Athenians represented Spartans, as speaking in the same way they did. But in doing so, they preserved stylistic decorum at the expense of the central historical principle of factual accuracy: "There are many inventions, and these include the speeches. A clear proof of this is the well-known fact that the Romans never spoke as some recent historian made them speak, and the Lacedaemonians never spoke in the way in which a certain Athenian made them argue."[87] Decorum was not a tool for understanding political and military situations in a different time and place, but a Procrustean bed on which the historian maltreated wildly divergent individuals, ignoring historical and cultural differences. A century and a half later, Le Clerc would wield exactly the same arguments against Curtius.

Again and again, authors of later *artes historicae* rebutted Patrizi. For the most part, they merely repeated the arguments that Pontano and others had advanced in favor of speeches before Patrizi wrote. Giovanni Antonio Viperano, Jesuit, historian, and bishop, had read and meditated on Pompeius Trogus's critique of the inclusion of speeches in histories.

---

[87] Patrizi 1560, in Kessler (ed.) 1971, 58 vo: "Le finte sono molte: et fra queste, le orationi. Et di ciò è argomento chiaro, il sapere, che non cosi parlarono gli antichissimi Romani, come gli fa parlare alcuno historico, de gli ultimi. Et i Lacedemoni non favellarono mai delle maniera, che gli fa alcuno Atheniese ragionare"; Wolf (ed.) 1579, I, 533: "Deinde multae inter caetera finguntur orationes: cuius rei manifestum argumentum est, quod nequaquam ita loquuti sunt olim Romani, quemadmodum eos quidam recentiores historici loquentes introducunt: nec Lacedaemonii ea utebantur oratione, quam illis Atheniensis quidam attribuit."

He also knew school rhetoric well enough to admit that flavorless scholastic speeches could make a history slow reading.[88] But he insisted on the value of the intellectual and stylistic exercise required to compose historical speeches. Nothing could be harder, nothing more rewarding than learning to understand the "decorum" of one's characters and their situation.[89] Clothing an actor's thoughts in one's own words did not amount

[88] Giovanni Antonio Viperano, *De scribenda historia liber* in Kessler (ed.) 1971, 40–41: "Non dicam quod haud scio qua ratione aliqui orationes funebres ab historia removendas esse censeant: quando pulcherrimum earum exemplum apud Thucydidem legamus. Sane Trogus (ut refert Iustinus) reprehendit in Livio et Salustio quod directas orationes operibus suis interserendo historiae modum excesserint: idem in Thucydide carpere potuisset. Vocant (ni fallor) directas orationes eas, quae per primam personam pronuntiantur; obliquas, quae per tertiam, ut illa Mithridatis est apud eundem Iustinum. Profecto mihi ut pro re, loco, et tempore breves et aptae conciones placent, sic nimium frequentes et prolixae ac quacunque de re susceptae orationes non admodum placent. Nam rerum gestarum cursum retardant, et multa praeter rem saepius amplectuntur. In quarum artificio multis mirus est Livius, nihilque mihi videtur eo inferior esse Thucydides. Contra sunt, qui eruditionis expertes, nec magni iudicii homines dialogismos quosdam et sermones intexunt, et hortationes loquacissimas et frigidissimas; insulsa omnia sine condimento, sine eruditione, sine acumine, sine iudicio, sine eloquentia, et ornatu orationis."

[89] Viperano in Kessler (ed.) 1971, 39–40: "Verumtamen ad amplificandum et rerum varietate distinguendum ornandumque opus, atque ad prudentiam et mores vim habent magnam conciones et cohortationes. Nec personam tamen ullam historicus effinget, sed loquentem modo interponet, ut credibile est illam fuisse locutam, cum eadem verba referri non possint. Id quod ingenium solers et acre iudicium et multarum rerum cognitionem quaerit, ut loquentium moribus et naturae conveniant, quae dicuntur. Quid enim magis arduum est, quam aliorum mores, animos, orationem induere? Et in illorum sese conformare voluntatem atque naturam? Qua quidem re nihil est in poesi difficilius:

to falsification. After all, one could rarely reconstruct them in detail; why not then follow probability, as one should when the course of events was obscure?

> Some deny that a historian may insert any speech, if he has to make it up; for history can admit no fiction. But events work in one way, words in another. The former can be described as they took place. The latter cannot possibly be reported as they were pronounced. And if it is acceptable to follow probability when recounting obscure events, why is that not permissible for words as well?

Five years later, the historian of Savoy and Genoa, Uberto Foglietta, directed even sharper rhetorical shafts against those who claimed that speeches destroyed a history's claim to truthfulness.

> Finally, these [critics] attack speeches. These men, the sharpest intellects ever reported, deny that direct speeches are acceptable in history, though they do not reject indirectly reported speeches. By direct speeches, they mean orations by individual speakers; by indirect ones, those in

nullusque locus mihi videtur historico relictus, in quo magis vim dicendi ostendere, rerum causas et consilia melius explicare, laudare, et reprehendere liberius possit, quam ubi alios dicentes imitatur. Primum igitur non quaecunque personae, sed illustres, praestantes, et dignae pro historiae gravitate inducentur non quacunque de re, sed de gravibus maximisque rebus concionantes sapienter et prudenter servato personarum decoro. Dicet graviter et severe Cato . . . Neque solum personae, verum etiam rei, loci ac temporis habenda ratio semper est"; 41: "Enimvero qui rerum, personarum, temporum, locorumque decorum non videt, is in omni re graviter peccat. Quod decorum contineri arte non potest: prudentia et iudicio tenetur."

which it is not the person himself who is brought on speaking, but when we narrate in our own words and person what someone said. They insist that direct addresses clearly violate the standard of truthfulness that ought to lie at the core of history.[90]

His intemperate tone revealed the identity of his adversary: the iconoclastic, self-consciously clever Patrizi. Foglietta criticized those who insisted that speeches should only be given in their actual wording as "superstitious," since no one could recall even an everyday conversation word for word.[91] Like Viperano, he

---

[90] Uberto Foglietta, *De ratione scribendae historiae,* in Kessler (ed.) 1971, 31: "Extremo loco in conciones invadunt, quas viri ex omni saeculorum memoria acutissimi in historia rectas ferendas esse negant, cum obliquas non reiiciant. Rectas voca<n>t Prosopopoeias; obliquas, non cum persona ipsa loquens inducitur, sed cum quae dixit aliquis, nos ipsi tamquam nostris verbis nostraque persona narramus. Veritati enim, cui rei studere in primis historia debet, prosopopoeiam perspicue adversari affirmant."

[91] Foglietta in Kessler (ed.) 1971, 31–33: "Quam vereor, ne eiusmodi homines, dum in veritate retinenda supra caeteras aetates religiosi volunt videri, ad superstitionem incubuerint. Nam cum historia non res tantum, quae manu geruntur, narret, sed consilia quoque, et caussas necessario cum illis connectat; neque enim alia res ab alia separari potest, consilia autem et caussae loquendo explicentur, non video quomodo magis a veritate recedat is, qui auctorem consiliorum ipsum sua persona loquentem inducit, prosopopoeiamque in historia inserit, quam is, qui Senatorem aut Ducem, non loquentem ipsum, sed haec illum dixisse ipse sua persona refert . . . Tum autem illud quaero, quamobrem a rectis concionibus tantopere isti abhorreant. Quod in illis, inquiunt, multa ponantur, quae ii, qui conciones habuerunt, ne somniarunt quidem. Ut hoc verum sit, idem vitium est in obliquis concionibus, quas si ipsas quoque tollere volunt, eadem opera et historiam tollant licet. Scribi enim sine illis prorsus non potest. Ex rebus

admitted that historians who did not understand the difference between their world and calling and those of a statesman could spoil a history by composing long and pedantic speeches.[92] On the whole, however, he showed even more enthusiasm for historical oratory than his predecessors, and devoted several pages to quoting and appreciating an exemplary speech from Livy. The Ferrarese scholar Alessandro Sardi, though less wordy than Foglietta, agreed on the main point. Careful attention to decorum could make speeches substantively truthful and rhetorically effective.[93] La Popelinière agreed: no one could possibly recall speeches word for word. Orators, he argued,

enim, quae manu geruntur, et quae sermone pronuntiantur, narratio historica constat. Omnino nugatorium est, verba aucupari, atque ad ea velle rem et veritatem deflectere. Quod si suscipitur, iam ne quotidianae quidem narrationes inter nos cohaerebunt. Nemo enim est tanta memoria praeditus, qui quae de altero audivit, ea ipse iisdem totidemque verbis expressa reddere memoriter possit. Sententia igitur inspicienda est, in qua veritas posita est. nam si verba sequimur, ad incertum fides revocabitur, neque ullus sermo verus erit."

[92] Foglietta in Kessler (ed.) 1971, 35: "... qui homines mihi non intelligere videntur quantum inter philosophum in scholis atque in coetu doctorum et ingeniosorum virorum disputantem, praeceptaque vivendi tradentem; et civilem virum in concione et in imperitorum turba verba facientem intersit; neque meminisse quantum utriusque munera inter se discrepent."

[93] Alessandro Sardi, *De i precetti historici discorsi, Discorsi*, in Kessler (ed.) 1971: 155–56: "Laudate sono le Concioni Cesariane, brevemente ristrette per relatione de i capi: le quali ne interrompono il corso della narratione, ne indarno affaticano il lettore, ne appaiono finte, come fanno, et come sono le altre Concioni, da alcuni vituperate per la fittione contraria sempre alle leggi della Historia. Pur ancora tali Concioni sono permesse in lei fatte da Capitani, da Consiglieri, et da Ambasciatori, et non troppo frequentemente. Perche cosi lo Historico sotto coperta di altra persona puo discoprire cause, consigli, attioni preterite, successi, giuditio, et

should not have the freedom to make up historical speeches as they liked, but "learned, experienced and judicious" historians should be allowed to insert speeches into their work.[94]

Vossius, then, followed majority opinion when he plumped for the tradition of speech writing, and devoted two chapters of his work to describing in detail how each of the Greek and Roman historians had practised it.[95] The main point he added was practical, the reflection of an experienced teacher of classical rhetoric who knew a great deal about ancient public life. Even if the historian could obtain stenographic transcripts of what his protagonists had said, Vossius argued, he would have to rewrite them in order to unify the style of his work. Otherwise its diction would be "hybrid and inconsistent."[96]

essempli, che non può fare per se stesso. I Capitani parlino a i soldati piu breve, o piu difusamente secondo la occasione, essortandoli alla vittoria, o per il numero o per il valore loro, per il sito del luogo, per la giustitia, per il premio, per la Gloria ... I precetti Rhetorici insegneranno di formare queste Concioni: io ben dirò, che esse verisimilmente rappresentino la persona indotta a parlare, non facendo che il Capitano philosophiche, il Principe theologizi, che il Prelato dica militarmente." See also Maccius 1593, 117–29.

[94] La Popelinière 1599, II, 75–81; see especially 77: "Qui dit autre chose ment, non celuy qui la rapporte d'une autre façon." For an interesting effort to defend the speeches in Thucydides as an adequate representation of Pericles's oratory, even though not an exact one, see Franckenberger 1586, 148: "Etiamsi autem nulla huius Oratoris pleni atque perfecti, quantum quidem in hac imbecillitate naturae humanae fieri potest, ad nos monumenta pervenerunt: tamen in primo et secundo libro Thucydidis specimen eloquentiae Pericleae occurrere omnibus notum est."

[95] Vossius 1699: Cap. xx, 31–34; Cap. xxi, 34–35.

[96] Vossius 1699, 31: "... si vel historicus nactus sit orationes, prout eas notarii exceperunt, necesse tamen erit, ut caeterae historiae stylo

For the most part, in other words, the waters of the *ars historica* closed over the great stone that Patrizi had hurled into them, and only the ripples that appeared as one authority after another briefly broke the surface and refuted his iconoclastic position revealed that he had ever written. To that extent, the discussions of speeches in the *artes historicae* illustrate the repetition compulsion that is one of the salient, and stranger, characteristics of the genre as a whole.

Yet at least one writer in the tradition responded to Patrizi far more edgily – and in a far more complex way – than his colleagues. Bodin had no love for speeches. When he rehearsed the ancient critiques of speeches that he turned up in Justin and Diodorus Siculus, he showed some sympathy for their authors. Even Thucydides had perhaps committed some oratorical excesses. Livy certainly had: remove the speeches from his history, Bodin joked, and only fragments would remain. That consideration, a reasonable one for once, had impelled Caligula to remove the works and images of Livy from all libraries.[97]

accommodentur, ne dictio sit hybrida, ac dissimilis sui." Also interesting is the rich but inconclusive discussion in Keckermann 1614, II: 1322.

[97] Bodin 1566, 57–58; 1572, 73–74; Wolf (ed.) 1579, 1, 50: ". . . concionum tamen apparatum tacite reprehendit Diodorus. Eadem reprehensione utitur Trogus Pompeius (ut est apud Iustinum) adversus Livium et Sallustium, quod directas et obliquas conciones operi suo inserendo, historiae modum excesserint [38.3.11]. Nihil est enim, ut ait Cicero, in historia pura et illustri brevitate dulcius. Sin conciones de Livio detraxeris, exigua fragmenta restabunt. Quae causa Caligulam impulit, ut scripta Livii et imagines de bibliothecis omnibus prope amoveret." Bodin may well
have drawn on Perotti's preface to Polybius, for which see Albanese 2003, 273.

Bodin also took care to make clear that he did not approve of Patrizi's radical iconoclasm. Even the greatest historians had faults. But all historians provided indispensable knowledge. And the *Ars historica* should provide rules not for devising some imaginary perfect history at a distant date in the future, but for reading the historians that existed in the present: "Let it seem madness to hope for better historians than those we have, criminal even to wish for them. I do not see any point in the work of those who create for themselves an ideal of a perfect historian, of a kind that has never existed and never can exist, but ignore the ones that we actually read and reread."[98] To carry out this scrupulous but pragmatic examination of the sources, Bodin explained, modern readers must abandon the prejudices natural to the time and place in which they lived. The great Hellenist Guillaume Budé had denounced Tacitus for writing against the Christians.[99] Bodin rejected this judgment: "Tacitus acted impiously, because he was not a Christian, but he was not impious when he wrote against us, since he was bound by the pagan superstition."[100] In fact, Tacitus

---

[98] Bodin 1566, 56; 1572 71–72; Wolf (ed.) 1579, I, 49: "Nunc optimi cuiusque delectum adhibeamus, meliores quidem iis quos habemus sperare amentiae: optare, sceleris esse videatur, nec eorum studia valde utilia duco, qui sibi fingunt ideam historici consummati, qualis nemo fuerit unquam, nec vero esse possit: eos autem quos in manib. terimus, omittunt."

[99] Bodin 1566, 75; 1572, 95; Wolf (ed.) 1579, I, 64: "Budaeus acerbe Tacitum scriptorem omnium sceleratissimum appellavit: quod nonnihil adversus Christianos scripsit."

[100] Bodin 1566, 75; 1572, 95; Wolf (ed.) 1579, I, 64: "ita quoque impie fecit Tacitus, quod non fuerit Christianus: sed non impie adversus nos scripsit, cum gentili superstitione obligaretur."

would have committed an impiety if he had failed to defend his own religion – especially when he was conditioned to do so by the sight of Christians and Jews, accused of abominable crimes and dragged off for punishment.[101] Modern scholars, in other words, needed to judge the texts and traditions they confronted in historical terms, the terms of their creators – not the anachronistic ones of their own, later times. Bodin could defend the historical tradition without claiming that it was perfect – just as Perizonius would, much later, in his reply to Le Clerc.[102] None of the authors of an *ars historica* anticipated the full, self-confident radicalism of Le Clerc's critique of tradition or the equally full, exacting traditionalism of Perizonius's reply. But Patrizi and Bodin forged the sharpest tools that Le Clerc and Perizonius wielded – including their proud assertions of the legitimacy of modern, critical forms of reading.

This single test case offers far too narrow a basis on which to judge the treatises *De arte historica*. But it is suggestive nonetheless. On the one hand, none of the authors of an *ars historica* anticipated the full, radical modernity of Le Clerc's work – his call for a kind of history that would emancipate itself

---

[101] Bodin 1566, 75; 1572, 95; Wolf (ed.) 1579, I, 64: "ego vero impium iudicarem nisi quancunque religionem veram iudicaret, non eam quoque tueri et contrarias evertere conaretur. Cum enim Christiani et Hebraei quasi venefici et omnibus sceleribus ac stupris infames ad supplicia quotidie raperentur, quis historicus a verborum contumeliis abstineret?"

[102] For a sharp rebuttal by a guardian of Catholic orthodoxy, which gives a sense of how shocking Bodin's treatment of Tacitus could seem, see Possevino 1597, 13 ro: "Quod sane impium per se est, neque vero a Christiano scriptore, et qualis haberi vult ipse Bodinus, est approbandum ... "

in every way, substantive and stylistic alike, from the classical tradition. On the other hand, Patrizi and Bodin forged the sharpest tools that Le Clerc and Perizonius wielded when they went to work, in their different context and for their different ends, to criticize the ancients. Bodin advanced a tolerant historicism that seems to have much in common with that of Perizonius. And both men appreciated, much as Le Clerc and Perizonius did, the idea that the best historian was not a participant in events but a critical reader who appeared when the tumult and shouting had died and recreated what had happened from the sources, critically assessed.

Much remains to be learned. Did later scholars read and apply the teachings of the *artes historicae*? Le Clerc referred to these works explicitly, Perizonius did not; and both referred with far more frequency to recent philological works, miscellanies, and commentaries on classical texts. Did they encounter the new principles and practices of Patrizi and Bodin in these intermediate sources? Or did the philologists they took such an interest in reformulate them independently? Did the *artes historicae* fall into oblivion before the new *ars critica* took shape? If so, why? These and many other questions need answers, and the case of Curtius – a minor and derivative historian – cannot yield enough information to solve them. Yet we are not quite finished with his story and its implications.

Part III: Curtius in the Quattrocento: back to the future in Ferrara

Most writers on the *ars historica* assume one point: that its creators devised the critical principles that they stated and

49

applied, and that readers of history before the sixteenth century could not have anticipated their hermeneutical subtlety. Yet one further source in which Curtius comes up for critical discussion – the *De politia litteraria* of the Milanese humanist Angelo Decembrio – calls these assumptions into question. Decembrio described, in concrete and often strikingly accurate historical detail, the discussions on literary questions that had taken place in the court of Ferrara in the 1440s, when Guarino of Verona and his pupils dominated scholarly life in the city and the marquess himself, Leonello d'Este, played an active role in learned circles. A hybrid modeled on Aulus Gellius and Quintilian, a madly energetic combination of nostalgic literary dialogue and grindingly detailed textbook on orthography, the *Politia litteraria* offers everything from instructions on the proper use of diphthongs to lively accounts of Roman inscriptions and the Vatican obelisk.[103] These vivid dialogues staged in Ferrarese libraries and gardens evoke both a particular, humanistic culture of texts and facts – chiefly ancient texts and facts – and a sharp modern ability to discriminate among them.[104]

Decembrio portrays Leonello and his friends as immersed in – almost obsessed with – ancient history and historians. By his account, they lost no opportunity to evoke the classical models whose actions great men should imitate. Leonello spent his winters in special quarters in the Este city palace,

---

[103] For a general introduction see Grafton 1997; on the Vatican obelisk see Curran and Grafton 1995 [1996]. The text has now received a modern edition: Decembrio 2002. Though unsatisfactory in some respects, it has the merit of existing, and I will cite it in what follows.

[104] Crisciani 2005.

their walls adorned with images of Scipio and Hannibal – the former equipped, appropriately, with a horse and a servant, the latter with an elephant bearing a castle and an Ethiopian guiding it.[105] In fact, Leonello took a special interest in the images of ancient heroes preserved in coins and statues. When a prosaic friend objected that he saw no intellectual merit in collecting works of art, as opposed to books, Leonello – at least in Decembrio's dialogue – joined the chorus of humanists that denounced the philistine. He took as much pleasure in seeing the faces of the ancient worthies, he explained, as in reading about them in texts "that are perceived only by the mind." In the same way, his friend Giovanni Gualenghi felt reverence every time he looked at his picture of Jerome and the lion, and the young poet Tito Vespasiano Strozzi renewed his mourning for a dead girl every time he looked at her picture in a locket.[106] Leonello,

---

[105] Decembrio 2002: 191 (2.14.1): "Memini siquidem iis aedibus Leonelli Ferrariae, ubi potissimum a genitore separatus, quanquam in eodem palatio, hibernare solebat, saepenumero vidisse Scipionis Affricani et Hannibalis imagines in pariete picturatas, *mutua* velut *admiratione*, ut apud Livium est [30.30.2], sese compellantes, Romanum equo comitatum et famulo, Poenum cum elephante cathedrato et Aethiope nigro gubernante, caeterum ipsos duces adstare pedestres."

[106] Decembrio 2002, 431–32 (6.68.20–22): [someone remarks] ". . . se quidem librorum copiam, sed nullam eiusmodi picturarum signorumve familiaritatem habere, quod ad legendum vel edocendum hominem nihil pertinere arbitraretur. Itaque se mirari, cur a Plinio minore, scribendi studiosissimo, signum illud Corinthium intra bibliothecam tanti fieret [*Ep.* 3.6 ff.]. . . . [Guarino replies: pictures induce one to study. He continues:] Sed nunquid effigies principum, seu exterorum sive nostrorum quoque, praecipue veterum, recognoscere manuque tractare, uti nunc ex his gemmis inspicimus, operae pretium credas atque iucundum in re litteraria? Tum Leonellus interdixit: 'Nempe

moreover, insisted that modern artists portray the ancients in historically appropriate clothing and settings, acting as they really had. Though he loved and collected Flemish tapestries, he denounced the weavers who indiscriminately included in their works apocryphal stories about the Roman emperors.[107] No

> Caesarum ego vultus non minus singulari quadam admiratione aereis nummis inspiciendo delectari soleo – nam idcirco ex aere frequentiores quam ex auro argentove superfuerunt – quam eorum staturas; uti Suetonii vel aliorum scriptis contemplari, quod intellectu solo percipitur' ... Tum Ioannes senior: 'Et ego Hieronymi praesertim effigiem spinam de manu leonis evellentis summa cum veneratione domi observo.' At Titus facete concludens adiecit: 'Et ego non ex Romanorum antiquis monumentis, sed ex Ferrarensium puellarum novis insignibus vultum habeo virginis, minima compactum in pyxide, aurea coma, pro cuius nuper interitu cum lacrymabile carmen excudissem, hoc quoque teneo perpetuae dulcisque memoriae testimonium, in quo nihil videtur praeter vocem deesse.' "

[107] Decembrio 2002, 427–28 (6.68.10): [Leonello speaks:] "Nam quid de pictorum ineptiis? Sunt et inter eos quoque, ut apud librarios ac scriptores ipsos, errores: nec in parietibus solum, dixerim, sed iis etiam vestibus, quas parietibus appensas cernitis ex transalpina Gallia deductis, in quibus ipsi textores pictoresque, quanquam id operis genus multi sit artificii, de colorum magis opulentia telaeque levitate quam picturae ratione contendunt. Ita vero regali luxuriae et stultae multitudini placent, cum in eis praesertim populares ineptiae depingantur, ut hinc Traiani principis fictam historiam cernitis: eius filium manibus propriis occisum, quod viduae filium interemisset; alii autem: pro defuncto eiusdem imperatoris filium mulieri substitutum. At quis haec scribit historicus? Tum ipsius parentis caput post saecula viventi rubentique adhuc lingua compertum, quod vera semper locuta fuerit: ac nonnulla de Gregorio pontifice anilia dictu figmenta, quae sic imperitis iactanda contigere, quod in eo principe mira constitit iusticiae pietatisque moderatio: inde Alexandri Bucephalum equum, non cuiusmodi Curtius exponit et animalis Graeca declarat appellatio, quod rictus bovis exhiberet, sed ut infernalem Plutonis vel Charontis equum;

wonder that he offered his support to Pisanello and Matteo de' Pasti, or that his court became the center of the new classicizing taste for medals.[108] The Ferrarese humanists, in other words, envisioned the ancient world in three dimensions, if not quite in living color.

In the end, as one might expect, Leonello, his teachers and their friends preferred texts to all other relics of the ancient world. And they preferred historical texts to most others. Decembrio describes Guarino as praising the fine three-volume manuscripts of Livy, their title-pages adorned with wreathed vine leaves and heroes on horseback, that were a specialty of the Florentine bookdealer Vespasiano da Bisticci – and that Leonello and his friends actually bought.[109] The dialogues in

aut Iasonis tauros ore flammas evomentes, cathenatos cruribus; et reliqua passim pro eius transalpinae gentis vanitate."

[108] On this chapter see the edition and commentary in Baxandall 1963. For antiquarianism in Decembrio see further Curran and Grafton 1995 [1996].

[109] Decembrio 2002, 459 (7.75.7) [Guarino is speaking]: "Solent igitur ex Hetruria Florentinaque civitate potissimum libri quam venustissime facti comparari, feruntque ibi Vespasianum quendam, eximium bibliopolam librorum librariorumque solertissimum, ad quem omnis Italica regio, longinquae etiam nationis homines confluunt, quicunque libros ornatissimos venales optant. Quem licet arbitremur Leonardi Caroliique Aretinorum diligentia exemplaria bona conquirere, tamen, ut antea dixi, cum alio modo exemplaria sint, alio librariis excribuntur. Quo satis eos percipitur neque syllabarum intensionem depressionemque cognoscere, quae productae vel breves, propter carminis ignorationem, per quam etiam alias geminari litteras, alias simplices relinqui opus sit, neque, quando cum *ch* vel *ph* seu *th* aut *y*, quod Graeci ypsilon vocant, scribi conveniat: ipsis duntaxat arbitrio suo describentibus. Ad quae incommoda sponte commissa accidit insuper incommodius in Graecorum sermonum defectiones frequenter incidere

the *Politia* make clear, moreover, that these books were not just treasures to be contemplated. Leonello's courtiers scrutinized them, criticized their spelling, and even played games of *sortes Livianae* with them, passing the triple-decker Livy from hand to hand as they tried to find by lucky dips in the text exactly the passages that verified their beliefs and prejudices (Decembrio shows one of Leonello's courtiers, Feltrino Boiardo, a great fan of Hannibal's, undergoing humiliation when he foolishly cites a passage that shows Hannibal acting in an undignified way when he is forced to leave Italy).[110] The study of history, in Leonello's Ferrara as in Alfonso's Naples, meant the reading of material texts, austere but luxurious, of great ancient writers.

Unlike Alfonso, however, Leonello did not find Curtius's history of Alexander the Great a sovereign remedy against ill health and that run-down feeling. When Leonello fell ill, he worked through historian after historian. Curtius interested him because he described Alexander, himself very ill, paying no attention to warnings of poison and boldly gulping down

---

quasi fenestras, sed contrario more obscuritatem legentibus opponentes, tum in sermones depravatos, nam de superfluo geminatis tolerabilius. Eninvero intelligere, quae pingit, non pingere tantummodo librarium decet."

[110] Decembrio 2002, 230–31 (2.24.4): "Iis ita recitatis paucioribus tamen Catonis commendatio, ut qui seniores extitere, pluribus autem, et quidem iunioribus, Caesarianae laudes placuerunt. Sed inter haec Leonellus ad visenda eius diei Baptistea sollemnia provocatus lectionem ocius expediri iussit. Quamobrem Feltrinus de bello Punico revolvens existimansque de Hannibale quicquam fortissimum invenire, quem miris semper laudibus extollebat, in id tamen egregium, licet minus felix, concidit, cum Hannibal invitus Italia decederet ... [30.20.7–9, on Hannibal's fury, like that of an exile, as he leaves Italy]."

a medicine prescribed by his doctor, Philip.[111] But the further Leonello read in Curtius, the more problematic he found the text.[112] It swarmed with contradictions. Why, after all, would Alexander drink a potion that he had been warned might be poisonous?[113] Why did Alexander find it impossible to get information about Darius's whereabouts? Curtius explained that no Persians ever deserted, and they kept the affairs of their rulers deeply secret. But he himself, a couple of books later, described a deserter informing Alexander about Darius's cavalry traps. Did the gods hide Darius, as if he were an Homeric hero having imaginary adventures?[114] And how could Curtius make Darius say, in his last speech, both that he had never

---

[111] Decembrio 2002, 411 (6.65.3): "Amicis itaque percunctantibus, quidnam potissimum per eam valitudinis intemperiem lectitasset, respondit historicos clariores diligentius tractavisse, Plinium maiorem, Livium, Salustium, commentarios Caesaris, Iustinum, sed Curtium quam antea studiosius. Cuius rei causa fuisset aegrotatio, ut de Alexandri modo disquireret: quam repente ob illius fluminis ingressum exanimatus, quanta mox fiducia, an temeritate magis, poculum sollicitudine plenum a medico suscepisset, utrum scriptoris de ipso rege an regis potius tam praesens, in dubio tamen eventu, sententia fuisset. Quanquam non in hac de Alexandro controversia solum, sed et aliis eius *historiae* locis Curtium sibi videri dicebat adeo contraria inter se protulisse, ut pene a naturali usu, ipsa etiam rerum veritate dissentire viderentur. Sperare aliquando ea demonstrandi tempus affuturum."

[112] Petrarch had similar problems with Curtius, which he solved by portraying Alexander as "an unbalanced youth protected by Fortune, vain, wild, almost insane; and the resultant picture of him in the *De Viris Illustribus* was unique for the age in its single-minded, deliberate abuse" (Cary 1956, 266). For recent efforts to make literary and cultural sense of Curtius see e.g. Atkinson 2000 and Spencer 2002, and cf. more generally Carney 2000.

[113] Decembrio 2002, 418–19.   [114] Decembrio 2002, 419–20.

contemplated running away, and that Alexander had twice put him to flight?[115]

Curtius contradicted the clear testimony of nature and reason. He described the Indians' bows as so long and heavy that one could shoot them only by resting one end on the ground – a technical error that Leonello found implausible, since it would have prevented bowmen from carrying out their natural task of shooting quickly.[116] He claimed that the Indians' elephants terrified the Greeks' naturally timid horses – an inaccurate description that Leonello, like all the Estensi a connoisseur of horseflesh, dismissed with disdain.[117] He even

[115] Decembrio 2002, 421–22.

[116] Decembrio 2002, 422–23 (6.67.19): [Curtius says that Indians' bows were so large that they had to rest one end on the ground to shoot them (8.14.19, 8.9.28)]: "Mirum est vel incredibile magis, quod ait historicus ... Quod teli vel balistae genus potissimum licet apud omnis gentes paululum forma vel qualitate sit differens, tamen ita fieri et excogitari solet ab hominibus, ut tractando feriendoque sit aptissimum." Ibid., 420 (6.67.11), on 8.14.23.

[117] Decembrio 2002, 420 (6.67.11), on 8.14.23 [At 8.14.23, Curtius describes how the trumpeting of the Indians' elephants "non equos modo, tam pavidum ad omnia animal, sed viros quoque ordinesque turbaverat"]: "Caeterum ex humano genere ad ferinum descendamus. Affirmat historicus animal equum esse ad omnia pavidum: cum forte aliquem equum iumentumve praecipue compertum sit ad omnia vel non visa prius vel non usitata pavidum et sternax, sicut experimur aliquando primis forte diebus desuetos famulantes, aliena stabula novos insessores abhorrere. At quidem de omni equorum genere, ut oratio scriptoris indicat, testatum non oportuit. Quorum magis proprium constat nihil expavescere, atque aliquos ita compertos, ut, si lancearum aciem contra se directam viderint, nihilo segnius praecurrere pergant. Ergo neque tubarum armorumve et horrisoni strepitus auditu non absterreri, sed audentius inflammari solitos accepimus. Inde est a poeta moraliter:

made fun of magic – not the ordinary, low sort well-known in Leonello's world, which supposedly involved crowds of dead people leaving their tombs to make music in the moonlight, or groups of living people whose spirits left their bodies, but the learned form of magic by which, as everyone knew, the ancient Egyptians and Persians had successfully predicted future wars, pestilences, and changes in regime and religion.[118]

frenos audire sonantes; fluviosque innare rapaces [Virgil *Georgics* 3.184; 142]. Ita, cum ante domandum audacissimi sint, postquam domiti sunt, non pavitare, sed obedire didicerunt, ideoque stimulis et habena gubernantur."

[118] Decembrio 2002, 424 (6.67.23–24), on 7.4.8 [Curtius derides the magic of the Mede Gobares at 7.4.8: "Erat in eo convivio Gobares, natione Medus, sed magicae artis – si modo ars est, non vanissimi cuiusque ludibrium – magis professione quam scientia celeber, alioqui moderatus et probus"]: "Demum magiam artem quamobrem palam ita confutet, ut eam nihil esse et ad hominis levissimi dicacitatem pertinere contendat, non minus admiror, immo vehementius, quod non ab aliis solum auctoribus, ut Herodoto in primis atque Iustino, sed a se etiam magorum officia memorentur. Nam apud Persas et Aegyptios eius artis fuit et astrorum non rarus eventus; indeque futura praedicere solebant, quae potissimum ad famem, sitim, pestilentiam et iis contraria, ut terrae vel aquarum ubertatem prosperam, mortalium valitudinem, animantium foecunditatem, ad haec bellicos tumultus, regnorum innovationes et quae ad deorum religiones pertinerent. Quorum ego virorum et scientiarum cognitionem haud magiam seu magicam artem appellare dubitaverim, ut philosophorum philosophiam; non cujusmodi vulgus existimat magicam dici peritiam, quam et Graeco vocabulo necromantiam nominant, sed Graeci a mortuorum divinatione vulgaverunt, variis inde fictionibus creditam, ut: mortuos in primis vivificatos incedere, loqui, in choreis ad lunam psallere cum eius quoque generis hominum turba, qui relictis domi corporibus per nocturna silentia evolare dicuntur: aliquando poetarum, ut fert opportunitas, sed muliercularum et puerorum vana figmenta."

Despite his grace and skill as a writer, Curtius posed special problems of credibility, at least to the reader whose sensibilities had been formed in this sharp-eyed, sharp-tongued Ferrarese circle. Leonello and his friends, immersed in the classics and committed to using them, acutely sensitive to the visual and material world which the ancients had inhabited, found themselves falling down a rabbit hole, shocked and sickened by the speed of their fall and the strangeness of what they saw on the way down, as they felt their way through passages that most fifteenth- and sixteenth-century readers traversed with pleasure and without incident.

Leonello skillfully traced these flaws in the text back to the writer's character and formation. Curtius, he argued, was really a rhetorician rather than a historian. That explained why he praised his hero's self-restraint and moderation, even though he knew perfectly well that Alexander had enjoyed nothing more than a bout of sex with eunuchs and male prostitutes: "Therefore he claims that Alexander never indulged in extravagance, or indulged in passion in a way that might be seen as unnatural. Note how this conclusion contradicts what he wrote before."[119] That explained, too, why Curtius absurdly described the habits and rituals of a single "king of India," even though his own account made clear that, then as in Leonello's own time, India had had many rulers. Curtius, as he himself admitted, was less a writer (*scriptor*) than a copyist (*transscriptor*) – and at that he did not believe everything he copied. Yet he took over the implausible with the plausible, the vague with

---

[119] Decembrio 2002, 423–24 (6.67.22), on Curtius's praise of Alexander's self-restraint (10.5.32).

the precise – so long as the accounts in question supplied the pigments for his flattering portrait of his hero.[120] Decembrio assures us that Leonello himself subjected the historian to this acid bath in historical and rhetorical criticism – one that ended, by his account, with the suggestive remark, unfortunately not pursued, that Herodotus too said many implausible things.[121]

---

[120] Decembrio 2002, 422 (6.67.16–17), on 8.9.23 ff. [a splendid description of how the king of India is preceded by attendants bearing silver trays of incense, while he reclines in a golden litter set with pearls, listening to the singing of trained birds]: "Neque enim vel Romanorum veterum, dum Curtius scriberet, seu Graecorum, si ad primos eius historiae scriptores intendimus, seu praesenti tempestate conveniunt, quae de Indorum rege memorantur. Quo satis perspicitur hunc Alexandrinae historiae transcriptorem potius, ut supra monstravi, quam scriptorem fuisse [note that the passage in question underlines Curtius's credulity: 9.1.34: 'Equidem plura transcribo quam credo; nam nec affirmare sustineo de quibus dubito, nec subducere quae accepi'], qui, uti ab historico Graeco scriptum invenit, de Indorum aliquo rege illius tempestatis ita transcripserit. Sed quisnam tandem ille rex fuit? Nempe non ab hoc historico percipimus. Qui sic regis Indi mores vitamque describit, hominis appellationem non producens, ut tanquam unicus Indiae rex eiusdem semper vitae consuetudinisque describendus videatur ut Phoenix, ac quemadmodum nos unum summum pontificem veneramur, cuius seu Hispani seu Italici ad divinum cultum spectantes ritus cum omnium fere summorum pontificum, qui fuerint quique demum insequantur, religione conveniunt. Sed quid ambio? Nec Alexandri quidem temporibus unicus Indiae rex fuit, si eius acta perspexeris, sed complures reges reginaeque traduntur, necdum omnes ab Alexandro superati. Quod idem auctor paulo supra manifestat *Indiae regum* inquiens, non *regis, luxuriam* ... [8.9.23: Regum tamen luxuria, quam ipsi magnificentiam appellant, super omnium gentium vitia]"

[121] Decembrio 2002, 425 (6.67.25): "Nam omisso nunc Curtio, de quo satis hodierna disputatione memoravimus: quis non apud Herodotum multo plura deprehenderit, ac magis, quam in hoc auctore

Leonello – and Decembrio – did not anticipate all the methodological questions and suggestions to be found in the *artes historicae*, any more than those treatises adumbrated all the bold ideas of Le Clerc and Perizonius. Yet it seems clear that fifteenth-century humanists began to pose new questions about history – questions about source criticism, about internal consistency, about the problems inherent in rhetoric as the central discipline of historical writing, about the relation between natural and technical knowledge and historical texts, and about the general status of ancient writers – before anyone began to draw up even the first, relatively traditional treatises on the subject. Leonello and his friends already saw the ancient historians less as inimitable, perfect accounts of events than as humans and historical sources, from whose accounts the modern scholar must reconstruct the past with the aid of philological and antiquarian learning. That fact, taken together with the divergences of opinion we have identified within the *artes*, signals us that this tradition needs another history.

A genial and helpful cicerone through the mansions of the Republic of Letters, Curtius has shown us much. By following him, we have learned to see past the deceptive smoothness of early modern rhetoric, to realize that novel ideas and practices took root and flourished in what scholars have often mistaken for a culture mired in tradition. He has led us

reprehendenda, hoc est minime credenda, quemadmodum historice referuntur? Quid ais, Guarine? At ille ita esse consentiens iandudum Leonelli subtilitatem iugemque memoriam, ut saepe alias, extollebat: adiecitque huius auctoris stilum inter caeteros interpretes perpolitum eminere ac eloquentiae cuiusdam separatae sic inter historicos, uti Plinii minoris esset in oratoribus."

from Leiden to Paris and from Paris to Ferrara, from the journals of the Republic of Letters to the disputations that took place in princely courts, and by doing so he has revealed the existence of microenvironments where the pursuit of *historia humana* involved the creation of new practices and the cultivation of a new critical sensibility. He has made us see that the history of historical criticism is a complex and indirect story, one step back for every two steps forward, punctuated by the appearance of wicked children who cry that the Ciceronian emperor has no clothes on, or that the Tacitean emperor has nicer clothes. Above all, he has taught us not to take the *artes historicae* for granted, but to look boldly for their connections to the practices of cutting-edge scholarship as well as their strange apparent continuity in form and content. In the next chapter, with regret, I shall leave his amusing company, to plunge more deeply into the turbid pools of the *artes historicae* themselves.

2

The origins of the *ars historica*: a question mal posée?

The English mathematician, magus, and antiquary John Dee did many things in a distinctive way. Most distinctive of all, of course, and most effectively ridiculed by Meric Casaubon and many others, was his habit of talking with angels. Dee did this with the help of scryers like Edward Kelly – a gentleman of ill repute who not only saw the celestial beings appear in the show-stone that Dee rested on a great seal of wax, but asked one of them, Madini, to lend him a hundred pounds. But when Dee set himself to read works of history, as he often did, he strictly followed standard practices. The Latin prose narratives of Troy's fall by Dares and Dictys – supposedly eyewitness accounts, the former written by a Trojan, but actually late works that circulated in Latin – fascinated Dee as they did many others. Nonetheless, he took care to establish their credibility. Dictys remarked that he could describe what Ulysses did at Troy "very precisely" because he himself had been present. Dee made an immediate inference: autopsy guaranteed authority. "The truth of this account," he wrote in the margin, "is certain."[1] Dictys

---

[1] Royal College of Physicians, 20cD139/7, 9959, 10: "Eorum ego secutus comitatum, ea quidem quae ante apud Troiam gesta sunt ab Vlysse, cognita quam diligentissime retuli: et reliqua quae deinceps insecuta sunt: quoniam ipse interfui, quam verissime potero, exponam." Dee remarks: "veritas huius historiae certa."

named heroes by their fathers' names as well as their own. Dee firmly believed, as so many of his countrymen did, that the British were descended from the Trojan Brutus. He used a second widely held principle to confirm the authority of his text. Each people had a fairly stable national character or "genius." Scholars, accordingly, could use modern evidence to confirm and elucidate ancient accounts of a given people: "Note in this passage," Dee remarked, "the British custom of naming by citing the patronymic or matronymic or both."[2] And once Dee had established that he could rely on these accounts, he used them above all as a source of prudent advice about political and military affairs. Dares explained that King Laomedon of Sparta had worried that it could be dangerous if the Greeks became too accustomed to sailing to Troy. "Note," wrote Dee, in his best vein as William Cecil's adviser on the theory of naval power, "it is not prudent to allow foreigners to know our coastline too well."[3]

Every one of the implicit canons Dee employed found explicit statement in the treatises on the *Ars historica* that Johannes Wolf collected in his famous two-volume collection of 1579, the *Artis historicae penus*. François Baudouin, the erudite jurist whose *Prolegomena* on law and history first appeared at Paris in 1561, stated clearly that "I would prefer that writers narrated only those things that they saw, and in which

---

[2] Ibid., 11: "Nota hic Brytannicum nominandi morem, per patrum etiam citata nomina, vel Matrum, vel vtrorumque."

[3] Ibid., 155: "Vbi audivit Laomedon rex, commotus est, et consideravit commune periculum esse, si consuescerent Graeci ad sua littora navibus adventare." Dee: "Nota, non esse consultum Littora nostra externis esse nimis nota."

they took part. Polybius professes that he desires this above all in history, and the ancients clearly demanded it."[4] Baudouin made clear that he too had learned, from its most dramatic ancient and modern sources, the rule that direct comparison between ancient and modern histories should yield political lessons: "What a certain Florentine tried to do in the last century to sections of Livy's history, for his own utility and that of his fellow Italians, we should do all the more intensively in universal history, especially where the matter deserves it, and a reasonable comparison comes to mind. Finally, the historical hypothesis should yield, so to speak, a political thesis."[5] Baudouin did not pay much attention to the genius of peoples. But Jean Bodin made it a central theme of his 1566 *Methodus ad facilem historiarum cognitionem*, that messy, mistitled masterpiece of historical geography, in which he traced the qualities of peoples to their lands of origin and later wanderings, and which formed the core of Wolf's anthology. When Dee read histories in a particular way, with schooled attention to their value as

---

[4] Baudouin 1561a, 54; Wolf (ed.) 1579, I, 634: "Equidem optarem, ut scriptores ea demum narrarent, quae viderunt, quibusque interfuerunt. quod et Polybius profitetur sese in historia imprimis desiderare, et veteres plane postularunt ... "

[5] Baudouin 1561a, 170; Wolf (ed.) 1579, I, 713: "Sicque historiae, quodammodo ut leges, legendae sunt, hoc est, ut priores ad posteriores, et rursus posteriores ad priores apta quadam collatione trahantur. Neque solum ubi posterior priorem laudat, id in lectione quoque prioris observare debemus, sed et παράλληλα (ut Plutarchi verbo utar) conferenda sunt. Saltem quod superiori seculo quidam Florentinus in Livianae historiae parte utiliter facere in rem suam suorumque Italorum conatus est: multo id magis faciundum esset in historia universa, praesertim ubi et res digna est, et non inepta occurrit comparatio: denique ex hypothesi historica saepe colligenda est politica veluti thesis."

testimonies and to their political applications, he showed that he was an apt pupil of the artists of history.

Dee's approach to his texts was by no means unusual, even in England. For a number of his countrymen cherished great enthusiasm for the *artes historicae*. One of them, Gabriel Harvey, has been more an object of ridicule than of respect in modern times. This outcome is perhaps connected with the fact that the only contemporary picture of Harvey, a woodcut, shows him taking down his codpiece to let fly "upon a jakes," terrified to the point of pissing himself by the announcement that Thomas Nashe's satire, *Have With You to Saffron Walden*, had reached the booksellers. Yet Harvey, as Lisa Jardine and I tried to show long ago, was taken seriously enough by higher-born contemporaries that they employed him in a post that Philip Sidney named: as a "discourser," a professional reader who could train the young in the formal lessons of history. Harvey read Livy's account of Hannibal with the young Thomas Smith before he went off to impose civilization on the Irish Ards, and studied Livy's books on early Rome with Sidney himself before the latter undertook his embassy to the imperial court in Prague.[6] In each case he deliberately calibrated the

---

[6] Princeton University Library (PUL) (Ex) PA6452 .A2 1555q, 93 (end of book III) : "Hos tres Liuii libros, Philippus Sidneius aulicus, et ego intimè contuleramus, qua potuimus politica analysi ultro, citroque excussos: paulò ante suam Legationem ad Imperatorem, Rodolphum II. Cui profectus est regineo nomine honorificè congratulatum; iam tum creato Imperatori. Summus noster respectus erat ad rerumpublicarum speties; et personarum conditiones, actionumque qualitates. De Glareani, aliorumque annotationibus parùm curabamus"; 269 (start of XXI): "M. Thomas Smith, & I reading this decade of Liuie togither, found verie good vse of M. Antonie Copes English historie of the two most noble

exercise to extract the same sorts of political lessons from the text that Dee did. He emphasized that he and Sidney paid little attention to the humanist commentaries in their search for political lessons, and that he and Smith, despite their low stature, made reading Livy an adventure in free criticism of the mighty dead. And though Harvey regularly disagreed on particular points with Bodin, he made no secret of the fact that the Frenchman, as he put it in a note, "wunne mie harte to Liuie."[7] When Bodin materialized in England during the

Captaines of the world, Annibal, & Scipio . . . Sed tamen, Dulcius ex ipso fonte bibuntur aquae. . . "; 518 (end of XXX): "Hanc Annibalis decadem vna hebdomade non magis raptim, quàm auidè, acriterque percurri cum Thoma Smitho, honoratissimi Secretarii regii, Thomae Smithi filio; paulo post Ardium Hybernicarum prorege; tam prudenti, quam animoso, validoque iuuene. Cum eramus liberiores, et aliquanto asperiores, Carthaginiensium, et Romanorum Censores, quàm decuerat homines nostrae fortunae, virtutis, aut etiam scientiae. Tantùm didiceramus nemini veterum, aut nouorum adulari; et aliorum facta si non solido iudicio, at integro arbitrio examinare. Aristotelis, Xenophontisque Politicis; et Vegetii libris de re militari, Frontinique strategematis multùm confidebamus. Nec semper aut Annibali, aut Marcello, aut Fabio assentabamur, aut etiam ipsi Scipioni."

[7] Princeton University Library (Ex) PA6452 .A2 1555q, [P ro]: "The notablest men, that first commended the often & aduised reading of Livie vnto mee, were theise fiue, Doctor Henry Haruey, M. Roger Ascham, Sir Thomas Smyth, Sir Walter Mildmay, Sir Philip Sidney: all learned, expert, & uerie iudicious in the greatest matters of priuate, or publique qualitie. Once I heard M. Secretarie Wilson, & Doctor Binge preferr the Romane his historie before the Greek, or other: and Liuie before anie other Romane historie. But of all other Sir Philip Sidney, Colonel Smyth, and Monsieur Bodin wunne mie hart to Liuie. Sir Philip Sidney esteemes no general Historie, like Justins abridgement of Trogus: nor anie special Roman historie like Liuie: nor anie particular historie, Roman, or other, like the Singular life, & actions of Cesar . . . "

negotiations for the Alençon marriage, Harvey hurled himself upon the Frenchman's bosom with a precise question about the best authorities in the complex and rebarbative realm of chronology.[8]

The *artes historicae* inspired reflections of many kinds in their English readers. For example, as Carlo Ginzburg has shown, it was Baudouin who taught Sidney, Daniel, and other theorists of poetry to reflect that it had served the primitive British and others as an early form of history – a point to which I will return at the end of this chapter.[9] But the basic story has remained rather fixed. Many Italian treatments of the *ars historica* contented themselves with detailed reviews of the uses and forms of history. They highlighted its pedagogical function as a source of moral principles exemplified in action, which could teach the intelligent reader prudence, and its literary nature as a genre that could not only inform, but move, its readers. Over time, they made impressive efforts, as Eckhard Kessler above all has shown, to wield the traditional principles and rhetoric and the *loci classici* from Cicero and Lucian to define history as a

8 Princeton University Library (Ex) PA6452 .A2 1555q, [P vo]: "Quanto fides Eusebio adhibenda; consulendi Neochronologi; praesertim Funccius, Crusius, Mercator. nam de authentico Synchronismo multi adhuc scrupuli. Quanquam mihi ualdè profuit cum duobus peritissimis Gallis, Joanne Bodino, et Petro Barone viua collatio. Qui plus industriae, certitudinisque tribuunt Glareano, Funccio, Mercatori, Crusio, quàm vlli veterum Chronologorum. Saluo tamen Cuiusque Classici auctoris iure." Harvey also knew Baudouin's work. See his note in the *Mosaicus* of Freigius (Freigius 1583, British Library C.60.f.4), [β 8 vo]: "Mosis Origines, vehementer perstrictae à Simplicio, et Galeno: De quo videndus Balduinus J.C. in extremo ferè lib. 2. De Coniunctione Historiae cum Jurisprudentia."
9 Ginzburg 2000.

genre and a domain with its own ends and rules.[10] In Germany
and France, by contrast, writers on the art of history concentrated less on how one would create a single perfect narrative
than on how one should assess the multiple conflicting narratives that actually confronted modern readers. Both Baudouin
and Bodin, after all, argued for a catholic history that would
include the ancient Near East and the recently discovered New
World, Asia and Africa, as well as the traditional territory of
learning, Greece and Rome. More important, both treated the
ars historica as a hermeneutical discipline, a set of rules for critical readers of history, rather than a set of canons for effective
writers. Both emphasized the need to read in a critical manner, with an eye always on the credibility of sources and the
proper ways to combine and reconcile their testimony. Both
assessed the value of the most prestigious ancient and modern historians – like Polybius and Guicciardini – in part by
their ability to draw on official documents and other reliable
sources. And both insisted that history could not be found in
any single narrative, but must be reconstructed by collecting
all the information yielded by all potentially relevant sources.
To that extent, both began to treat history in a new way –
as a comprehensive form of inquiry that ranged across space
and time, and as a critical discipline based on the distinction
between primary and secondary sources.[11] Wolf emphasized
the similarities between the two men – and the importance he

[10] Kessler (ed.) 1971; Kessler 1982.
[11] See esp. Brown 1939; Klempt 1960; Franklin 1963; Huppert 1970; and
     Couzinet 1996.

attached to their work – by placing them prominently in his anthology.

Both Baudouin and Bodin, as is well known, were jurists by profession. Both traced their intellectual ancestry to earlier legal humanists, such as Alciato and Budé. These men had insisted that the Roman *Corpus iuris* was not a timeless body of principles that could be applied to any modern situation, but a product of history in its own right – a compilation of legislation and jurists' opinions drawn from many centuries of Roman history, which Tribonian had ruthlessly excerpted and reorganized. And they had claimed to offer a radically new way of interpreting the law. They began by sorting the individual components of the *Corpus* by their periods of origin and then interpreted them by reference to their original historical contexts. Baudouin and Bodin argued that the jurist must be a historian, if he was to avoid humiliating errors of chronology and interpretation. As or more important, the historian must be a jurist, if he was to set events into their political and legal contexts and to understand their bearing on the evolution of the Roman state. These claims made excellent sense – especially from the historians' standpoint. As practitioners of the elementary art of rhetoric they enjoyed, as we do now, low salaries and modest status. Jurists, then as now, stood out for the exalted status embodied in their robes and the high financial rewards allotted to them by society. A marriage with the law – even a forced one – could only benefit the humanists, and several of the north European artists of history called for such a match. Reasonably enough, historians have classified the most influential of the *artes historicae* as the theoretical component of a "revolution in the methodology of law and history" – to quote the title of a justly influential book by Julian Franklin.[12] To ask where the *ars historica* came from, for generations, has meant to ask about its origins in a new, humanistic approach to Roman law.

This framework for inquiry has yielded splendid results. But it has also set the *artes historicae* in general, and Baudouin's *Prolegomena* in particular, into too narrow a context – one that omits some of the crucial conditions that brought them into being and some of the central ways in which contemporary readers used them. In this chapter I shall concentrate on Baudouin (1520–73), partly because his work had a powerful impact and partly because I am hooked on the challenge of this brilliant man. A refugee at different times from what he saw as the intellectual corruption of Catholicism and the terrible simplification of Calvinism, Baudouin had a distinguished career that took him from his native Arras to Louvain, where he was educated, Geneva, where he served as Calvin's secretary, and Heidelberg, where he taught Roman law, before trying to help resolve the French wars of religion at the Colloquy of Poissy.[13] His 1561 *Prolegomena* on universal history formed, as their title indicates, an introductory statement, offered before his course at Heidelberg on the law.

In many respects, Baudouin fits the bill drawn up by his best modern students. Again and again, he explained that the marriage of history and jurisprudence was ancient, natural,

---

[12] Brown 1939; Franklin 1963; Kelley 1964; Huppert 1970; Kelley 1970; Kelley 1971.

[13] On Baudouin see the classic article by Kelley 1964 and the full-length treatments by Erbe 1978 and Turchetti 1984.

and necessary – the only way to make history provide profound lessons about the state. Like Machiavelli and many others, Baudouin took Polybius and Tacitus as his examples of profound history – the history that revealed the hidden laws of human history.

> But even if the world is immobile, yet how admirable is the revolution – if I may use Polybius's term – of events that take place in it? It is certainly true, as Cornelius Tacitus once wrote, that there is a kind of revolution in all things, and that as times change, so do customs. Those who feigned that the heavens stand still and the earth revolves were fools. But just as this is an absurd dream, so when we turn over the pages of history, we are forced to recognize that the motion of the earth is just as varied and full of changes as the state of the heavens is stable and constant, so to speak, and we learn that Plato and Aristotle spoke the truth: there are also natural changes in states.[14]

Like Polybius, whose favorite term he borrowed, Baudouin called for a history that would not narrate events, but also lay bare their causes: "The ancients applied the term

---

[14] Baudouin 1561a, 4; Wolf (ed.) 1579, 1, 601: "Sed sit licet immobilis,tamen earum, quas dixi in ea geri moverique rerum, quam est admirabilis (ut Polybii [6.9.10] verbo utar) ἀνακύκλωσις? Certe vetus est, quod dixit olim scripsitque Cornelius Tacitus, rebus cunctis inesse videri quendam veluti orbem: et quemadmodum temporum vices, ita et morum verti. Ac inepti quidem nimium illi fuerunt, qui caelum stare, terram volvi finxerunt. Sed ut ridiculum hoc somnium est, sic cum historiam volvimus, non minus terrae varium et volubilem motum, quam caeli stabilem ac constantem (ut ita dicam) statum agnoscere cogimur: verumque esse experimur, quod Plato et Aristoteles dixerunt, naturales quoque esse Rerumpublicarum conversiones."

'pragmatic' to the form of history that exerts itself to explain and wisely and usefully demonstrates what it narrates, so that it describes not only events, but their causes, and gives events with their counsels."[15] Unlike most of his forerunners, who kept up a repetitive drumbeat of quotations from Cicero and Livy on *historia magistra vitae*, Baudouin cited Livy only to cap him with Polybius: "This is a grave preface, one worthy of a Roman writer, and the advice it offers is useful and necessary to one who is about to read Roman history. But this praise of history seems feeble when we consider its scale and value. What then? Let Livy stand aside without complaint, when I say that Polybius, whom he generally follows and imitates, made this much clearer by his silence."[16]

Unlike Polybius, however, Baudouin deliberately defined "pragmatic" history in what he saw as Roman terms, as history inextricably combined with law: "As Cicero writes to Atticus in Book 14, 'You, if you have anything pragmatic to report, write it down.' Here he calls anything that took place in the forum or the Senate pragmatic. So I believe that anything of this kind belongs to the writing of history. In addition, the

[15] Baudouin 1561a, 29; Wolf (ed.) 1579, I, 618: "Veteres appellarunt historiam πραγματικὴν, quae quod narrat, diligenter exponit, et sapienter utiliterque demonstrat, ut non solum eventa, sed et causas eorum, et cum consiliis facta describat. Talem ergo πραγματείαν esse eius universitatis, de qua loquor, partem praecipuam profiteor."

[16] Baudouin 1561a, 15–16; Wolf (ed.) 1579, I, 608–09: "Gravis profecto est et Romano scriptore digna haec praefatio: et historiam Romanam lecturo utilis atque necessaria cautio est. Sed quam tenuis tamen est haec historiae commendatio, si quid praeterea illius amplitudo et dignitas mereatur, consideremus. Quid igitur? Feret aequo animo Livius, si dicam Polybium, quem sequi et imitari solet, magis hoc indicasse silendo."

matters that are called in legal texts pragmatic constitutions or sanctions should also be included in history, so that it may be truly pragmatic, as it should be."[17] Baudouin simply transformed Cicero's demand for information about current legal events into the demand that scholars assemble information about past ones. True history must include detailed accounts of legislation. True legal scholarship must set each law into its context: "The so-called Corpus iuris that Justinian left to us was assembled from the whole vast range of Roman laws thrown up in the 1,300 years that separated Justinian from Romulus. Not only do they say that old, new, and middle jurisprudence differed from one another, but jurisprudence changed almost every year, and the condition of these laws is such, by law, that a later law invalidates an earlier one. What would happen then, if we do not use history to observe the order of times, and establish something like a chronology of the laws?"[18]

Baudouin's declaration that legal scholarship must become historical rested on his own practice. In a long series of

[17] Baudouin 1561a, 117; Wolf (ed.), 1579, I, 677: "Atque ut Cicero ad Atticum lib. XIIII [14.3.2]. Tu (inquit) si quid pragmaticum habes, scribito: pragmaticum vocans, quod fiebat in foro vel in Senatu: sic et quae sunt eius generis, ad historiae scriptionem omnino pertinere puto: ut et quae in libris legum appellantur pragmaticae constitutiones vel sanctiones, in eam referantur, quo magis sit, esse quae debet, historia πραγματική."

[18] Baudouin 1561a, 127–28; Wolf (ed.), 1579, I, 684: "Corpus illud Iuris (ut appellatur) quod Iustinianus nobis reliquit, conflatum est ex ea legum Romanarum varietate, quae annis mille et trecentis iactata est abs Romulo usque ad Iustinianum. Neque modo alia esse dicitur Iurisprudentia vetus, alia nova, alia media: sed et quotannis prope est mutata. harumque legum ea est conditio, ut etiam lex sit, posteriorem derogare priori. Quid igitur fieret, nisi si ex historia, temporum ordinem observemus, et aliquam veluti Chronologiam legum teneamus?"

books beginning early in the 1540s, he had elucidated the history of the Roman law and edited and explicated the early laws of Romulus, the Twelve Tables, and the laws made by Roman emperors – especially Constantine, to whose special role in making the empire Christian he devoted a book. Again and again he suggested that one could trace – as he put it in 1545 – "the history of our civil law, that is, its origins, growth, travails, and various fates."[19] Again and again he made clear that the those who threw together the Corpus Iuris "had twisted and perverted" the texts in it. They had done so that they would serve the current needs of the Empire, but had failed to

[19] Baudouin 1545, 30: "Videamus nunc tandem reliquam Iuris nostri civilis historiam, hoc est, eius originem, incrementum, iactationem, variaque fata: in quibus rursus deprehendemus admirabilem divinae providentiae rationem." Cf. also Baudouin 1542, Pii ro: "Post absolutum Pandectarum, prioris Codicis, Institutionum, et alterius Codicis opus, sensim rerum usu exigente emanarunt *nearai*, hoc est, Novellae constitutiones, propriae ac veluti privatae (ut testatur Agathias Graecus rerum Iustiniani scriptor) ipsius Iustiniani leges, quae veluti extremam Iuri Civili manum imposuerunt, quaeque in eo desiderari docuerat quotidiana experientia, sarcierunt, emendaruntque ea quae esse emendanda iudicabat ille gravissimus legum omnium censor et explorator usus. Fueruntque harum Iustiniani constitutionum plures scriptores, quod indicat ipsius Graecanicae phraseos diversitas subindeque varians stylus. Postea in unum volumen omnes congestae sunt. Quod etiam testatur Constantinus Harmenopulus . . . "; 1560a, 5: "Cum ergo posterior lex priori deroget, atque eam quoque abroget, valde est necesse legum tempora observare, et quosdam earum habere veluti Fastos, annales, diaria, praesertim cum versamur in iis quos Iustinianus collegit libris: qui quidem ita sunt conflati ex multiplici varietate Iuris novi et veteris, nulla ut initio magis in re laborandum nobis sit, quam ut discernamus quid prius, quid posterius sit. Atque hoc quidem illud est, quod in primis in Iustiniano nostro, eiusque voluminibus observandum est."

indicate what they had added and what was old.[20] Only a historical approach, one that dissected the *Corpus Iuris* and other ancient legal works into their components, could clarify the circumstances that had led emperors to make their decisions. Constantine, he noted, "used to hear his beloved Lactantius preach that the only author of brothels was Satan – so far from acceptable was it for a Christian ruler to permit them to exist." Yet he did not close the stews. This decision reflected the wider context in which he worked, the pressures exerted by the society in which even an emperor had to live: "the times were so given over to every sort of shamelessness that they could not immediately be recalled to productive activity and subjected to the strict discipline of chastity."[21] A modest man, Baudouin regularly insisted that he "was not writing a history of the

---

[20] Baudouin 1557b, 30: "Caeterum consarcinatores Pandectarum longe audacius interpolarunt quod describebant, ut ad id quod volebant, inflecterent atque detorquerent. Et vero hoc erat plerunque necesse, ut ius ederent, quo resp. tunc uti commode posset. Verum illud omnia interturbat, quod nullam adiiciant notam, qua discernamus, quid eorum sit, quid abs veteribus acceptum . . . "

[21] Baudouin 1556, 236–37: "Quid faceret? Publica lupanaria et Romanorum et Graecorum veteres leges tolerabant. At divinae non tolerant. Has profecto potius, quam illas, sequi pius castusque princeps debebat: praesertim cum videret, cuius intemperantiae non modo exemplum, sed etiam licentiam Romae dedisset libidinosus Maxentius. Sed ut Constantini hac in parte non excusem indulgentiam (neque enim quae vitiosa sunt, excusari debent) certe tam erant ea ad omnem impudicitiam proiecta tempora, ut statim ad meliorem frugem revocari, et casta disciplina arctius coerceri non facile possent.

Audiebat Constantinus suum Lactantium concionantem, lupanaria non alium habere autorem quam Satanam. Tantum abest ut a Christiano principe permitti recte possint. Sed non efficiebat, neque fortasse poterat, quaecunque volebat."

law" or even of Constantine, only a limited study of jurisprudence.[22] In fact, however, anyone who knew his work could see that his vision of history and law grew from his own work as a legal scholar. The historical approach to law established, for the first time, the principle that Bartholomäus Keckermann would state, more generally, half a century later: "Circumstances are to history what modes are to chant. For modes are like rules, that give order and direction to harmony, as Glareanus teaches." From Baudouin's point of view, the legal historians did even more than the rhetoricians had to formulate the discipline of contextual reading.[23]

Yet if Baudouin's legal expertise was a necessary condition of his accomplishments as a theorist of history, it was not sufficient. The standard account neatly explains why Baudouin and Bodin, both jurists, hoped to connect law with history, and why they saw history itself as the path to a reform of the state. But for the content of Baudouin's vision of history and the palette of methods he applied, as he made clear, to the careful and informed contemporary reader, he drew on other traditions as well. Again and again, Baudouin invoked with impressive eloquence a vision of history as a kind of world theater – a

---

[22] Baudouin 1545, 29; 1556, a 8 ro: "Etsi nunc non institui aut Constantini vitam conscribere, aut eius generis historiam aliquam edere: tamen ut id quod nunc instituo, planius intelligatur, breviter hic notabo nostri Legislatoris aetatem, genus, et cognationem ... "

[23] Keckermann 1614, II, 1314: "Circumstantiae id sunt in Historiis, quod in cantu modi. Modi enim sunt instar regulae, cuius ductu harmonia dirigitur, ut inter alios late docet Glareanus in Dodechordio: Ita in Historiis circumstantiae arg. veritatem Historicam et illustrant et confirmant, simulque efficiunt, ut certam ex Historiis utilitatem percipiamus."

spectacle that had lasted for centuries, and that every modern Christian must strive as hard to watch as ancient Christians had striven to avoid the Roman theater.[24] Here he drew, as he himself indicated, on Polybius and Diodorus Siculus – the Hellenistic and later Greek historians who had made a point of expanding the stage on which political history unrolled to the entire Mediterranean world and beyond.

In this case and others, Baudouin made clear that he drew not only on legal scholarship, but also on the classical scholarship of his time. Far to the north, in Rostock, David Chytraeus, classicist, theologian, and jurist, was also lecturing on history. In the broadsides that he had printed to advertise these, he made clear that he too saw the Greek historians as offering powerful guidance for modern life. Chytraeus culled what he called *gnomai*, sententious maxims, from Thucydides, and laid them out as rules that could offer guidance in the present as they had in the past: "Thucydides," he explained in 1562, "not only sets out many prominent examples of counsels and virtues and events, but also fits them to rules or γνῶμαι which are standards for action."[25] When Baudouin took Polybius as his model Greek historian, as Arnaldo Momigliano and Carlotta Dionisotti have taught us, he was not innovating, even within the confines of the learned world. Rather, he followed a tradition founded by

[24] Baudouin 1561a, 9–10; Wolf (ed.) 1579, I, 599–601.
[25] David Chytraeus, introductions to his Thucydides lectures, in Wolf (ed.) 1579, II, 546, 554: Book 1 (12 April, 1562): "non exempla tantummodo consiliorum et virtutum et eventuum multa et illustria integre exponuntur: verumetiam plerumque ad regulas seu γνώμας quae sunt normae actionum vitae accommodantur." Book 5 (5 December 1563) "…colloquium Meliorum et Atheniensium, in quo multae dulcissimae γνῶμαι et dignissimae memoria ponuntur."

Machiavelli's *Discourses* and established in academic practice at one of the most advanced centers of classical teaching in Europe, the Collège Royal in Paris, where Jean Strazel held public political lectures on Polybius.[26]

But Baudouin adopted much more than individual authors from the specialists on the ancient world. Though he did not bother quoting Cicero's description of history as *nuncia veritatis, testis temporum* and the rest, he did repeatedly depict Cicero and his contemporaries engaged in the practice of history. In fact, Baudouin drew from Cicero's letters something like the first history of historical scholarship in late Republican Rome.

> In *Ad Atticum,* book 16, he writes "I am burning with the desire for history. Your exhortation moves me deeply." And he did not only recognize Atticus as his master in history. He also consulted him regularly about Roman chronology and magistrates. He not only allowed Atticus to correct his books, but begged him to do so. And he gladly entered into precise discussion of many details – as when he discusses Fannius, Tuditanus, Carneades, and the Athenian embassy which came to Rome because of Oropus. And when he had heard the judgement of Atticus, who responded to questions like these, he cried out: "You have given me the perfect gift." And at the same time Cicero's brother Quintus consulted him in a similar way. "My brother Quintus (Cicero writes to Atticus) asks me to correct and publish his Annals." And Aemilius Probus also belonged to this seminar.[27]

---

[26] Dionisotti 1983.

[27] Baudouin 1561a, 66; Wolf (ed.) 1579, 1, 643: "Nam et libro decimo sexto ad Atticum, Historiae (inquit) studio ardeo. Incredibiliter enim me

By piecing together every reference to history in Cicero's works, Baudouin revealed that Cicero did more than praise the subject. He also practised it. Like the great twentieth-century Cambridge scholar Elizabeth Rawson, Baudouin saw Cicero as a proficient historian and antiquary in his own right, and reassembled testimonies from many sources to reveal the nature of his interests and methods.[28]

Baudouin also assembled fragments and quotations to recreate the scholarly practices of Cicero's friends and contemporaries. He knew from Cicero's *Brutus*, for example, that Atticus had compiled a great work on Roman history, the *Liber annalis*, which did not survive. Drawing on a second source, he argued that it had adumbrated his own vision of a unified law and history: "What Atticus accomplished in this area, I do not know, since his commentaries have perished. But Nepos says that that every law, every peace, every war, and every illustrious deed of the Roman people was set down, with its date, in the volume in which Atticus laid out all of

---

commovet cohortatio tua [16.13a (b).2]. Neque tamen non lubenter ipsum Atticum in historia suum veluti magistrum agnovit. Quam enim eum et saepe et lubenter consulit de temporibus Magistratibusque Romanorum? Quam suos ab eo libros castigari non iam dico patitur, sed petit et cupit? Quam diligenter etiam disputat, et curiose singula scrutatur? Vt cum de Fannio [16.13a (b).2], de Tuditano [13.6.4, 13.4.1], de Carneade et ea legatione Atheniensium, quae Romam venit Oropi causa, quaerit [12.23.2]. Denique ubi Attici talibus quaestionibus respondentis iudicium audiisset, exclamat, Habeo a te munus elaboratum [13.4.1]. Simul autem et hunc suum Fratrem Quintus simili ratione consulebat atque appellabat. Quintus Frater (inquit Marcus ad Atticum) me rogat, ut Annales suos emendem et edam [2.16.4]. Sed et huic collegio adiungebatur Aemylius Probus ... "

[28] Rawson 1972.

antiquity."[29] Here Baudouin worked at, or even ahead, of the cutting edge of classical philology. Though the early humanists had made a start at collecting the fragments of lost writers like the poet Ennius, their efforts remained modest in scale. In 1557, when Henri Estienne published the section of Ctesias's work on Persia preserved in the Byzantine *Library* of Photius, he remarked that "I had always had a special passion for Persian history, which led me to make a very accurate collection of everything related to it. Hence I collected everything that Greek and Latin writers said about under a single heading, as an aid to memory." But even the hyperenergetic Estienne found it too hard to assemble so much material, and cut his plan down to a collection of the fragments of Ctesias alone – only to abandon that when he found what he took to be the complete text in Photius.[30] Estienne would not produce the

---

[29] Baudouin 1561a, 117–18; Wolf (ed.) 1579, I, 677: "Quid olim praestiterit in hoc genere Atticus, nescio, quia eius commentarii interierant. Sed Cornelius Nepos ait nullam fuisse legem, neque pacem, neque bellum, neque rem illustrem populi Romani, quae non in eo volumine, quo Atticus omnem antiquitatem exposuit, suo tempore notata sit."

[30] Ctesias, ed. Henri Estienne (1557): "Quum igitur Persica historia nescio quomodo impensius quam alia delectarer ulla, accuratissime quae ad eam pertinebant omnia semper conquisivi: iis etiam quae de ea passim apud authores Graecos pariter atque Latinos leguntur, unum in locum, in memoriae subsidium, collectis. Quum autem res Persicas cum ab aliis, tum vero a Dinone et Ctesia memoriae mandatas fuisse, ex Strabone, Plutarcho, Athenaeo, et quibusdam aliis intellexissem, utrunque illorum scriptorum, aut saltem ex utroque aliquid consequi mihi semper optatissimum fuit. Sed quum timerem ne voti immodicus, ut quidam dixit, iudicarer: illius vela contrahens, meam, quae antea circa duos occupata erat, ad unum, videlicet ad Ctesiam, coepi restringere diligentiam. Qua quidem tantum effeci tandem, ut ex hoc authore non

first great fragment collection – an edition of early Roman poetry – until three years after Baudouin wrote. Carlo Sigonio and others were hard at work assembling the fragments of Cicero's *De republica* – not to mention the pseudo-Ciceronian *Consolatio* that Sigonio used his mastery of quotations and testimonia to forge.[31] Only in the 1570s would Antonio Riccobono compile the first full-scale collection of the fragments of lost Roman historians. Though he argued forcefully that critics must "gather into one place the lovely remains of the ancients, which have lain for so long, despoiled of rank in honor, in the most varied shadows," and then do their best to correct and explicate them, he did not argue that the evidence he collected about the work of Cato, Claudius Quadrigarius, and others shed a new light on the development of historical method or its modern practice.[32] Nicolaus Krag did not argue

plura equidem quam olim concupivissem, sed plura quam sperare mihi fas esse iam putarem, et ea etiam de quibus ne cogitaram quidem, nanciscerer. Etenim quum primo quidem περσικά eius integra in manus meas pervenire valde optavissem, mea postea sic ratio fuit, ut si vel qualescunque ex illis scriptis ἐκλογάς (quales ex nonnullis aliis authoribus, quorum libri sunt amissi, habebam) adipisci possem, praeclare mecum agi existimare deberem."

[31] See McCuaig 1989. For Baudouin's appreciation of Sigonio see 1561a, 111–12; Wolf (ed.) 1579, I, 673: "Equidem (cur enim dissimulem) nuper legebam perlubenter novos de antiquo iure civium Rom. et Italiae commentarios doctissimi hominis Caroli Sigonii, qui de historia Rom. praeclare meritus est."

[32] Riccobono 1579, 80: "Quibus omnibus malis illi mederi aliquantulum meo iudicio videntur, qui cum pulcherrimas veterum reliquias dignitatis atque honoris expertes diversissimis in tenebris diutius iacentes in unum redigunt, tum vero locos corruptos corrigunt, obscuros illustrant, et difficiles ita diligenter exponunt, ut maximum eis lumen afferant et

that the fragments of Nicolaus of Damascus (first century BCE) that he found in Stobaeus, which he edited and translated into Latin, could really fill the place of Nicolaus's lost universal history; nor did he add the other fragments he had found in Athenaeus and elsewhere.[33] This was a wise decision, as the fragments he published mostly came in fact not from Nicolaus's *Histories* but from a separate work on strange peoples. Baudouin's strenuous efforts to use and interpret the fragments he collected placed him at the forefront of philological research.[34]

ornamentum . . . Quamobrem mihi consilium accidit non modo aliquot historicorum, et praecipue Catonis, Quadrigarii, Sisennae, Sallustii, et Varronis, in hoc de historia commentario, quas potero, reliquias colligere, verum etiam pro viribus in ordinem redigere et aliquibus scholiis illustrare."

[33] Krag (ed.) (1593), 4: "Quorum [the Peripatetics] e numero est Nic. Damascenus haud postremus, qui ad exemplum Aristotelis ac Theophrasti huius generis scripsit libros octoginta καθολικῆς ἱστορίας, ut vocat, seu de moribus gentium universarum, plenos haud dubie bonae frugis et multiplicis doctrinae. Utinam extarent tantummodo, tum huius, tum istorum auctorum quos dixi, scripta, non esset ista eruditae doctrinae pars a cultoribus adeo deserta: sed inveniret complures tui similes vere nobiles, id est ad virtutis gloriam recta via grassantes, quorum animis efficacissimum sui amorem excitaret. Sed quia manca praeceptorum aliquatenus philosophia et historia huiusmodi politica destituimur, haud nullo in operaepretio studium ab iis occupari putandum, quibus ad curam est haec qualiacunque veterum Rerumpub. monumenta conservare. Quapropter quae istius Nic. Damasceni in collectaneis apud Stobaeum reperi, placuit descripta et seorsum excusa hoc tempore evulgare, ac quod ad Gnomas seu sententias proprie non pertineant, suo quasi auctori ex aliena possessione asserta restituere. Nam quae apud Athenaeum sunt, vel quae alia eo pertinentia observare licuerit, alias additurus."

[34] For the larger context see Most (ed.) 1997.

Baudouin's dialogue with this erudite tradition was not confined to the study of ancient historians, preserved or fragmentary. From the early fourteenth century onwards, a second kind of classical scholarship had grown up alongside the first – a scholarship concerned less with texts than with objects. Antiquaries from Petrarch to Poggio and beyond paced the dark, filthy streets of Rome, hemmed in by medieval arcades that projected from the house fronts and stumbling over animal carcasses, as they tried to establish the identity of monuments and buildings in the teeth of would-be helpful locals who assured them that every one was a bath. This new scholarship often stimulated fakery – but it also provoked some of its practitioners to new kinds of critical thought.[35] The principle of *historia magistra vitae* could lead humanists to deal with their sources in a strikingly careless way. The early-fifteenth-century scholar Poggio Bracciolini decided that Xenophon's idealized *Education of Cyrus* made a fine contribution to the library of Latin historiography. Worse still, he explained in the preface to his translation of the text, which he abridged and altered, that "I did not translate the individual words, the little aphorisms, the discussions that appear throughout, since I know that there are many things that can be eloquently said in Greek and that Latin scholars could not read without distaste. So I followed the history, omitting those things which did not detract from the truth and seemed hard to say in proper Latin."[36] Baudouin,

[35] See in general Weiss 1988; Herklotz 1999; Miller 2000; Miller 2005; and Stenhouse 2005.
[36] Princeton University Library (PUL) MS Kane 22, 1 vo: "Non autem verba singula, non sententiolas omnes, non collocutiones, quae quidem frequentius inseruntur, expressi: quippe qui sciam multa graece haud

who larded his legal histories with direct quotations from the sources, each supplied with a marginal source reference, would have been horrified by Poggio's easy decision to sacrifice precision in order to produce an attractive and instructive Latin text.

Yet Poggio showed a radically different attitude when he fought his way through brambles to read the inscription on the Pyramide of Cestius at Rome. Preening fastidiously, he praised himself in the best academic way, by noting the failures of his most distinguished predecessor: "I am all the more surprised, since the inscription is extant, that the learned Petrarch described this, in a letter, as the tomb of Remus. I believe that he followed popular opinion, and did not consider it important to examine the inscription, covered with brambles. In reading this, his successors have shown greater diligence, if less learning."[37] The antiquarians, with their passion for exact information about material objects and inscriptions, called for new levels of precision in both the work of research and the details of reporting. Flavio Biondo wrote with apparent modesty in the preface to his *Italy Illustrated* that he had only "hauled

---

infacunde dici: quae apud nos non absque fastidio legi a doctis possent: sed historiam sum secutus: ea quandoque omittens: que nec veritati rerum detraherent et concinne dici latine vix posse viderentur." Cf. Albanese 2003, 163.

[37] Poggio, *De varietate fortunae* I, in D'Onofrio 1989, 69: "Quo magis miror, integro adhuc epigrammate, doctissimum virum Franciscum Petrarcham in quadam sua epistola scribere, id esse sepulcrum Remi; credo, secutum vulgi opinionem, non magni fecisse epigramma perquirere, fruticetis contectum, in quo legendo, qui postmodum secuti sunt, minore cum doctrina maiorem diligentiam praebuerunt."

FIGURE 1. A Caesar in full medieval dress.

FIGURE 2. A Milanese courtly Suetonius. Caesar is depicted as a medieval knight, but the smaller images that surround his central figure indicate a new interest in such antiquities as the Vatican obelisk (top right). Legend held that Caesar's ashes were preserved in the metal ball at its top.

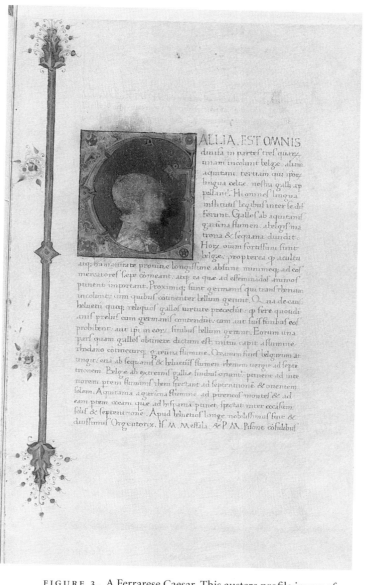

ALLIA. EST OMNIS diuisa in partes tres quarū unam incolunt belgæ, aliam aquitani, tertiam qui ipsorū lingua celtæ, nostra galli appellantur. Hi omnes lingua instituti legibus inter se differunt. Gallos ab aquitanis garūna flumen, a belgis matrona & sequana diuidit. Horū omnium fortissimi sunt belgæ, propterea q̃ a cultu atq; humanitate prouintiæ longissime absunt, minimeq; ad eos mercatores sepe cōmeant, atq; ea quæ ad effeminandos animos ptinent important. Proximiq; sunt germani qui trans rhenum incolunt, cum quibus cōtinenter bellum gerunt. Qua de causa heluetii quoq; reliquos gallos uirtute precedūt, q̃ fere quotidianis preliis cum germanis contendunt, cum aut suis finibus eos prohibent, aut ipsi in eorū finibus bellum gerunt. Eorum una pars quam gallos obtinere dictum est, initiū capit a flumine rhodano, cōtinetur, garūna flumine, Oceanum fine belgarum, attingit, et a sequanis & heluetiis flumen rhenum uergit ad septentrionem. Belgæ ab extremis galliæ finibus oriuntur, ptinent ad inferiorem prtem fluminis rheni, spectant ad septentrionē & orientem solem. Aquitania a garūna flumine ad pireneos montes & ad eam prtem ocean quæ ad hispaniā ptinet, spectat inter occasum solis & septentrionē. Apud heluetios longe nobilissimus fuit & ditissimus Orgentorix. Is M. Messala & P. M. Pisone cōsulibus

FIGURE 3. A Ferrarese Caesar. This austere profile image of Caesar gives a sense of what the erudite patricians of Leonello d'Este's court had in mind when they argued about the merits of ancient Roman leaders.

FIGURE 4. Caesar's bridge. This woodcut, from the Aldine edition of Caesar printed in 1513, represents a much discussed effort by the antiquary Giovanni Giocondo to reconstruct the sort of wooden bridge, two of which Caesar built to cross the Rhine.

FIGURE 5. The siege of Vxellodunum, as recreated by
Giocondo, with full details of the city's defenses and Caesar's
siege engines.

FIGURE 6. Caesar crosses the Rhine: in his 1575 edition of Caesar, the great architect and antiquary Andrea Palladio and his sons dramatically recreated many scenes of combat in three dimensions.

ashore some planks from so vast a shipwreck, planks which were floating on the surface of the water or nearly lost to view, rather than be required to account for the entire lost ship."[38] In fact, however, he was referring to a set-piece analysis that appeared within his chapter on Latium. After giving a thrilling account of how Leon Battista Alberti had tried, and failed, to raise one of the two Roman ships sunk in Lake Nemi, in the Alban Hills, Biondo analyzed the larchwood planks that Alberti did manage to bring up, layer by layer, describing the pitch, lead, bronze nails, clay, and chalk that had made them waterproof.[39] Between them, the preface and this dramatic section of the text highlighted the new kind of attentiveness, the new set of skills, that antiquaries could bring to the task of reading the material records of the past.

Through the fifteenth and sixteenth centuries, the new approaches of the antiquaries gradually infiltrated the manuscripts and editions of the ancient historians. Reading about Caesar, for example, became a new experience: educated sixteenth-century aristocrats whose ancestors had consumed vernacular accounts with splendid miniatures, which depicted Caesar as a medieval ruler, now read his own words in the handy pocket form of an Aldine octavo, made more vivid by the illustrations of the great antiquary Giovanni Giocondo. Baudouin drew on the work of Biondo's successors, the specialist

---

[38] Biondo 2005, 4–5: "Nec tamen ipsam omnem nominum mutationem temeraria et inani arrogantia indicare spoponderim: sed gratias mihi potius de perductis ad litus e tanto naufragio supernatantibus, parum autem apparentibus, tabulis haberi, quam de tota navi desiderata rationem a me exposci debere contenderim."

[39] Ibid., 190–93.

antiquaries of the sixteenth century, in his histories of Roman law. Giovanni Marliani supplied him, for example, with both a problematic text of the "laws of Romulus," from an inscription, and vivid images of the Lupa and other Roman antiquities.[40] Another set of antique materials and modern comments inspired him with a special interest. In the 1540s, the fragments of the Roman *fasti* – lists of the magistrates and triumphs, year by year, through Roman history – came to light in the forum. After a long debate between Michelangelo and Pirro Ligorio, Michelangelo received the contract to set them up and restore them on the Capitoline. Initially, the *fasti* inspired enthusiasm because they seemed to provide authoritative dates for all of Roman history. Gradually, however, Ligorio and the other scholars who examined and commented on the fragments – Ligorio himself, Antonio Agustín, Carlo Sigonio, Onofrio Panvinio – realized that they were not an official record but the work of Roman scholars – perhaps the Augustan antiquary Verrius Flaccus.[41]

Like all writers on the *ars historica*, Baudouin insisted that history had two eyes: chronology and geography. A bit of a sceptic as to the claims of the former subdiscipline to precision, he expressed no dismay whatsoever at the fact that "doctissimi homines" had conjectured that Verrius set up the *fasti*, "inscribed on a marble wall in a hemicycle," in the time of Augustus or Tiberius. Instead, he imagined what the "four great marble tables" had looked like, as the jurisconsults strolled

---

[40] Baudouin 1554, 6.
[41] See McCuaig 1989, Schreurs 2000, and Stenhouse 2005. Cf. also Gaston (ed.) 1988 and Coffin 2004. The older account by Mitchell in Ligorio 1963 retains considerable interest.

among them, listening to their city speak of its own past: "was this not a superb academy and civil school of jurisprudence and history?"[42] In the fifteenth century, the pioneering antiquary Cyriac of Ancona had boasted that he could speak with the dead. A little over a century later, Baudouin could imagine early Imperial Rome as a speaking city, a metropolis whose walls and inscriptions addressed and informed its visitors.[43] At the same time, he drew another, more important moral from these materials as well. Sigonio and Panvinio made clear that the *fasti* represented only a backbone for Roman history – and only a conjectural one at that, the work of scholars trying to recreate the city's early history. Even the material records of Roman history were the fallible products of scholarly industry.

---

[42] Baudouin 1561a, 131–32; Wolf (ed.) 1579, 1, 686–87: "...aliae Tabulae aliorum Fastorum, qui non, ut illi priores, singulorum dierum conditionem, sed annorum singulorum Magistratus notabant, tandem coniunctae fuerunt. quales eae fuerunt, quarum nuper fragmenta Romae reperta, et ruinis Capitolii rursus affixa sunt, historiaeque Romanae lucem maximam intulerunt: illas dico, quas Verrius Flaccus (sic enim doctissimi homines coniiciunt) temporibus Augusti vel Tiberii, in foro publicavit, marmoreo parieti incisas in hemicyclo, quemadmodum is scribit, qui vitas illustrium Grammaticorum olim scripsit, sive Plinius, sive Suetonius, sive eius aetatis alius fuerit. Erant eae quatuor Tabulae magnae, quae ab urbe condita usque ad Augusti obitum, quinam singulis annis Consules, Dictatores, Censores, Pontifices, quae bella, qui triumphi fuissent, breviter indicabant, et ad Hemicycli formam erectae atque compositae prostabant. Erat profecto res praeclara ... nonne excellens erat haec Academia et schola civilis, Iurisprudentiae et historiae?"

[43] Baudouin 1561a, 132; Wolf (ed.) 1579, 1, 687: "Certe forum Romanum non modo statuis refertum, sed et inscriptionibus et literis et tabulis, quae Iuris et antiquitatis indices essent, conspersum atque ornatum erat." For interesting discussions of the uses of antiquarianism in a later *ars historica* see Possevino 1597, 27 vo, 95 vo–96 ro.

"Historia integra" – the perfect history that Baudouin called for – had to combine the study of past historians with that of "things that talk"[44] – but it must integrate both of these strains of evidence with information derived from a vast range of other texts. Nepos had suggested that Cicero's letters to Atticus offered a very good history of his time.[45] Baudouin went much further. Cicero's letters, orations, and other works could offer a substantial "correction" to Roman history – so long as scholars bore in mind that the great orator sometimes lied or exaggerated. And this was only a beginning to the comprehensive research project that Baudouin called for. A century before, Biondo had remarked that he had had to compile his *Decades* by "laying out in order excerpts from the writings of many others, who set out to describe things other than these events" – that is, by systematic compilation of every relevant piece of information, whatever its source. Baudouin not only stated the same point, but also drew some of its wider implications:

> As Cicero's books could provide rich and ample matter for Roman history, so testimonies on many points that now escape us could be derived from other writers, even if they do not claim to be historians. Therefore I must rebuke the negligence of those who do not look in this direction when they are seeking histories. And why confine myself to

[44] See Daston (ed.) 2004; cf. Daston (ed.) 2000.
[45] Nepos *Atticus* 16.2–3: "quamquam eum praecipue dilexit Cicero, ut ne frater quidem ei Quintus carior fuerit aut familiarior. ei rei sunt indicio praeter eos libros, in quibus de eo facit mentionem, qui in vulgus sunt editi, sedecim volumina epistularum, ab consulatu eius usque ad extremum tempus ad Atticum missarum: quae qui legat, non multum desideret historiam contextam eorum temporum."

books and parchments? Everywhere ancient statues and paintings, and inscriptions carved on stone slabs and coins, and woven into tapestries and coverings, provide us with historical materials of every kind.[46]

Francis Bacon noted, in *The Advancement of Learning*, that "Letters of Affaires from such as Manage them, or are priuie to them, are of all others the best instructions for History, and to a diligent reader, the best Histories in themselves."[47] This comment caught the attention of a reader expert in the *ars historica*, Isaac Dorislaus, who energetically underlined it in his copy of the book.[48] Yet Bacon only reiterated what Baudouin had written, and he relegated the broad-gauged form of research that Baudouin placed at the center of history as useful only within narrow limits: "Antiquities, or Remnants

---

[46] Baudouin 1561a, 70–72; Wolf (ed.) 1579, 1, 645–47: "Dixit olim Cornelius Nepos, eum, qui legit Ciceronis epistolas ad Atticum, non multum desiderare historiam contextam eorum temporum . . . Neque vero ex epistolis modo, sed et ex Orationibus, et ex aliis Tullii commentariis praeclaram historiae Ro. emendationem repeti posse sentio. quanquam sit aliqua cautio adhibenda, ne protinus rem aestimemus ex iis, quae forte oratorie dixerit, ut foro et causae serviret . . . Vt autem ex Ciceronis libris dico amplissimam et uberrimam historiae materiam repeti posse: sic etiam ex aliorum scriptorum, etsi historicos se esse non profiteantur, commentariis excerpi multarum maximarum rerum testimonia possunt, quae alioqui nos fugiunt. Itaque non possum non eorum reprehendere negligentiam, qui cum historias requirunt, eo non respiciunt. Quid de libris aut chartis loquor? Nonne et veteres statuae ac picturae, et lapidibus aut nummis insculptae inscriptiones, et denique quae aulaeis vel peristromatibus intexta sunt, historiae argumentum undique nobis suppeditant?"

[47] Bacon 1605, Bk II, 17 ro.

[48] Cambridge University Library LE 7.45; see Maccioni and Mostert (1984), 431–33.

of History, are, as was saide, *tanquam Tabula Naufragii*: when industrious persons, by an exact and scrupulous diligence and obseruation, out of Monuments, Names, Wordes, Prouerbes, Traditions, Priuate Recordes, and Euidences, Fragments of stories, Passages of Bookes, that concerne not storie, and the like, doe saue and recouer somewhat from the deluge of time."[49] If some amateurs of the ancients believed that they offered full and perfect histories of their world, Baudouin drew a very different lesson from the scholarship of his time. Ancient history could not be found in the text of any writer. Rather, modern scholars must reconstruct it, using every possible source of evidence, textual as well as material. Baudouin's *ars historica*, then, reflected not simply a development of the legal tradition, but a fusion of legal with philological and antiquarian scholarship and a new approach to written sources. In theory as in practice, Baudouin defined history as an interdisciplinary task that required not only artistic composition, but systematic assembly and interpretation of the evidence.

At times, Baudouin drew attention to the fact that some ancient historians had already raised the problem of trying to determine which earlier sources to believe. In particular, his favorite Hellenistic and Imperial historians, given their cosmopolitan interests, had done so: "I remember that Polybius wrote that the largest and hardest part of the historian's task is making correct judgments about historical writers. I refer not to their language, but to their testimony and the credibility it bears, if any."[50] Drawing on the traditional rules of

---

[49] Bacon 1605, II.2.3, 11 ro.

[50] Baudouin 1561a, 51; Wolf (ed.) 1579, I, 632: "Memini Polybium scripsisse maximam et difficillimam partem historici operis esse, recte et sapienter

jurisprudence and rhetoric, Baudouin noted that the wise judge always looked for a reliable witness – someone whose status and integrity endowed what he said with authority.[51] As he put it in another context, "it is an ancient rule that one should believe witnesses, not witnessings (*testibus, non testimoniis*)."[52] But he knew that this principle was inadequate, since no witness always told the truth. As he wrote, ironically quoting the *Scriptores Historiae Augustae* – a set of imperial biographies ascribed to six authors, but now known to be the work of a late fourth-century forger – "When Flavius Vopiscus set out to write a history, he did not blush to confess that there is no writer of history who has not told at least one lie. But he certainly did not think that this fact should make us reject the writings of all of them, and he did not pronounce all histories to be what Iulius Capitolinus terms 'mythical histories.'"[53] How then to sort the reliable from the unreliable?

iudicare de scriptoribus historicis. De eorum oratione non loquitur, sed de testimonio et ea, qua digni sunt, fide."

[51] Baudouin 1561a, 50–51; Wolf (ed.) 1579, I, 632.

[52] HAB MS 11.20 Aug. fol. 39 ro: "Regula est vetus testibus non testimoniis credendum esse: idest videndum non tam quid quave ratione dicatur, quam quis testetur, an sit bonae malaeque fidei, rei de qua testatur peritus vel imperitus." Cf. on this point Serjeantson 1999 and 2005.

[53] Baudouin 1561a, 44; Wolf (ed.) 1579, I, 628: "Non erubuit olim Flavius Vopiscus, cum historiam alioqui scribere institueret, confiteri, nullum historae scriptorem esse, qui non sit aliquid mentitus [*Scriptores Historiae Augustae* (*SHA*) *Div. Aur.* 2.1]. Sed minime nos abduci propterea ab omnium scriptis debere iudicavit: neque omnes historias, Iulii Capitolini verbo, pronunciavit esse mythistorias [*SHA Quad. tyr.* 1.2: 'Marius Maximus, homo omnium verbosissimus, qui et mythistoricis se voluminibus implicavit.']."

The humanists of the fifteenth century had already worried about these issues. Leonardo Bruni preferred to follow – and rewrite – a single source in his histories of Florence and of Rome's wars with Carthage and the Goths. Though he noted that the extant writers on Roman history, Polybius and Livy, had drawn on divergent sources no longer extant, he did not make a systematic effort to compare and assess the information they offered. Only when he confronted a particularly controversial problem – like the question of the origins of Florence, or that of whether Totila had really destroyed the city – did he take time to lay out the evidence and arrive at a formal solution.[54] Poggio roused himself to take an interest in the assessment of sources when, in the course of a lively debate over the merits of Scipio and Caesar, his opponent, Guarino of Verona, attacked him for failing to take Greek writers into account. Poggio retorted that the Latin ones deserved more credence, and found an elegant, characteristically Florentine way to criticize his enemy for failing to examine all of them: "Guarino seems not to have read the passages in which Cicero gave his true and frank view of Caesar. What happened to him is what happens to careless or tricky merchants. After they have read the one page of their account books where the debtors are recorded, they hide the next, which contains their creditors. This is the origin of the proverb 'Turn over the next page.'"[55]

---

[54] See esp. Phillips 1979, Cabrini 1990, and Ianziti 1998 and 2000, which substantially revise the picture given in the classic study by Santini 1910. Cf. also Fryde 1983. On early discussions of the nature of history see more generally Grafton 1999.

[55] Poggio, "Defensio," in Canfora 2001, 146: "Nam, quid Cicero de eo vere et ex animo senserit, non videtur legisse, cui evenit quod neglegentibus

Lorenzo Valla, as Carlo Ginzburg has shown, drew on the techniques of classical rhetoric, which included training in the assessment of documentary and narrative evidence, in his attack on the *Donation of Constantine*.[56] In his commentary on Quintilian's handbook of rhetoric, he made clear that ancient historians, like witnesses in court, were fallible. Like Baudouin, Valla cited Flavius Vopiscus on the fallibility of historians. But he also piled up evidence to show that Livy himself had repeated incredible stories and made basic mistakes.[57]

None of the best-known fifteenth-century scholars, however, drew up a full set of rules for the assessment of older sources. Baudouin, by contrast, offered three distinct solutions to this problem, each of which drew on a particular scholarly tradition and set of practices. First he took aim at one particular target – a very revealing one: "As to the fact that some years ago, a certain monk named Annius published fragments ascribed to Berosus, I am surprised that he was able to fool so many so easily." In 1498, as Baudouin and everyone else knew, the Dominican Giovanni Nanni of Viterbo, Annius in Latin, had published a magnificent book. In it, twenty-four interlocking histories of ancient kingdoms appeared, ascribed to authors – mostly ones whose works were indirectly known, but thought to be lost: the Chaldean Berosus, the Egyptian

aut captiosis solet mercatoribus, qui, cum unam paginam in libris rationum suarum, in qua debitores conscripti sunt, legerint, reliquam, quae continet creditores, occultant: ex quo proverbium est exortum: 'aliam paginam evolve.' "

[56] Ginzburg 1999; cf. Camporeale 1996, and for the larger story see especially Setz 1975, Webb 1981, Levine 1987, Black 1995, Regoliosi 1995b, Fubini 1996, Delph 1996, Kablitz 2001, Hiatt 2004.

[57] Valla 1981, 52–54.

Manetho, the Persian Metasthenes, the Romans Fabius Pictor, Cato and Propertius (whose work, exceptionally, was genuine). Nanni embedded these texts, printed in a large and gothic type reminiscent of the Bible, in a massive commentary. Here he argued that the ancient kingdoms had appointed priests to keep and oversee their archives. Their accounts, vested with "publica et probata fides," deserved belief, while those of individual Greeks like Herodotus did not. Nanni drew his notions about how these writers worked, and about why they should be believed, mostly from the Jewish historian Josephus, who had cited them at length.[58] As Baudouin explained, Josephus "claimed that Berosus's work was not fabulous, since it has much in common with Jewish history, and agrees with the ancient archives of the Phoenicians."[59] Baudouin found it easy to reject Annius's work, since, as he noted, it contained many

[58] See most recently Stephens 1989, Rowland 1998, Curran 1998/9; and Fubini 2003.

[59] Baudouin 1561a, 48–49; Wolf (ed.) 1579, I, 630–31: "Sed quae superioribus annis, Annius quidam monachus protulit fragmenta Beroso inscripta, miror tam facile multis etiam doctis imponere potuisse. Berosum Chaldaeum, qui fuit sacerdos Beli (ut ait Tatianus) tempore Alexandri, saepe meritoque laudari a veteribus scio: quem quidem Iosephus libro 1. contra Apionem, narrat descripsisse res Babylonicas abs Diluvio usque ad Iudaeorum in Babyloniam abductorum captivitatem: asseritque eius non esse fabulosam historiam, quae et cum Iudaica historia habeat multa communia, et cum antiquissimis Phoenicum Archivis consentiat, et quam comprobari ait Tatianus ex Iubae Regis historia de Assyriis. Sed tanto magis doleo, cum illius commentarios intercidisse, tum vero eorum loco adulterinas quasdam rapsodias suppositas esse. Nam etsi in iis agnoscam nonnulla, quae notha non esse ex Iosepho intelligo: tamen plura sunt supposititia, quae alioqui abs Iosepho non fuissent praeterita: quaedam etiam in illa farragine video esse praeterita, quae Iosephus ex Beroso recitat. Itaque in lectione adhibere oportet iudicium et delectum:

100

inventions not found in Josephus and omitted much that Josephus included in his quotations. For one thing, Josephus noted
that Berosus had written three books, while the Annian wrote
five; for another, Josephus offered little support for such central
pillars of Annius's views as the theory that Viterbo, founded by
Osiris, had been the center of ancient civilization. In doing so
he joined a number of other critics who, in the mid-1550s, tried
to drive Annian bad money from the historical marketplace –
scholars as varied as the Portuguese historian Gaspar Barreiros,
the Spanish Dominican Melchior Cano, and the Flemish polymath Goropius Becanus, who demolished Annius's forgeries
to make room for his own theory that the Dutch had been the
inhabitants of the garden of Eden. Even before these men deconstructed Annius's edifice stone by stone, moreover, Pietro
Crinito, Juan Luis Vives, and Beatus Rhenanus had proclaimed
his texts forgeries.[60] Why then did Baudouin train his guns on
so easy a target?

The answer is clear. When Annius argued that Berosus and his friends deserved credibility, he did more than describe them, as Josephus had, as priests with access to ancient
records. He elevated their supposed status as public "notaries"
and priests to the status of formal criteria for credibility. Only
those historians who met this standard, he argued, deserved
trust. As a good Dominican – or at least a well-trained bad Dominican – Annius was steeped in formal theology, and he drew
on his training to offer the first formal principles of historical

ut neque confuse (quod quidem faciunt) vera cum falsis repudiemus:
neque rursus temere (quod hac aetate plures illius Berosi lectores
fecerunt) falsa cum veris complectamur."
[60] See Grafton 1991.

criticism ever elaborated in print. For a century to come, anyone who hoped to formulate rules for assessing historical *fides* had to come to terms with these influential precedents.

Annius's approach reflected not only the personal prejudices of an opponent of the new Greek scholarship of the humanists, but also the wider Roman environment in which he operated. Annius worked in the papal Curia – a court, and one linked to many satellite courts in the palaces of cardinals and ambassadors. In this environment, as in Naples or Ferrara, radical hypotheses could induce a patron to swing his ear trumpet in the direction of their creator. More particularly, Annius enjoyed the patronage of the powerful Spanish Cardinal Carvajal – a grandee in search of an ancient pedigree as glorious as Spain's new imperial claims. This fact helps to explain why he folded Spain, at the last moment, into his history, and traced the Catholic kings' genealogy back to Isis and Osiris.

Another influential humanist, Giulio Pomponio Leto, also worked for Carvajal. And in the same years in which Nanni devised and printed his *Antiquities*, Leto offered his students – presumably the advanced ones – what may have been the first formal lectures on the art of history. Copies of Sallust now in the Vatican library and the Pierpont Morgan Library, New York, contain formal notes, by both Leto and one of his students. These show that Leto too took an interest in the credibility of historians. He told his students that in writing both history and biography, "truth is more important than eloquence." Like Baudouin he recommended writers like Suetonius, Iulius Capitolinus and Elius Lampridius (mostly the forged *Scriptores historiae Augustae*), who "speak more truly than eloquently."[61] When Leto discussed such vexed questions as the origins of Rome, he drew on the same sources that Annius did, such as the work of Dionysius of Halicarnassus, studded with antiquarian detail and recently translated into Latin. Leto stated that some problems – like that of the date of Rome's founding – were very difficult, since ancient authorities disagreed, as his Greek texts made clear.[62] As he reflected when discussing the question of who first settled Italy, "who can make a positive assertion about so ancient an event?"[63]

---

[61] BAV, Inc. Ross. 441, [VI vo]: "*Veritas in historia queritur. IN scribenda historia et potissimum vitis clarorum virorum veritas magis quam eloquentia requiritur ut in Mario Maxumo: Suetonio Tranquillo: Fabio Marcellino Gargulio Martiale, Iulio Capitolino, Helio Lampridio hi omnes magis vere quam diserte locuntur:- Historia non ostentationi sed fidei veritatique componitur: nec debet egredi veritatem ut cecilius ait et honeste Factis brevitas Sufficit: In historia requiritur Brevitas Lux Suavitas Splendorque et Sublimitas in narrando.*" On Leto and his teaching of the *ars historica* see the splendid study of Osmond 2003.

[62] BAV, Inc. Ross. 441, C vo: "*CONDITA EST VRBS ROMA* ut M. Porcius Cato Diligentissime scribit Ante XI Kal. Mai. Anno Quadringentesimo XXXIII post res Troianas: Polybius anno ii° viie olympiadis. Heratosthenes anno primo vii olymp: L. Cincius Anno iiii XII olymp. Timeus Siculus scribit conditam Romam xxxviii anno ante primam olympiada et eodem Anno edificatam fuisse Carthaginem alii iii° anno vi olymp. tradunt Initium iaciendi fundamenta fuisse inter [primam et crossed out] secundam et tertiam Horam diei ex observatione T. Aruntii ma*the*matici qui collegit etiam Anno iii secund. olymp. mense decembr. pr. Kal. Ianuarii Hora iii diei Iliam compressam a marte et peperisse ante XI Kal. Octobr. post solis ortum. Romulum et Remum [Dionysius of Halicarnassus *Roman Antiquities* 1.74]."

[63] BAV, Ross. Inc. 441, F ro: "De re tam vetusta quis adfirmare potest: cum et arcades ferantur ante troianos venisse et palatium incoluisse [cf. Dionysius of Halicarnasses *Roman Antiquities* 1.45]."

Both Nanni and Leto combined philological with antiquarian methods. Nanni wielded not only a wide range of texts to support his history of the ancient world, but also a marble frieze, which he claimed Osiris had left to record his founding of Viterbo – the first time that actual material evidence was cited in a published work of history.[64] Leto was the dominant expert in his day on Roman antiquities, and offered expert patter on every site as he led visitors through the city. Nanni famously decided, drawing on Genesis 6, that all men before the Flood had been giants – a view that had immense influence, and that explains, among much else, why Rabelais gave his characters such great stature. Leto also found ancient giants fascinating – so much so that when he found the "immense bones" on the acropolis at Pozzuoli, he wrote a verse inscription to them, which identified them as those of one of the giants who piled Pelion on Ossa in their assault on Olympus.[65] The point here is simple: the *ars historica* advocated, among other things, conscious and systematic efforts to discriminate between historical sources. This part of Baudouin's enterprise had its roots not in the world of learned jurists but in that of courtly scholars and antiquaries at Rome, half a century earlier. One point emerges with special clarity. It was no accident that Angelo Decembrio – whose Ferrarese friends also studied texts and objects with equal passion – could stage a scene in which Leonello d'Este deconstructed an ancient historian. These court environments proved an ecological niche in which a new, critical history could take shape in practice and even in theory, long before

[64] The fullest study of this episode is Curran 1998–99.
[65] Pisano 2003, especially 28–29.

humanists and lawyers began their slow courtship. Baudouin's call for a cosmopolitan history was genuinely cosmopolitan in its sources.

A second set of practices and traditions – one quite distant from the High Renaissance Rome of Annius and Leto – mattered even more to Baudouin and his fellows. In the *Prolegomena*, Baudouin made clear more than once that what he called *historia integra* had to take in far more than battles and politics. It must describe and analyze the history of the church, and in doing so it must offer more than lists of popes, prelates and heresies. Many humanists agreed. Even when they read pagan historians, they sometimes found ecclesiastical lessons in what now seem strikingly secular passages. Thucydides, in his description of the revolution in Corcyra, explained that language itself degenerated under the impact of civil war: "The received value of names imposed for signification of things, was changed into arbitrary. For inconsiderate boldness was counted true-hearted manliness: provident deliberation, a handsome fear: modesty, the cloak of cowardice: to be wise in every thing, to be lazy in every thing. A furious suddenness was reputed a point of valour" (3.82.4, tr. Thomas Hobbes). Lorenzo Valla, who translated Thucydides into Latin, felt an immediate shock of recognition when he contemplated this passage: "All this neatly fits the corruption of our times as well."[66] The Lutheran Chytraeus made clear what Valla probably also had in mind: Thucydides's "very learned description of the revolution at Corcyra shows the clear image of our modern

---

[66] Vat. lat. 1801, 66 vo: "Pulchre et ad nostri temporis corruptelam omnia hec congruunt."

revolutions and internal struggles in the church. In these, many fight with words about the true nature of heavenly doctrine and the health of the church – but in fact they are fighting about their private hatreds and interests, and about primacy."[67]

But Baudouin had more than analogies in mind. In his view, true history must describe the "ceremonies, discipline, order and governance of the church," century by century: must recreate the church, in each period, as it had really been. Over the years, Baudouin had made clear in passing that he knew that the explicit citation of documents – a central practice of his own work on Constantine – had its roots in the practices of Eusebius and the traditions of Christian historiography.[68] More important still, he identified church history as a special, central field of research and insisted that secular historians need to master it (as ecclesiastical historians, in his view, needed

---

[67] Chytraeus in Wolf (ed.) 1579, II, 551: "Tertius locus est eruditissima descriptio seditionis Corcyreae, expressam imaginem referens praesentium in Ecclesia seditionum et certaminum intestinorum, in quibus, verbis quidem de veritate coelestis doctrinae et salute Ecclesiae, sed re ipsa de privatis odiis ac commodis et primatu multi dimicant."

[68] Baudouin 1556a, 16: "Si quis illa quae dixi Constantini edicta requirat, quibus et populum Christianum libertate donat, et ad veri Dei purum cultum invitat: extant apud Eusebium, multis illa verbis tam religiose descripta, ut Ecclesiasticae conciones esse videantur. Quibus adiungi etiam poterunt, eiusdem Principis ad regem Persarum literae pro Christianis deprecatrices." For the connection between legal and ecclesiastical history in Baudouin's work see also 1557a, 17: "Hanc eo nunc historiam totam describere non institui: Sed interea dum instituitur integra descriptio historiae Ecclesiasticae, facio non invitus, ut eam nunc partem attingam, quae ad Iuris Ro. memoriam propius accedit: et veterum Imperatorum usque ad Constantinum leges, vel privilegia potius, de Christianis continet."

to master secular history).[69] His own specialized studies on Constantine and his edition of Optatus had established him as an expert in the field. In the *Prolegomena* Baudouin recalled, almost in passing, that he had served as a consultant to a major contemporary enterprise in this field, though with characteristic modesty he played down his own role: "I remember that when a group of five men at Magdeburg, some years ago, had undertaken to compose a history of the church, they asked my advice, and I explained my views on that matter in a long letter. But it is much easier to say what needs to be done, than to do it."[70]

The enterprise Baudouin referred to – the Magdeburg Centuries – began to take shape early in the 1550s, when the South Slav Matthias Flacius Illyricus began to rally support for a Protestant church history. He collected a vast amount of information himself, so ardently that librarians throughout Europe came to fear the *culter Flacianus* ("Flacian razor") with which he supposedly slit the heretical texts and liturgies of the Middle Ages, the sources and ancestors of Protestantism, from

---

[69] Baudouin 1561a, 30; Wolf (ed.) 1579, I, 618: "Ac nescio quomodo acciderit, ut quemadmodum, qui civilem historiam susceperunt, neglexerunt Ecclesiasticam: sic qui huic se dediderunt, illam praeterierunt, cum haec tamen divisio utramque prope corrumpat."

[70] Baudouin 1561a, 109; Wolf (ed.) 1579, I, 671–72: "Non minor eius historiae pars est posita in quaestionibus inter ipsos Christianos agitatis de ceremoniis, disciplina, ordine, formaque gubernationis Ecclesiasticae ... Memini, cum superioribus annis vviri Magdeburgenses historiae Ecclesiasticae descriptionem suscepissent, meumque consilium expetiissent, longiori me ad eos epistola, quid ea tota de re sentirem, exposuisse. Sed dicere quid facto sit opus, multo, quam id facere, est facilius."

their bindings. And he wrote to friends and acquaintances, urging them to join him. A lively discussion ensued, which focused on the form and method of the projected history. Flacius emphasized that it must show "not only what sort of doctrines existed in the church in individual centuries, but also what sort of ceremonies and liturgies – though briefly – for these things are all organically connected."[71] But he and his correspondents paid even more attention to the problems of gathering material. A history of the ancient church must necessarily rest on ancient sources – many of them apocryphal or polemical or otherwise problematic; a historian of the church necessarily worked as a critical reader both of other historians and of other texts. These had been the standards of ecclesiastical history, in fact, for millennia, ever since Eusebius, emulating Josephus, compiled his own history of the early church and his life of Constantine. He studded both with long extracts from primary sources, quoted in their own words, and set out not only to tell the particular stories of saints and martyrs, but also to give his readers a sense of the condition of the church in past times.[72]

[71] Flacius to Philo Lotharius, 9 September 1555, Österreichische Nationalbibliothek MS 9737b 14 vo–15 ro (holograph): "Scribis cerimonialia et cantiones Ecclesiasticas nihil ad nos. Nos vero omnino cupimus ostendere non tantum qualis doctrina singulis seculis in Ecclesia fuerit sed etiam quales cerimoniae et cantiones, tametsi breviter, nam illa omnia inter sese coherent connexaque sunt. Quare ex istis omnibus nos aliqua sumere necesse erit, si vel [MS vel vel] nos scire vel aliis indicare qualis quoque tempore Ecclesiae status fuerit oportet. Optarim vero et ego esse qui ex professo historias Martyrum, item ceremonias ac cantiones Ecclesiasticas insertis etiam prolixe ipsis precibus cantilenis ac rubricis exponere vellent."

[72] See Momigliano 1963 and Grafton and Williams 2006.

Baudouin did more for this project than he admitted. He offered both advice and criticism, and the "long letter" he referred to in his *Prolegomena* mutated, in the hands of Flacius and his collaborators, into standing instructions for the critical use of sources. Greg Lyon has elegantly traced these connections in a recent article.[73] Baudouin made an appropriate consultant for the project, moreover, because he had dedicated himself to ecclesiastical history throughout his career. As early as 1545, in his first effort at a history of the Roman law, Baudouin made clear that he knew the literature of ecclesiastical history – and that much of it, like much of legal literature, had to be re-constructed from citations in surviving compendia: "What remains to us today," he asked, "of all those ecclesiastical writers

---

[73] Compare, for example, a passage from Baudouin's letter to the Kollegium in Magdeburg, 13 June 1556, HAB Cod. Guelf. 11.20, 137–42 (holograph): "Nam quid olim factum sit, non modo incerta plerumque est divinatio, sed etiam est obscura, et non raro nulla memoria. Cumque veterum scriptorum veluti consignata testimonia legerem, cogitabam quid Prudentes de testibus et eorum fide olim responderint. Testibus (inquiunt) non testimoniis credendum esse: perpendendam quoque esse fidem testimonii, quod integrae frontis homo dixerit" with the corresponding passage in the "Regulae Balduini" that the Magdeburgers boiled down from it, ibid.: "Regulae: V. Testes igitur factorum gestarumque rerum expendendi sunt, ut scire possimus quatenus eis fides haberi debeat, aut non.

VI. Regula est vetus Testibus non testimoniis credendum esse: idest videndum non tam quid quave ratione dicatur, quam quis testetur, an sit bonae malaeque fidei, rei de qua testatur peritus vel imperitus etc.

VII. perpendenda quoque est fides testimonii, quod integrae frontis homo dixerit, quod et in eo error hallucinatiove esse potest, ut infra 19 prolixius dicetur." See Lyon 2005.

that Eusebius and Jerome cite?"[74] His own work as a scholar concentrated at least as much on the history of the church as on civil law. In his study of Constantine, for example, he elaborately reconstructed not only what the emperor did for the church, but also such complex and controversial chapters as the careers of Donatus and Arius. Both here and in his pioneering edition of Optatus, Baudouin revealed deep knowledge of the late antique Mediterranean world and the development of the Christian church within it. He knew that the African church had played a particular and vital role in the history of Christian culture and practice. Baudouin cited numismatic and epigraphic evidence, as well as texts. But he took care to indicate that he was applying antiquarian methods to a separate enterprise. The ecclesiastical historian Sozomen noted that Constantine had eliminated crucifixion, to honor the Christian Cross. "If I were writing antiquities," Baudouin remarked, "I would say (what many perhaps do not know) what the form of the cross was, and what sort of punishment the Romans imposed with it. But at the moment I am moving quickly in another direction."[75] The moral was clear. Baudouin's massive works on imperial legislation and the church were not legal

---

[74] Baudouin 1545, 84: "Quid hodie nobis superest ex tot ecclesiasticis scriptoribus, qui commemorantur ab Eusebio et Hieronymo?"

[75] Baudouin 1556, 350–51: "Constantini leges et iudicia de criminibus missa faciam, si illud addidero, quod Sozomenus scriptor Ecclesiasticae historiae commemorat: illum, cum de poenis ageretur, lege lata sustulisse vetus supplicium crucis. Existimavit enim, propter honorem crucis Dominicae et Christianae, tale animadversionis genus in usu amplius esse non debere. Si antiquitates scriberem, dicerem (quod multi fortassis ignorant) qualis forma crucis olim fuerit, et quale hoc supplicium apud Romanos. Verum nunc alio propero."

scholarship solely, but novel a fusion of legal with ecclesiastical history. Their contents and their form came from both traditions.

Ecclesiastical history, as practised from late antiquity through the Byzantine and Western Middle Ages, was in many ways the richest form of historiography: the one that paid the most attention and gave the most space to documentation, that covered the widest range of topics, and that used the evidence not only to establish the order of events, but also to recreate past social and cultural conditions. This is what Campanella had in mind when he wished that some bold scholar would produce "a Baronio for the whole world, and not just for Christianity."[76] Christian humanists and Protestant Reformers reconfigured the history of the church as a story of decline. Some of them, like Luther, admired Constantine as a model of the engaged Christian ruler. Others, like Thomas Müntzer, condemned him, and took Eusebius's stories of persecution as the model for the church in its pure state. Catholics, by contrast, defended Constantine and his successors. As churches formed and controversies erupted over doctrine, liturgy, and institutions, ecclesiastical history became a highly popular field. Editions of Eusebius and other older writers multiplied.[77] In the middle of the sixteenth century, the Marian exile and the concentration of militant Protestants in Switzerland made Zurich and other cities into laboratories of martyrology. The heavily documented, if sometimes uncritical, form of historical writing

---

[76] Campanella 1954, 1254: "Utinam quis Baronius fiat mundi, et non Christianae solius nationis!"

[77] See in general Ditchfield 1995, Backus 2003, Benz 2003, and for the related field of hagiography Frazier 2005.

practised by John Foxe and many others was clearly a branch from the great tree Eusebius had planted.[78] It was only natural that these traditions and developments – especially the massive team project in Magdeburg, the first expensive, grant-supported historical enterprise in modern times, and one that provoked acid criticism from Flacius's enemies in Wittenberg – played a central role in the creation of the *ars historica*.

Baudouin also urged historians to draw on a third form of inquiry and a third set of sources. In long and eloquent passages on the wealth of historical sources still available, he urged his contemporaries not to turn up their fastidious humanist noses at histories of medieval European nations or of the contemporary Turks. Indeed, he pointed out, many archives – like those in Paris and in the Vatican – offered rich possibilities for future research. Much that now seemed lost, moreover, could be recovered by sufficiently imaginative research in these remains of barbarian tradition.

> What happened to the Germans must have happened to many peoples. Tacitus says that the ancient Germans did not know the secrets of letters, but used ancient songs, and this was their one form of public memory and annals ... Eginhard – clearly a good witness for the point in question – remarks of his Charlemagne: "He wrote down and memorized the barbarous and ancient verses in which the acts and wars of the ancient kings were sung." I will give another example, and one no less noble. In the new,

---

[78] The fullest source of information on Foxe's methods and their ongoing analysis by scholars connected to the British Academy John Foxe project is to be found on the World Wide Web at http://www.hrionline.ac.uk/foxe/foxe_project/index.html.

that is, newly discovered islands of the West Indies, there are said to be men who are illiterate, and who yet adore letters as if they were gods. When they heard that our fellow Christians there could converse with one another through letters, while at a distance, and understand one another, they worshipped the sealed letters, in which they said some sort of divine spirit must be enclosed, that reported the message. Those men, for all their illiteracy, have conserved in memory the history of their people's past for many centuries, partly with certain arbitrary symbols, as the Egyptians did with hieroglyphs; partly with their songs, which they teach one another, and sing in their choruses; and they call these choruses *areytos*. And now I understand that those of us who live there have recorded in writing histories derived from these songs.[79]

---

[79] Baudouin 1561a, 73–74; Wolf (ed.) 1579, I, 648–49: "Quid dicam, multos populos scribi noluisse multa, quae fideli memoriae cuiusque mandare et veluti imprimere volebant? Quid dicam, carminibus tantum, quae ediscerentur, et cantionibus quae iactarentur, vulgata diu fuisse, quae postea tandem literis consecrata sunt? . . . Verum etsi obliviosae et mutae posteritatis silentio sepulta multa perierint, tamen non dubito pleraque in literas esse relata: et quod Germanis (ut de aliis nunc non loquar) olim accidit, multis populis accidisse. Corn. Tacitus ait [*Germ.* 2, 3]: veteres Germanos ignorasse quidem secreta literarum: sed antiquis carminibus usos esse, fuisseque hoc unum apud eos memoriae et annalium genus. Vnde et lib. II [*An.* 2, 88, 4] loquens de Arminio: Canitur (inquit) adhuc barbaras apud gentes, Graecorum annalibus ignotus. Quid igitur tandem? Eginhardus, bonus profecto eius rei, quam dicere nunc volo, testis, de suo Carolo Magno [*Vita Karoli Magni* 29]: Barbara (inquit) et antiquissima carmina, quibus veterum regum actus et bellica canebantur, scripsit memoriaeque mandavit. Recitabo alterum non minus nobile exemplum. In novis, hoc est, nuper repertis Indiae Occidentalis insulis, tam dicuntur esse homines illiterati et literarum

Baudouin derived his information on the *areytos* from Fernandez de Oviedo, who described them in his history of the first decades of European activity in the New World. Oviedo also remarked that they provided a sort of "image of history," comparable to that offered to Europeans by songs and romances. Even illiterate Spaniards knew, after all, about how don Alonso, in the noble city of Seville, decided to go to Algeciras.[80] But Baudouin did something more radical than to accept the simple possibility that oral traditions could convey

tamen, tanquam Deorum, cultores: ut cum audirent nostros ibi Christianos alioqui absentes sic inter sese per epistolas colloqui, ut alter alterum intelligat, epistolas illas clausas adorarint, in quibus dicebant inclusum esse aliquem divinum internuncium genium. Illi (inquam) tam illiterati homines multorum seculorum historiam suae gentis memoriamque conservarunt, partim quibusdam temere effictis symbolis, ut Aegyptii notis hieroglyphicis: partim suis cantionibus, quas alii alios docent, et in suis choraeis cantillant: quales Choros vocant Areytos. Nunc etiam audio nostros, qui illic habitant, in literas referre talem et ex talibis carminibus repetitam historiam. Non dignarer illorum barbariem meminisse, nisi si nostram nobis barbariem exprobrare maiorem illi possent, si simus ἀνιστόρητοι et nos ab iis discere possemus atque deberemus diligentiam conservandae publicae memoriae."
[80] Fernández de Oviedo 1851–55, 5.1: "... esta manera de cantar ... es una efigie de historia ó acuerdo de las cosas pasadas, así de guerras como de paçes, porque con la continuaçión de tales cantos no se les olviden las hazañas é acaesçimientos que han pasado. Y estos cantares les quedan en la memoria, en lugar de libros, de su acuerdo; y por esta forma resçitan las genealogías de sus caçiques y reyes ó señores que han tenido, y las obras que hiçieron ... No le parezca al letor que esto que es dicho es mucha salvajez, pues que en España é Italia se usa lo mismo, y en las más partes de los cristianos, é aún infieles, pienso yo que debe ser así. ¿Qué otra cosa son los romançes é cançiones que se fundan sobre verdades, sino parte é acuerdo de las historias pasadas? A lo menos entro los que no leen, por los cantares saben que estaba el rey don Alonso en la noble

information. Like Oviedo, he compared modern Indian to ancient and modern European ways of passing on information. More radically than Oviedo, moreover, he noted that not only modern illiterate Spaniards, but ancient and literate Romans and Germans had done the same: "I confess that much has been lost. Cicero writes in the *Brutus*: 'I wish those poems mentioned by Cato in his *Origines*, which the guests at banquets sang about the praises of distinguished men, were still extant.'"[81] In doing so, as Carlo Ginzburg has shown, Baudouin revolutionized historical criticism. He took a more favorable view of Indian pictorial codices and oral traditions than the most influential historian of the Indies, José de Acosta, would, a generation after Baudouin. Juan de Tovar, who knew native practices at first hand, assured Acosta that Indians could recall events and speeches with astonishing accuracy.[82] But Acosta disagreed,

ciudad de Sevílla, y le vino al corazón de ir á çercar Algeçira. Así lo dice un romançe ... "

[81] Baudouin 1561a, 74; Wolf (ed.) 1579, I, 648: "Fateor tamen multa esse amissa. Cicero in Bruto [19.75]: Vtinam (inquit) extarent illa carmina, quae multis seculis ante suam aetatem in epulis esse cantata a singulis convivis de clarorum virorum laudibus, in Originibus scriptum reliquit Cato: quia talibus deliciis veteres sua convivia condirent. Historias quoque olim vocatas esse bellaria scribit Plutarchus."

[82] José de Acosta and Juan de Tovar, exchange of letters in García Icazbalceta 1947, 89–93: Acosta: "Mas deseo me satisfaga V.R. a algunas dudas que a mí se me han ofrecido. La primera es, ¿qué certidumbre y autoridad tiene esta relación o historia? La segunda, ¿cómo pudieron los indios, sin escritura, pues no la usaron, conservar por tanto tiempo la memoria de tantas y tan varias cosas? Le tercera, ¿cómo se puede creer que las oraciones o arengas que se refieren en esta historia las hayan hecho los antiguos retóricos que en ella se refieren, pues sin letras no parece posible conservar oraciones largas, y en su género elegantes?"

and influentially assured his readers that Indian writing was "less adequate" than its alphabetic, European counterpart.[83] More remarkably still, Baudouin reduced the Romans – who for centuries had used songs to transmit the traditions about their past, and had lost many of them – to the level of barbarians. Ancient Europeans, he suggested, were in some respects as primitive as modern Americans.

Baudouin's bold comparison inspired his readers to rethink many commonly accepted truths. Lipsius incorporated it in his vastly influential commentary on the *Germania*.[84] Soon sharp-eyed students of Roman history like the well-named

Tovar: "Vi entonces toda esta historia con caracteres y hieroglíficos, que yo no entendía, y así fue necesario que los sabios de México, Tezcuco y Tulla se viesen conmigo … y con ellos, yéndome diciendo y narrando las cosas en particular, hice una historia bien cumplida … digo, como queda referido, que tenían sus figuras y hieroglíficos con que pintaban las cosas, en esta forma: que las cosas que no había imagen propia tenían otros caracteres significativos de aquello y con estas cosas figuraban cuanto querían … Pero es de advertir que aunque tenían diversas figuras y caracteres con que escribían las cosas, no era tan suficientemente como nuestra escritura, que sin discrepar, por las mismas palabras, refiriese cada uno lo que estaba escrito; sólo concordaban en los conceptos; pero para tener memoria entera de las palabras y traza de los parlamentos que hacían los oradores y de los muchos cantares que tenían, que todos sabían sin discrepar palabra, los quales componían los mismos oradores, aunque los figuraban con sus caracteres; pero para conservarlos por las mismas palabras que los dijeron sus oradores y poetas, había cada ejercicio dello en los de los mozos principales que habían de ser sucesores a éstos y con la continua repetición se les quedaba en la memoria, sin discrepar palabra … "

[83] Acosta 1590, VI. 7, 408.
[84] Lipsius on Tacitus *Germania* 3.2: "Uti apud barbaros fere omnes et rudes litterarum. Nec Hispani aliter comperere apud novos Indos." See esp. Landucci 1972, who traces the impact of Lipsius's comment.

chronologer Ioannes Temporarius and Philip Cluver drew radical, even destructive inferences. Roman tradition, based as it was on orally transmitted information, was a fabric of legends that deserved no credibility. "I deny," Temporarius proclaimed, "that Romulus ever existed."[85] By the end of the sixteenth century, English intellectuals from John White to Francis Bacon were making sharp, precise comparisons between New World Indians and ancient Europeans – White in his drawings, Bacon in his compressed, pregnant remark that "Antiquitas mundi juventus seculi" and in his many demeaning comments on the parochialism and ignorance of the ancients.

Baudouin drew a somewhat different moral from this leveling of the historical playing field. His intellectual cosmopolitanism was by no means absolute: "We cannot," he wrote, understand our own history

> without that of the so-called barbarians. If we are French, or British, or German, or Spanish, or Italian, we cannot speak of our countrymen if we do not know the history of the Franks, the Angles, the Saxons, the Goths, the Lombards. And since our countrymen have often encountered Saracens and Turks, we dare not be ignorant of Saracen and Turkish history. We must not immediately classify as barbarous or condemn as unknown everything that is alien from our customs or from the eloquence of the Romans and the Greeks.[86]

---

[85] See Erasmus 1962; Grafton 1983–93, II.

[86] Baudouin 1561a, 36–37, Wolf (ed.) 1579, I, 623–24: "Valerius Maximus de antiquis Romanorum institutis loquens, Maiores natu (inquit) in conviviis ad tibias egregia superiorum opera carmine comprehensa pangebant, quo ad ea imitanda iuventutem alacriorem redderent.

Yet even this qualified argument for the importance of non-European history – along with his discussion of oral tradition – identified the final, indispensable source for Baudouin's *historia integra* – the vast and proliferating literature of travel.

Through the fifteenth and sixteenth centuries, antiquaries like Cyriac of Ancona traveled the world to find

Deinde exclamat: Quas Athenas? Quam scholam? Quae alienigena studia huic domesticae disciplinae praetulerim? Non dissimilem fuisse veterum Germanorum morem, testis est Tacitus. Sed multo magis fuisse veterum Gallorum, Amm. Marcellinus significat, cum ait, eorum Bardos fortia virorum fortium facta, heroicis composita versibus, cum dulcibus lyrae modulis cantitasse ... Et nos erimus tam degeneres, ut ne audire quidem velimus patriae historiae carmen? Caeterum id intelligere non possumus, nisi si et eorum, qui Barbari dicuntur, memoriam teneamus. Si Galli, vel Britanni, vel Germani, vel Hispani, vel Itali sumus: ut de nostris loqui possimus, necesse est nos Francorum, Anglorum, Saxonum, Gothorum, Longobardorum historiam non ignorare: cumque nostri cum Saracenis et Turcis saepe congressi sint, ne nescire quidem licet Saracenicam et Turcicam. Neque vero quaecunque res a nostra consuetudine, vel Romanorum Graecorumque facundia abhorrent, eas propeterea res aut barbaras statim iudicare aut ignotas damnare debemus. Cicero lib. 5. de Finib. loquens de philosophia, quae etiam ad rerump. gubernationem refertur, Omnium (inquit) fere civitatum non Graeciae solum, sed etiam barbariae, ab Aristotele, mores, instituta, disciplinas: a Theophrasto, leges etiam cognovimus." Note that Gabriel Harvey, in his notes on the *Mosaicus* of Freigius (Freigius 1583, British Library C.60.f.4), remodels this fairly conventional world history into an enthusiastic account of how the Patriarchs learned by traveling. See e.g. his notes on 83 ("Antiquissima Apodemica, et Odyssea; à Noacheis usque temporibus. Postea Abrahamidae, et Hebraei, Magni Apodemici. Novissimis etia[m] temporibus, Apostoli, et primitiui Christiani, summi Apodemici. Diuinus semper populus, maximè omnium Apodemicus"); and 85 ("Hebraei, peregrinatores, Apodemici . Etiam Pelasgi, πολυπλάνητον ἔθνος"; "Hebraei, maximi Apodemici").

inscriptions and sketch monuments. They risked sunstroke, capture by pirates and, perhaps worst of all, derision from attractive young women and ignorant old men, as they regularly complained. Meanwhile their armchair-loving colleagues basked vicariously in the Turkish suns described by Busbecq and shivered luxuriously as they read in Acosta of chilly weather at the Equator. Adventurers and readers sought the same sorts of information: knowledge of how it really is, over there, formed the traveler's equivalent to the antiquary's knowledge of how it really was, back then.[87] Both drew on ancient precedents and models. And both insisted that intelligent men must systematically seek, process and assess the information they collected. Theodor Zwinger and others wrote formal manuals for travelers, as Justin Stagl, Joan-Pau Rubiés, and Paola Molino have taught us, and these closely resembled the *artes historicae* in the demands they made on the intelligent consumer of information.[88] Zwinger's *Art of Travel*, as Molino has shown, rested in part on the ideas of the traveler and polymath Hugo Blotius, who conceived the Imperial Library in Vienna as a vast enterprise in the study of universal history. The book offered readers systematic outlines and questionnaires. By filling these out as they made their grand tours, they could produce total accounts

---

[87] Cf. Bann 1994.

[88] See Stagl 1983 and 1995, Rubiés 1996, 2000a, and 2000b, Elsner and Rubiés (eds.) 1999, the pioneering comments in Manley 1995, and the brilliant analysis of Hugo Blotius and Theodor Zwinger in Molino forthcoming. For the classical background see also the important articles in Alcock, Cherry, and Elsner (eds.) (2001). An especially attractive treatise on learned travel, by an author with practical experience, is Erpenius 1721, the results of a conversation conducted "inter pocula."

of the towns they visited, complete with descriptions of lay-
out, the names and locations of public buildings, churches or
temples, and private houses and a full analysis of the customs
practised in all of them. Like other writers, Zwinger also made
clear that one could make an informed journey of this kind
either in space or in time. The four towns for which he offered
exemplary analyses were modern Basle, Paris, and Padua, and
ancient Athens, whose gymnasia, to which young men flocked
for exercise and sophists for argument, he evoked in detail.[89]

Contemporaries recognized the connection between
critical history and learned travel. Possevino, who wrote a famous first-account of Muscovy, knew what he was talking about
when he told his presumably Catholic readers that travel might
verify what seemed the tallest of Herodotus's tall tales:

> As to the fabulous things that Herodotus is accused of
> inventing: first, I say that those who have never set foot in
> foreign lands find many things incredible. Once they have
> traveled in Asia, Africa, and India, they will change their
> opinion. It would be truthful to say that this has happened
> to me more than once just in my European travels. For as a
> youth in France, reading about Gothic matters in Olaus
> Magnus, I thought he was relating mere dreams. When I
> went on a number of missions to Gotland and Sweden,
> many years later, I found that much that I had thought
> invented was true. The same thing happened to me when I
> had to do with Muscovites, Tartars, Turks. Therefore what
> we read in Herodotus must be weighed in a fair scale.[90]

[89] Zwinger 1577.
[90] Possevino 1597, 39 ro–vo: "Iam de fabulosis ac mendaciis quae Herodoto
obiiciuntur: primum, aio multa videri posse incredibilia iis, qui pedem

At the other end of the world of learning, the statutes for Brooke's readership, the first official teaching post in history at Cambridge, expressed a preference for candidates who "have travelled beyond the Seas, and so have added to their Learning knowledge of the modern tongues, and experience in foreign parts, and likewise such as have been brought upp and exercised in publique affairs." They also stated that the incumbent could, if he chose to do so, "dwell beyond the Seas" for two out of every five years.[91]

Evidently the convertibility of time and space – often thought of as a discovery or invention of the Scottish Enlightenment – was bound up with the rise of antiquarian scholarship and the new travel writing of the early modern period. The new information brought back to Europe by travelers played a substantial role in inducing Baudouin and his colleagues to think new thoughts about the meaning of the past. History expanded dramatically. Campanella, as often, put the matter crisply:

> Read the individual histories of all the nations, French, Spanish, German, British, and Ethiopian (for you will find

domo in alienas regiones non extulerint. Quod si Asiam, Aphricam, Indiam peragraverint, eos sententiam mutaturos. Id mihi non semel si dixero accidisse in ipsius tantum Europae peragratione, haud mentiar. Adolescens enim in Gallia Olai magni de Gothicis rebus historiam perlegens, quasi somnia esse putabam. In Gothiam et Suetiam post multos annos haud semel missus, comperi plura esse vera, quae existimaveram esse commenta. Idem contigit mihi, dum cum Moscis, Tartaris, Scythis agerem. Quamobrem aequa lance pendenda sunt quae in Herodoto leguntur." On the other hand, Olivieri 2004, 305–09, shows in detail how writers used Herodotus as a model for travel narratives.
[91] Cambridge University Library MS Mm. 1.47 (Baker MS 36), 147, 150; Maccioni and Mostert 1984, 422–23.

this too) and Turkish and Moorish. You must receive the traditions of the New World from their inhabitants, for they lacked writing. Likewise what the Chinese, Japanese and Tartars, the inhabitants of Ceylon, Persia, India and other nations record in writing or by memory of their origins and their deeds. Jesuits and voyagers have written much about this. But this should really be a task for kings, especially the Spanish one ... Whatever the pretenders claim, universal history is not yet complete, but only partial.[92]

The *ars historica,* as exemplified by Baudouin, was nothing if not cosmopolitan. An intellectual crossroads laid out on coordinates drawn from both the humanistic and the legal traditions, it gave multiple methods and practices a place to meet, as antiquarianism intersected with ecclesiastical history, both collided with law, and all of them in turn experienced the shock of the new as travelers described unknown worlds to the east and, even more surprising, the west. This next chapter will suggest that, in some cases, these methodological collisions turned into something like intellectual earthquakes. This one should at least have suggested why so illustrious and daring a seeker after new truths as John Dee found intellectual nourishment in the *ars historica.*

[92] Campanella 1954, 1254.

3

Method and madness in the *ars historica*: three case studies

When E. H. Carr counseled his listeners to "[s]tudy the historian before you begin to study the facts," he made clear, by a homely analogy, that the best historians were an eccentric breed, each of whom harbored a quite distinct set of interests and obsessions: "the intelligent undergraduate...when recommended to read a book by that great scholar Jones of St. Jude's, goes round to a friend at St. Jude's to ask what sort of chap Jones is, and what sort of bees he has in his bonnet. When you read a work of history, always listen out for the buzzing. If you can detect none, either you are tone deaf or your historian is a dull dog."[1] In this chapter, we will visit three of the artists of history. All three were strong-minded and artful writers and exceptionally original scholars. In each case, we will listen for the buzzing. But I also hope we can do something more: that we can use these three cases to see how strong individuals found very different meanings in, and advanced very different theses with, the *ars historica*. The genre was marked, as we have seen, by striking continuities in form and concern. Whether you were Protestant or Catholic, cleric or layman, engaged sixteenth-century jurist or dryasdust seventeenth-century polymath, if you chose to write an *ars*

[1] Carr 1962, 26.

historica, you committed yourself to explaining how to learn the truth about the past, how to reduce its lessons to systematic form, and how to apply them to the present. Your reader knew, before he turned the first page, that he would encounter quotations from Cicero, praise of Polybius, discussion of speeches and battle scenes, and – in almost every case – texts forged by Annius of Viterbo. Every author responded to others who had written before him and drew on what rapidly became a standardized international range of traditions.

Yet every author also worked with a defined set of local resources, had support from a distinct patron, institution, or readership, and experienced a particular set of local constraints. Watching three of them compose their *artes historicae* will provide a privileged way to trace the interactions, in a particular late humanist world of exuberant learning, of tradition and the individual talent. Francesco Patrizi (1529/30–97), a renowned anti-Aristotelian philosopher from Dalmatia who studied at Padua and retained deep roots in the Paduan Aristotelian tradition, taught at Ferrara and then, less happily, at Rome.[2] Reiner Reineck (1541–95), a pupil of Melanchthon, worked his way, usually as a tutor to young nobles, through such centers of Protestant learning as Wittenberg and Frankfurt an der Oder. He wound up teaching at Helmstedt and serving as court historian to the house of Braunschweig-Lüneburg.[3] Jean Bodin (1530–96) studied and taught Roman law at Toulouse, practised law at Paris, worked as a secretary to the Duke of

[2] On Patrizi see Kristeller 1964; Bolzoni 1980; Vasoli 1989; Leinkauf 1990; Deitz 1997 and 1999; Castelli (ed.) (2002); and Mulsow (ed.) 2002.
[3] On Reineck see *Allgemeine Deutsche Biographie*, s.n., and Herding 1965, by far the fullest treatment.

Alençon, fought for the privileges of the governed at the 1576 Estates General in Blois and argued against many of the privileges of the governed in his classic *Six Books of the Republic*, which appeared in the same year. He ended up as a royal officer in Laon, a participant in the Catholic League, a speculative philosopher and a particularly rabid demonologist – the only one of all his tribe who believed that witches could physically remove the genitals of their male victims.[4] All of them enjoyed great esteem from colleagues, publishers, and readers. All of them helped to make the genre they practised relevant to circles across Europe. And none of them was a dull dog.

Patrizi played a critical role in making the *ars historica* a success. *Artes historicae* were written everywhere in Europe. But it was at the great cosmopolitan publishing center of Basel that Joannes Wolf, in 1576 and 1579, created the anthology of these texts that made them a canon and carried them into studies and libraries across Europe. His interest in the texts needs little explanation. Swiss scholars and publishers like Conrad Gesner, Theodor Zwinger, and Heinrich Petri took advantage of their central position in the international book trade, their contacts with both Catholic and Protestant centers, and their articulate, well-informed local communities of exiles to make their cities central nodes in the sixteenth century's international web of information-gathering institutions. They assembled and published not only the *artes historicae*, but also the *artes peregrinandi* and the *bibliotheca universalis*. Typically, a

---

[4] For guidance to the vast literature on Bodin see the excellent critical bibliography by Couzinet 2001. The most recent systematic study of the *Methodus* is Couzinet 1996. Also important are Franklin 1963, Kelley 1971, Muhlack 1991, and Blair 1997a.

cosmopolitan Protestant emigré from Italy, Jacopo Aconcio, brought news of the new genre to the north. Reading Patrizi's work set him afire, as he explained in a phosphorescently enthusiastic letter of 20 November 1562 to a Zurich scholar, also named Joannes Wolf: "To leave out everything else," he wrote, "I was astounded recently when I read the *Ten Dialogues on History* and, after them, ten *On Rhetoric* written in Italian by Francesco Patrizi of Dalmatia. Would you believe it? He practically makes me despise Plato and Aristotle. His brilliance is unbelievable, his judgement most polished, and he writes with such charm that no passage, however prolix, causes satiety. He dares great things, but provides them so deftly that we would believe him if he promised even greater things."[5]

Patrizi is best remembered now as a late herald of the *prisca philosophia*. He devoted his brilliantly contorted late work as an editor and interpreter, the modestly titled *Nova de universis philosophia*, to the dialogues of Hermes Trismegistus, whom he ardently defended against the first doubters of his deep antiquity. But he was also a theorist and practitioner of historical scholarship, and one who took his conclusions wherever they led him.[6] His brilliant, ferocious work of 1560, *Della historia diece dialoghi*, more than lived up to Aconcio's

---

[5] Aconcio 1791, lv–lvi: "Vt alia praeteream, stupore affecerunt me non ita pridem dialogi decem de historia et nuperrime totidem de rhetorica nostrate lingua a Francisco Patricio, homine, ut audio, Dalmata conscripti. Quid quaeris? Nihil hercle est propius, quam ut omnes iam Platones atque Aristoteles contemnam. Acumen est incredibile, iudicium politissimum: lepore ita condit omnia, ut satietatem afferre prolixitas nulla posse videatur. Magna audet, sed ita praestat, ut si multo maiora polliceatur, facile sit fidem habiturus."

[6] Vasoli 1989, 25–90.

advance billing. In it Patrizi made clear to what good effect he had studied Plato, in the workhorse Latin version of Marsilio Ficino and in the original Greek. Like Plato, he staged his ten dialogues vividly, offering readers something like a tour of Venice. He and his friends argued about history as they walked to the Palazzo of San Marco, as they rode in a gondola, as they confronted the vast historical library of Niccolò Zeno, with its "more than 1,600 historians, most of them inaccurate or prejudiced", and as Patrizi himself lay on a sickbed.

Modeling his persona on that of Socrates, Patrizi made his book an ironic commentary on himself – the self-portrait of an annoyingly committed historical sceptic who bothered every Venetian patrician he could find with his doubts about history and would go to any lengths to keep his interlocutors engaged. When one young man tries to leave him after explaining the relationship between events on earth and the planets in heaven, Patrizi complains that he will be left lifeless on the ground. The young man, stunned, asks why. "Because," Patrizi replies, "I know for certain that if you depart, my spirit is so desperate to learn this lesser form of history, that it will leave me and follow you. And it's possible that it will enter your body, and some evil will result."[7] Terrified that he has encountered a magus, the young man speeds away. Only another friend's

---

[7] Patrizi 1560, 38 vo: "Stupì egli alhora, et disse, morto? et perche morto? Percioche io so, risposi io tutto tremante, ch'alla partita vostra, l'anima mia portata dal disiderio di intendere piu avanti della minore historia, s'uscirà di me, et correravvi dietro: et potrebbe ella entrarvi addosso: et avverrebbevene forse qualche male. Sbigottì tutto à queste parole il giovane, et ritirossi immantinente un passo adietro: et temendo non forse egli si fosse abbattuto in alcun mago incantatore, subito s'usci di chiesa di gran passo": Wolf (ed.) 1579, I, 486: "Obstupuit ille ad hoc, et exanimem?

arrival consoles Patrizi and enables him to carry on the conversation. Like the sophists in Plato's dialogues, the interlocutors in Patrizi's often seem ready to tear their own heads off rather than face another round of full and frank discussion.

Their nervousness is natural. Patrizi learned from Plato that mocking, carefully sequenced questions can do powerful intellectual work. In the first dialogue, Patrizi confesses to two friends that he has never quite understood what history is. The answer is obvious, one of them replies: as Cicero said, history is the memory of events remote from our own memory. But, Patrizi objects, what of Aristotle's history of animals, Theophrastus's history of plants, Pliny's history of nature itself? Could one not write a history of Pope Paul IV's war with the Duke of Alba, which had taken place only a year before? The other participant tries to save the definition by drawing limits: history deals with what public men do. Well then, asks Patrizi, what of the history of Thales, who fell into a ditch while contemplating the heavens? "Enough jokes," the friend replies, "I think Cicero means by history a narration of things done by men in politics." But, Patrizi objects, would that not exclude Plutarch, who described the war machines built by Archimedes to resist the Romans at Syracuse? And what of the narratives in which the Portuguese and Spanish described their voyages of discovery? Losing patience, one of his friends says

qua de causa exanimem? Quod certo scio, inquam trepidus, fore tuo discessu, ut animus meus addiscendae minoris historiae studio, te sequatur, hic relicto corpore: fierique posse, ut in tuum corpus intret, et aliquid illinc mali oriatur. Hisce verbis perterrefactus iuvenis, subito uno atque altero passu recessit, metuensque ne forte in magum quempiam incidisset ex templo bene celeri gressu properavit."

baldly: "History is a narration of things done by kings or states." But by now Patrizi has converted the other one, who objects on his behalf: "Did not those who wrote navigations to India and lives of hermits compose histories? You would be wrong to deny this."[8] Patrizi and his friend produce in turn every

---

[8] Patrizi 1560, 1 vo–2 vo, esp. 2 ro–vo: "PATR. Nò? et come adunque ci narrano che Talete contemplando i cieli, cadde in una fossa? GIG. Hor non piu ciancie; io credo che Cicerone intendesse per historia la narration di quello che fanno gli huomini civili. PATR. et i Contadini; i naviganti, i romiti, et altre simiglianti creature vi sono per nulla? GIG. Stravaganti sono coteste vostre cose. et si le escludo io tutte dall'historia, et che? PATR. Alinomo, quello che Alessandro trovatolo povero hortolano fece Re di Pafo, non poteva per cotesta ragione entrare in historia, et Plutarco non fece bene à raccontarci in historia quelle macchine che operò Archimede al tempo dell'assedio in Siracusa? et i Portughesi et i Castigliani, non doverebbono farci historia delle loro navigationi: et quegli altri che ci scrissono le vite de S. Padri, si prenderono fatica invano a farci historia di quello, che in essa non puo secondo voi venire. GIG. Egli si mi par bene hormai, che voi me la andiate sofisticando questa cosa. Ma per finirla, io vi dirò brevemente, che historia è quella che si fa raccontando cose fatte da Re, o da Republiche. BID. Et dir cotesto, è nulla o Compare, et vi dira il Patritio: Adunque costoro ch'io v'ho detto che scrivono i viaggi delle Indie, et le vite de romiti, non fanno historia? et se voi glie le negaste, havreste il torto"; Wolf (ed.) 1579, I, 398–401, esp. 400–01: "PAT. Quomodo igitur de Thalete historia refertur, quod dum ambulando coelum contemplaretur, in foveam inciderit. GIG. Satis nugarum iam, Ciceronem puto historiam appellare narrationem rerum ab hominibus politicis gestarum. PAT. Agricolae vero, nautae, et alii eius generis homines, frustra erunt? GIG. Aliena sunt haec a nostro proposito, adeoque omnia ab historia excludo, ecquid tibi vis? PATR. Alinomus hoc modo, quem ex pauperis hortuli cultore Alexander regem Paphi creavit, non caderet in historiam: neque recte fecisset Plutarchus, qui machinas ab Archimede, in Syracusarum obsidione artificiose excogitatas, recensuit. nec Portugallenses et Castellani navigationum suarum historiam nobis relinquere debuerunt: inepteque et frustra laborem

commonplace of the *ars historica* – but they wither, one by one, in the harsh glare of his dialectic. No wonder that an electric shock went through Aconcio – himself an expert on history – as he saw the best-loved bromides of Cicero and Livy fall like dandelions before a sickle.

Patrizi felt able to mount his ferocious attack on contemporary practices in part because he was conscious of his powers as a philosopher – a breed that had been ready to flog historians without mercy ever since Plato and Aristotle, in their different ways, first questioned the value of historical research. But he was also a historian in his own right. He knew the rich and profound Venetian literature of political analysis, the works of Gasparo Contarini and other patricians who had been trained since youth to observe the foreign nations to which the republic sent them and to draw the lessons of history by comparing the Venetian constitution to a range of others.[9] Such men, Patrizi noted, "write in a certain novel way about the magistrates of the Romans and the Greeks, and others about the form of the Roman Republic, and those of the Athenians, the Lacedaemonians, the Carthaginians, and the Venetians. As you know, this is a most useful kind of writing." He also knew the innovative practices of contemporary antiquaries, who had

susceperunt, qui sanctorum patrum historias scripserunt, quod haec in historiam non cadant. GIG. Iam nimium sophistice negotium implicare videris, uno verbo dico: Historiam esse narrationem rerum gestarum a Regibus aut Rebuspublicis. BID. Et hoc ipso nihil dicis. Obiiciet enim Patritius, qui Indicas navigationes et Vitas Eremitarum scripserunt, an non historiam composuerunt? Quod certe si negaveris, facies inique ... "

9 See esp. the studies of Venetian political writing in Gilbert 1977.

taught him to see history as thick description rather than taut narrative: "Some historians," he explained,

> have not so much described events as customs, ways of life, and laws ... And there is another sort, those who, especially in our day, write in another way about the clothing of the Romans and the Greeks, the forms of armament they used, their ways of making camp, and their ships, their buildings, and other things of this sort, which are necessary for life.[10]

Patrizi himself became a skilled and influential antiquarian. He did pioneer work on the military affairs of the Greeks and the Romans, comparing them to those of the moderns, long before Justus Lipsius made the subject fashionable.[11]

---

[10] Patrizi 1560, 11 ro: "PATR. Et e' vi sono alcun'altri anchora, et hoggidi massimamente: i quali di una quinta maniera di cose ci scrivono. Si come è della forma de' vestimenti Romani et Greci; della foggia dell'armi; del modo dell'accamparsi; delle forme delle navi, et degli edificii, et di altri stormenti di ogni fatta della lor vita, et de lor mestieri. BID. Et questo è vero. PATR. Et alcun'altri scrivono di una sesta maniera di cose, si come de' magistrati Romani et de' Greci. Et alcun'altri il fanno, della maniera del governo delle Republiche di Roma, o di Athene, o di Sparta, o di Cartagine, o di Venetia. La qual cosa sapete voi, che è util molto"; Wolf (ed.) 1579, I, 421: "PAT. Accedit huc aliud genus, eorum qui alio quodam modo, et maxime nostris temporibus, scribunt de Romanorum Graecorumque vestimentis, armorum forma, ponendorum castrorum ratione, deque eorum navibus, aedificiis, aliisque eius generis rebus ad vitam necessariis. BID. Verum est. PAT. Et alii iterum nova quadam ratione, scribunt de Magistratibus Romanorum atque Graecorum, alii de forma Reipublicae Romanae, Atheniensium, Lacedaemoniorum, Carthaginensium, Venetorum, quod proinde genus scriptionis perutile esse scitis."

[11] Patrizi 1583; Patrizi 1594.

Joseph Scaliger – never unhappy to leave a dent in Lipsius's reputation – even told his Leiden pupils that Lipsius had plagiarized his famous *De militia Romana* of 1596 from Patrizi.[12] By his emphasis on the importance to the historian of material remains and his appreciation of the antiquaries' and theorists' analytical, monographic forms of history writing, he made clear that he was more than a passive witness of his period's new forms of historical and philological writing.

Students of the *ars historica* have emphasized the originality of Patrizi's fifth dialogue.[13] Here he and his friends develop a strong argument against the credibility of history. Historians, they argue, are either private or public men. But private men watch great events from the outside, and can report only the sort of hearsay one picks up in a barber's shop. Public men, by contrast, write from the inside, and since they do so *parti pris*, they take sides instead of reporting just the facts. Only kings and their intimate counselors know the reasons for their actions – and they, as all habitués of courts know, never disclose these, since they wish to be known as they should be, not as they are. History, in other words, could not be written – not, at least, in a way that would be both impartial and informed. These arguments would reappear again and again, in the seventeenth-century heyday of historical scepticism, which Patrizi's work did much to inspire.

In later dialogues, however, Patrizi used his mastery of new forms of historical writing to offer a partial solution for these dilemmas. By combining narrative with the sorts of

---

[12] Scaliger 1740, II, 431: "Lipsius libro de Militia Romana omnia cepit ex Francisco Patritio qui Italice scripsit ea de re."
[13] Scheele 1930; Franklin 1963.

anaytical history practised by antiquarians, the historian could give his readers useful information:

> The quantity of the public expenditures should be set down, similarly, both those made in the ordinary course of events and the extraordinary ones. After all, if we compare our times with antiquity, we are bowled over. In the first Punic War, when the Roman empire did not yet extend outside Italy, the Romans armed 330 quinqueremes at public expense. Nowadays the Turk, a great monarch whose eastern empire is as great as that of the Romans, can barely equip half so many modern ships.

Readers must know if a state uses money or public discipline to mount its military forces. If Polybius had only made this clear, readers would understand how the Roman republic had raised so great an army against Carthage.[14] In passages like these, Patrizi resembles Baudouin, and like him

---

[14] Patrizi 1560, 34 vo–35 ro: "Et sarà forse bene che parimente ci accenni la quantità delle spese, o ordinarie, che fossero, o peraventura anco straordinarie. Et cio dico per questa cagione; che paragonandosi i nostri tempi in ver gli antichi, l'huomo stupisce ad udire, che i Romani nella prima guerra contra a Cartaginesi, a spese publiche spignessero in mare trecento et trenta quinqueremi, non havendo per anco l'imperio loro posto [ed. porto,] il piede fuor d'Italia. Et hora il Turco cosi gran Signore, il qual possiede tutto cio che essi nella lor maggior grandezza tennero in Levante, non possa cacciare la metà tante galee di nostro uso, le quali pure armano meno della metà degli huomini, che armarono le Romane. La terza cosa è la forza dell'imperio, laquale dall'historico ci dee essere ricordata. Et è principalmente posta ne soldati, et nella maniera della militia, appresso poi nell'armate, et negli altri stormenti da guerra, et nelle munitioni. Lequali anchor che per lo piu senza dinari non si possano haver molte; sono pero diversa cosa tutte da dinari. Percioche egli è molte fiate avvenuto, che senza dinari gran forze si sono poste

calls for the creation of a radically modern *historia integra*, a discipline that manages to fuse antiquarian precision in the use and citation of evidence with formal narrative.

insieme, si come fu nella guerra, che contro à Cartaginesi fecero Matone e Spendio. Et tale è hoggidi la militia de Persiani, et de Circassi, et in parte de Francesi. Sono adunque le forze veramente negli huomini, o per natura, o per disciplina, o per numero arditi et forti. Et deeci l'historico accennar talhora, se essi sono o tutti, o parte, o pagati, o commandati, et in qual guisa et l'uno, et l'altro. Pero che dal non ci haver Polibio detto questo, a gran ragione l'huomo stupisce come sia che i Romani della Italia sola, fuor anco la Liguria, la Lombardia, la Romagna, et la Marca piana, mettessero insieme presso ad ottocento mila pedoni, et molti piu di sessanta mila cavalli: et hor di tutta insieme non se ne possa in tutto, ne anco la decima parte trarre"; Wolf (ed.) 1579, I, 477–8: "Debent etiam redditus ac vectigalia reipublicae vel saltem obiter annotari, quo pacto paulatim creverint, una cum aucto imperio: nec inepte etiam narrabuntur sumptus publici, et alia hisce similia. Atque hoc quidem eo magis faciundum est, quoniam si nostra tempora cum antiquis illis conferamus, non possumus non obstupescere, Romanos primo bello Punico, cum nondum extra Italiae fines eorum imperium extenderetur, trecentas et triginta quinqueremes publicis sumptibus armasse: cum tamen Turcus tantus Monarcha, quique maius in Oriente imperium obtinet, quam ipsi cum in vigore essent: iam vix queat instruere mediam partem earum navium, quae nostro tempore in usu esse consueverunt, dimidio scilicet minorem, iis quas in usu habuere Romani. Tertio minime praeteriri silentio debent in historia, imperii cuiusque vires, cum ceterae, tum quae in copiis et militiae peritia consistunt, aliisque bellicis instrumentis. Quae, etsi absque opibus et pecunia raro comparari queant, tamen ab opibus separamus, quod magnae quandoque copiae sine pecuniis comparatae sint, sicuti in bello accidit, quod adversus Carthaginenses gessere Mathon et Spendius. Talis etiam hodierno die est militia Persarum, et quandoque etiam Gallorum. Omnis autem vis copiarum, aut in militum disciplina consistit, aut numero, aut robore. In cuius rei descriptione, debet historicus diligenter annotare, pecuniane an magistratus iussu aliove modo sit exercitus comparatus. Dum enim istud Polybius neglexit, effecit ut hodie non

Elsewhere, however, Patrizi's radicalism was nourished by very different sources, and took radically different, very individual forms. In his third dialogue, Patrizi tells a particularly revealing story. Antonio Patrizi, the brother of his grandfather, had visited Egypt in the course of a pilgrimage to the Holy Land. There he had met a holy hermit named Hamon, who explained to him that

> our country has been given many privileges by the heavens, more than all the rest of the universe. For it produces in large quanitity every kind of fruit, and is healthy, and has excellent air. Moreover, it has men of the highest intellect. In the past they discovered all the most vital and valuable arts in the world, and all the sciences. Accordingly, men of lofty mind have come from that Europe of yours, and elsewhere, to learn our sciences. And the Egyptians are the most ancient of all the rest, and they remember two universal corrections, and two universal rebirths of the whole mechanism of the universe. All in all, Egypt's unique gifts and divine attributes have always made it the temple of all the world, and the image of heaven.[15]

immerito omnes admiremur, Romanos olim ex Italia reliqua, praeter Longobardiam, Liguriam, Insubriam et Flaminiam octingenta circiter millia peditum, et sexaginta equitum millia coegisse: quod nunc ex Italia universa, vix decima tanti exercitus pars possit comparari."

[15] Patrizi 1560, 15 ro–vo: "Sappi, disse il Romito, figliuol mio, che il nostro paese, ha dal Cielo molti privilegi sopra à tutti gli altri dell'universo havuto. Percio che oltre che egli è ferace d'ogni maniera frutti, et salubre, et d'ottima aria; egli ha gli huomini suoi d'ingegno elevatissimo. I quali per lo passato, sono stati ritrovatori di tutte le piu necessarie, et piu pregiate arti, che habbia il mondo, e di tutte le scienze. Si che sono venuti huomini d'alta mente della vostra Europa, et d'altre parti, ad apparare le

Hamon also insisted on the cultural inferiority of modern Europe to Egypt, the ancient birthplace of all the arts and sciences: "you Europeans always remain childish, and have not yet mastered erudition in its fulness."[16] Asked what he meant, Hamon replied that Egypt, unlike other parts of the world, escaped the universal fires and floods brought about periodically by the stars, thanks to the Nile and the desert climate. Egyptians, unlike the other inhabitants of the earth, were never reduced to living like beasts of the field, and never had to reinvent their arts and sciences. Moreover, a Saitic priest called Bitis had discovered a square column, decorated with "holy characters," which described not only the past, but also the future, through

> scienze nostre. Et sono stati quei di Egitto sempre antichissimi di tutti gli altri; si come quelli, che hanno havuto memoria di due universali correttioni, et di due universali rinascimenti di tutta la machina mondana. Et in somma, è stato l'Egitto per le rarissime doti sue, et per le divine cose, che egli ha sempre havuto in se, tempio di tutto il mondo, et imagine del cielo"; Wolf (ed.) 1579, I, 432: "Nolim enim te ignorare fili, inquit Hamon ad eum, nostram hanc regionem prae caeteris omnibus, permultis privilegiis caelitus esse donatam. Nam praeter id, quod ferax est omnis generis fructuum, habetque aerem saluberrimum: homines quoque progignit summi ingenii, quique elapsis seculis necessarias quasque artes et maxime utiles ad hanc vitam sustentandam invenerunt. Vt saepe magni nominis viri ex vestra Europa capessendi animi cultus gratia ad nos hucusque pervenerint. Fuereque Aegyptii semper omnium antiquissimi: ut qui binos totius mundi interitus totidemque illius restaurationes meminerint: adeoque ob insignes quasdam planeque divinas dotes, quibus excellit Aegyptus, semper fuit veluti templum totius universi caelique ipsius imago."

[16] Patrizi 1560, 15 vo: "Ma e' si par bene, che voi huomini di Europa, siete stati sempre giovanetti, et non sapeste mai scienza canuta veruna"; Wolf (ed.) 1579, I, 432: "Tum Aegyptius, apparet, inquit, vos in Europa semper iuveniles fuisse, necdum maturam scientiam didicisse."

the course of the "great year" of 36,000 solar years. Egyptians accordingly knew history, both back to the beginning of time and forward to its end. Before the end of the last Great Year, an Egyptian who "knew the powers of stones, herbs, animals, and the heavenly bodies" worked out, by experimenting with animals, how to call the dead back to life. He then made preparations, enclosed himself in a large vessel, had it buried deeply, and then killed himself. Once the new great year started, the powers of the stars and the magical characters that he had inscribed brought him back to life, exactly as he had been, and he renamed himself Seth. He then recorded this history in two columns, one of bronze and one of brick, which served as the source of the later Egyptians' knowledge of the past.[17]

To weave this bold tapestry Patrizi drew strands from several distinct reels. In the *Timaeus* and the *Critias* he had read Plato's argument that only Egypt, with its ancient temple records, preserved true memories of the ancient past. The bare, mountainous countryside of Greece – where generations of modern travelers and ethnographers have hunted for survivals of ancient customs – housed only ignorance and oblivion, and the Greek cities preserved only myths about the past. Egypt, with its written tradition, served Patrizi – as it had served Plato – as a powerful rationalist tool with which he could gain leverage against ethnocentrism and self-delusion, and Hamon's speech explicitly recalled the similar speech of an Egyptian priest to Solon in the *Timaeus*.[18] In the *Jewish Antiquities* of that honorable traitor Josephus, Patrizi found the story of the Patriarch

---

[17] Patrizi 1560, 15 ro–18 ro; Wolf (ed.) 1579, I: 432–9.
[18] Plato *Timaeus* 22b; see Veyne 1988.

Seth, who erected two columns, one of stone and one of brick, on which he had recorded antediluvian knowledge – and thus transmitted true, revealed knowledge of man and nature to those who came after the Flood, which one of the columns survives.[19] Like more than one seventeenth-century free-thinker, in other words, Patrizi more or less identified the culture of ancient Egypt with that of Israel. Anti-Aristotelian that Patrizi was, finally, he drew his cosmological information from the radical forms of astrological theory espoused by the Paduan thinker Pietro Pomponazzi and some others. These men held, in theory, that the stars had the power to determine everything on earth, from the power of prayer to the stigmata of St. Francis – though Pomponazzi hastened to explain that, in practice, divine intervention actually caused those particular phenomena. They also speculated that the world might last not the seven thousand years dictated by biblical prophecy, but the 36,000 years of a Platonic Great Year. Patrizi thus melded history with prophecy, as many had done before him – but prophecy of a particular, local, and theologically problematic kind. His fusion caught the eye of more than one radical reader – notably Giordano Bruno.[20]

Yet Patrizi's central source was far less respectable than Plato and far less radical than Pomponazzi.[21] In his fifth dialogue, Patrizi made clear that another ancient tradition of

---

[19] Josephus *Jewish Antiquities* 1.67–71; see Popper 2006 for a lucid discussion of this story.

[20] See Garin 1983; Copenhaver 1992 offers a searching recent discussion of Pomponazzi's natural philosophy. On the diffusion of Pomponazzi's views see Zanier 1975 and Brosseder 2004.

[21] Vasoli 1989, 67 n. 24.

historiography had existed, alongside the rhetorical one he rejected. "The ancient priests," says one character, "the holiest of men, recorded everything that happened in individual years, and preserved them in the shrines in their temples. These served as the sources from which histories were later composed. It seems that the histories of Berosus were of this kind, and also those of Metasthenes the Persian, and Manetho the Egyptian."[22] Patrizi treats this argument with characteristic independence and reserve. Another character points out that priestly annals record only bare names and dates – and that even such bare accounts could be falsified. He was right: the Spanish humanist Juan Luis Vives apparently devised a wonderful set of Roman annals, covering an eventful week in which stones rained from the sky, fires blazed, ambassadors left the city, and the two sons of Marcia, Q. and L. Metellus, gave the people a banquet to celebrate their mother's death.[23] Elsewhere Patrizi himself discusses the ancient annals with a sharp cynicism worthy of Voltaire. "Berosus notes that Iove Belus was the second king of Babylon, and ruled there for 62 years. In the third year of his reign, the city of Veii was founded in Italy. Tyrus the founder

---

[22] Patrizi 1560, 29 ro: "I sacerdoti delle genti, seguitai io, santissimi huomini, faceano le memorie di tutto ciò, che avveniva ciascun'anno, et le riponeano ne i lor sacrarii. Et di quivi poi lo historico cavava le sue historie. Et si vede, che cosi fece Beroso in Assiria, et cosi Metastene Persiano, cosi anco Manetone Egittio"; Wolf (1579), I, 465: "Eorum sacerdotes, inquam, sanctissimi homines in monumenta litterarum referebant, quae singulis annis accidissent, eaque in templorum adytis conservabant: ex quibus deinde historiae a scriptoribus contexebantur. Apparet enim tales esse Berosi historias, sicuti etiam Metasthenis Persae et Manethonis Aegyptii."

[23] See Lintott 1986.

of Tyre was the creator of the Thracians." What use, he asks, is all of this information, dry as Alice's Anglo-Saxon history, for life?[24]

But he never questions the value or genuineness of the texts themselves. The names of their authors reveal the source in which he found them: the very ones which Baudouin severely attacked. In fact, Patrizi reared his vision of Egyptian knowledge and tradition on the foundations Nanni laid. When Patrizi imagined Seth, predicting the end of the world and surviving it, he echoed Nanni, who had his forged Berosus claim that Noah had foreseen the Flood by astrology and discussed the columns of Seth in his commentary.[25] And when Patrizi stated that only Egyptian tradition preserved the vital fact that "in those early years, men had such large bodies that when their feet touched the ground, they touched the heavens with

[24] Patrizi 1560, 22 vo: "[PATR.] . . . Diciamo cosi. Conta Beroso, che Giove Belo fu secondo Re di Babilonia, et regnò sessantadue anni; et l'anno terzo di lui si edificò in Italia, alla maniera di Scitia, di carri la citta, che poi si chiamò Veij. Et Tira, poi che fondò Tiro, fu autor de Traci . . . SCOL. Bene, io l'crederò, ma che è perciò? PATR. Questo, ch'io vorrei, che voi mi dimostraste, quale ammaestramento possa io alla mia vita trarre da questa historia?"; Wolf (ed.) 1579, I, 449: "[PAT.] . . . Ecce enim Berosus commemorat, Iovem Belum fuisse secundum regem Babyloniae, et ibi duos et sexaginta annos regnasse: cuius regni anno secundo condita in Italia fuerit civitas Veiorum. Tyrum Tyri conditorem fuisse Thracum autorem . . . SCOL. Credo, sed quid tum? PAT. Quod vellem edoceri, quid hinc utilitatis ad vitae meae institutionem desumere queam."
[25] For astrology and the Flood see Berosus's account in Nanni 1545, 8 vo: "is [sc. Noa] timens quam ex astris futuram prospectabat cladem, anno .78. ante inundationem navim instar arcae coopertam fabricari coepit," and the splendid discussion in Schmidt-Biggemann 2006; for the columns of Seth see Nanni 1545, 6 ro, Stephens 1979, Stephens 1989, and Popper 2006.

their heads, and were called Emephim," he made clear that he accepted Nanni's reading of Genesis 6, according to which all men had been giants before the Flood.[26] History and philology served, in Patrizi's case, not to convince him that Hermes and other representatives of Near Eastern wisdom were dubious, but to open his imagination. He not only qualified the radical scepticism of his first five dialogues with five more in which he made far more positive arguments, but also wrote an influential form of speculative history himself. By studying the past with the most up-to-date tools at his disposal, historical and scientific, he found himself drawn irresistibly to the belief in an ancient barbarian wisdom. This conviction would, in later years, underpin his unremitting critique of Aristotle as well as his passionate, untroubled faith that the *Hermetica* were genuine. The most trenchant sixteenth-century defense of the *prisca philosophia* had its roots in Patrizi's *ars historica*, in which he grafted the ideas of a forger onto the most innovative methods of contemporary antiquaries and connected both to the most radical materialist cosmology.[27]

Patrizi's career, like Galileo's, would lead him to Rome and into a conflict with the papacy, which censured his efforts

---

[26] Patrizi 1560, 17 vo: "Si habbiam ben noi quello, ch'io ti dirò in memoria, che nella piu vecchia rivolutione, gli huomini erano grandissimi, si che con piedi calcando la terra, toccavano con capi il Cielo, et chiamavansi Emephim"; Wolf (ed.) 1579, 1: 437: "Istud certe adhuc memoriae proditum conservamus, quod in primo illo annorum ambitu homines fuerint usque adeo grandi corpore, ut pedibus in terram nixi, capita inter sydera conderent, et Emephimos fuisse appellatos." On Nanni and the giants see the wonderful account in Stephens 1989; equally excellent on the ancient background is Adler 1989.

[27] See now the studies and documents collected in Mulsow (ed.) 2002.

to defend the antiquity and authority of Egyptian wisdom.[28] Reineck, by contrast, led a relatively peaceful life in the small, obsessively erudite academic communities of Protestant north Germany.[29] He summarized his beliefs about history not in passionate dialogues but in a modest *Oratio* and *Methodus*, published in 1580 and 1583. Like Baudouin, Reineck found it easy to penetrate to the true nature of the false Berosus and his author: "A good many grounds exist to make us doubt whether that fragment is legitimate. Wacky and stuffed with fables as it is, its interpreter Annius – if I may use a word from comedy – is wackier still. All he does is to pile unbelievable fables on still more unbelievable ones."[30] Unlike Baudouin, Reineck proved too cautious to reject these texts entirely. Like Baudouin, however, he celebrated the range and breadth of sources on which the modern historian might draw. He too praised Charlemagne for his interest in ancient German songs and histories.[31] Like Baudouin, too, he urged the surly purists

[28] Firpo 1950–1; Gregory 1953.
[29] See generally Wegele 1885, 344–5, 435–6, 440, 461–2, the fullest and best account is given by Herding 1965.
[30] Reineck 1580a, 7: "Reliquum est solius Berosi fragmentum. Tametsi is non primam, sed tertiam Monarchiam attigerit. Vixit enim temporibus Alexandri Magni: suntque Plinii et Iosephi de eo testimonia in medio. Attamen idem fragmentum γνήσιον sit, quae dubitare nos cogant, causae plurimae sunt. Quod ut per se mirificum plenumque fabularum est, ita mirificissimus (liceat enim mihi Comici vocem istam retinere) interpres Annius. Quippe qui id tantum agat, ut fabulas prodigiosas adhuc prodigiosioribus accumulet. Et ut semel dicam, plane novus Berosus ille videtur, et sunt ita paucis veris falsa plurima immista, ut cum probare omnia nequeas, reiicere tamen penitus vix audeas."
[31] Reineck 1580a, 22: "Carolus Magnus, ut mirifice studuit lectioni librorum Augustini, ita praecipue iis delectatus est, qui de civitate Dei

among his readers to abandon their stylistic prejudices and plunge into the rich histories of the German Middle Ages.

Like Baudouin, finally, Reineck based his recommendations for the study of history on his own extensive experience as a practitioner – a practitioner of a kind of scholarship widespread among German, as among French and British and Spanish scholars, all desperate to establish their own nation's place among the ancient peoples. His work, like Baudouin's and Bodin's, reflected his active engagement with forms of scholarship well outside the tradition of political history. During the late 1570s and early 1580s, he edited a whole series of medieval historians: Ditmar of Merseburg, Widukind, Helmold.[32] He searched for manuscripts, collated them with the existing editions, and equipped each edition with a detailed preface explaining his editorial procedures and a fully documented life of his author. Reineck's methodological grasp often exceeded his reach. Though he claimed that he did not try to improve the Latinity of his authors, he could not in fact restrain his chastening pen, and turned every improper *quia* he found in Widukind into a *quod*. After speculating interestingly about the manuscript tradition of Helmold's work, he ended up by suggesting that a friend's manuscript, shorter than the received text, represented both a first draft and an epitome

inscripti sunt. Idem hanc summam diligentiam adhibuit, ut vel inter coenandum praelegi sibi historias et antiquorum regum gesta voluerit. Nec minus in universam patriae historiam consuluit: Nam barbara et antiquissima carmina, quibus veterum regum actus et bella canebantur, scripsit, memoriaeque mandavit, teste Eginharto, qui alumnum se Caroli profitetur, et tam cum illo quam cum liberis amicitiam praedicat."
[32] Reineck (ed.) 1577, 1580a, 1580b, 1581.

of the chronicle. Sadly, as Helmold's twentieth-century editor Bernhard Schmeidler plaintively complained, these two arguments squarely contradicted one another.[33] Yet Reineck also made his expertise on these texts and their contexts clear. Sigismund Schorckel, the Naumburg medical man who published a moderately careful edition of Helmold in 1556, anticipated Reineck in warning readers not to let the author's stylistic crudities put them off.[34] But Reineck carefully noted the ways in which Helmold's account stood out – for example, his fair-minded explanation of the reasons for the break between Henry the Lion and Frederick Barbarossa, and his peculiar insistence that Henry's later life turned out exactly as he himself had wished.[35]

---

[33] See Helmold 1937.

[34] Schorckel (ed.) 1556, [A6 vo]: "Ac manifeste in hoc ipso historico apparet, quantum posteriorum temporum Ecclesiae et Episcopi a prioribus degenerarint. Has maximarum rerum, religionum videlicet atque imperiorum, mutationes consyderare, excellentibus ingeniis et Principibus viris digna cura est. Cumque talia multa in hoc historico extent, spero eius editionem candidis lectoribus non fore ingratam. Etsi autem stylus est incultior, et alicubi non satis Latinus (quod quidem vitium non tam authori quam temporibus est imputandum, scripsit enim ante annos pene 400. regnante Imperatore Friderico primo, quo tempore et Latina lingua, et omnes bonae artes foeda barbarie contaminatae atque obrutae iacuerunt, nec est cur quisquam Livianam aut Salustianam eloquentiam in homine Saxone, illius aetatis atque loci requirat) tamen historica multa, bona atque utilia continet, et quae in aliis scriptoribus non habentur."

[35] Reineck (ed.) 1581b, iii ro: "Videbatur et alterum istud mentione hic nostra ex Helmoldi historia repetendum, et cuiusdam quasi cautionis loco commonendum ac discutiendum, quod Henricum Leonem, cum is proscriptione Imp. Caes. Friderici Barbarossae dignitate et fortunis suis excidisset, recuperasse tandem universa, seu, ut ipse loquitur, cessisse

The openness that Reineck showed when dealing with the German Middle Ages was characteristic of his work as a historian. He also took an interest in the very earliest histories – for example, those recorded by Seth on his columns of brick and stone. In particular, he noted that the ancient Greeks, though they often spun fables about the early past, had done so in a systematic, allegorical way. Christian learning, he insisted, could provide the light that would guide the student through the Cimmerian shadows of early times. "For to touch on the matter briefly, and start from the religion of the Greeks, it is clear that their names have Hebrew meanings... Athene matched Adonai, Lord. Nor can I distinguish the name of Apollo, which

omnia iuxta placitum eius, et ereptum fuisse a circumventione Principum absque omni sui diminutione, affirmat [Helmold cap. 107 = 2.11, 210 Schmeidler: Et cesserunt omnia iuxta placitum ducis, et ereptus est a circumventione principum absque omni suimet diminucione. Schmeidler notes, ibid n. 2, that 'ante reditum imperatoris principibus inferior fuit, quod Helm. dicere noluit.'] Id enim perpetuo omnium qui eandem historiam monumentis commendarunt, repugnat consensui. Neque obscurum est, quibus Principis potentissimi exuviae cesserint. Quare hoc vel auctoris σφάλμα vel libri mendum ducamus. Est enim parte illa expositionis series perturbatior. Interea tamen Helmoldus proscriptionis Henrici Leonis causam προηγουμένην, ut Arnoldus προκαταρκτικήν, quemadmodum Dialectici vocarunt, enodare recte videtur. Nam quod alii de Principis illius perfidia, alii de elati animi fastu et morum perversitate inculcant et criminantur, locum habere non debet. [In capp. 103 (2.7) – 107 (2.11) Helmold ascribes the duke's problems to the other princes' envy of him.] Longeque tutius mea sententia sequemur omnium oculati testis Arnoldi auctoritatem, quam eos, qui post aut hisce nostris temporibus scripsere. Hos enim nescio quo partium studio multa saepe temere finxisse aut pleraque ignorasse, res docet."

145

the Latins used, from Baal." [36] Anyone who used his method and set out to combine Greek with sacred history, Reineck promised, would "find it easy to stride past the rough patches" in ancient tradition.[37] He was right, too – as more than one polyhistor would show in the seventeenth century, when erudite spiders crouched in their dark dens from Uppsala to Naples spun gossamer webs of genealogical conjecture, based on similar principles, that tied the original inhabitants of the Americas to the Laps, the Chinese, and many others, and proved that

[36] Reineck 1580a, 8: "Tametsi in his ipsis fabulis saepissime historia lateat. Quam ut absque Ecclesiae doctrina et scriptis elicere neutiquam licet, ita ubi illa tanquam ansae quaedam, ἢ χειραγωγίαι apprehenduntur, facilis se ad veritatem via pandit, et pro Cimmeriis tenebris clarissima se lux offert. Nam ut breviter saltem rem delibemus, et a religione Graecorum ordiamur, certum est, Deastrorum nomina Ebraeas habere notiones, et de appellationibus veluti per prosopopoeias numina conficta. . . . Ἀθήνη convenit cum Adonai, Dominus. Nec discerno Apollinis nomen, quod Latinae linguae in usu fuit, a Baal, non item Cerberi, quem canem inferorum tricipitem Poetae fingunt, ab Ebraeo Scorpher, ut cum sanctissimae memoriae maximique ingenii viro, Luthero, capita eius tria, peccatum, legem, mortem statuamus."

[37] Reineck 1580a, 9: "Caetera de mortalium primordiis a Graecis tradita, demto fabularum tanquam involucro, ferme eadem, quae sacris litteris commemorantur, reperimus. Quae nos hic singulatim retexere, adeoque ad vivum resecare, nec temporis nec instituti πρέπον ferebat. Vnum id dico, quae in Biblica historia extant Iapheti et Iavanis nomina, etiam ab utriusque linguae Poetis celebrari, sed modica inflexione mutata. Et si quis hoc iam nixus fundamento, Graecam historiam cum sacra coniunxerit, vix quicquam invium habebit, sed pleno gradu extra salebras procedere poterit. Sic enim res se habet, ut antiquitatis fontes e sacrarum litterarum veritate, rivuli vero atque corrugi a Graecae historiae auctoribus, quique vestigiis horum insistunt, petendi ac deducendi sint . . . "

Plato's Atlantis had been – who could doubt it? – Sweden.[38] And if Reineck's historical allegoresis provokes mockery now, he showed a more independent and critical attitude elsewhere – as when he argued, against Josephus, that the Greeks must have been literate in Homer's time, and pointed out that Josephus had adopted this extreme argument not because he believed it, but in his zeal to crush his learned opponent Apion.[39] In a century when Nanni and many other influential historians could have adapted Erasmus's famous prayer to Socrates and sighed, "Saint Josephus, pray for me," Reineck had the courage to see the rock on which Christian chronology rested as a human being capable of exaggeration and error.

Reineck defined the central purpose of history, however, in a distinctive way: not as pragmatic instruction of the sort Polybius and others had praised, but as another, apparently distinct realm of historical work. Genealogy, he claimed, "illuminates all the other parts of history, and without it they bear basically no fruit at all." After all, he pointed out, "anyone can see that histories chiefly deal with the persons who did

---

[38] See Allen 1970 and Mulsow 2005.

[39] Reineck 1580a, 10: "Audet denique hoc etiam affirmare, Graecos Troianis temporibus litteris caruisse: ideoque Homeri Poema non litteris sed cantibus conservatum. Verum ut in his aliquid Iosepho demus, ita res tamen per se propterea non ruit. Nec mihi dubium est, magis hoc auctorem illum egisse, ut adversarium Apionem, contra quem illa scripsit, quemque Eusebius lib. 10. de praeparat. Evang. cap. 3. Grammaticorum omnium diligentissimum historiae perscrutatorem nominavit, quam historiam Graecam everteret. Nam eam ad rem talibus quasi machinis opus erat. Et longe cautior, ideoque verior eiusdem Eusebii in Chronologia, quam de praepar. Evang. ibidem ex Africani annalibus assertio est. Neque enim omnem Graecae historiae fidem derogat, sed temporibus discrimen facit."

things, and that they must be separated out into familes." Like states, moreover, families had set periods of existence, during which they grew from humble origins to positions of power and then declined and died. "Knowledge of this," Reineck insisted,

> must be very pleasant for kings and others who steer the ship of state, and very useful for everyone. For if we consider the matter rightly, the ornament of nobility itself rests on this as if on a foundation. For if we are to believe Aristotle – since we cannot and should not debate this point precisely here – it is the antiquity and integrity of the breed, or its rank, attained by the services of its ancestors to the state.[40]

[40] Reineck 1580a, 24: "Libet nunc partes disciplinae istius perstringere, ut hinc porro planum fiat, e qua plurimum commodi expectandum sit. Nominavit autem has Eustathius, Dionyisii interpres: τὸ τοπικὸν τὸ πραγματικὸν τὸ χρονικὸν τὸ γενεαλογικὸν [cf. Herding 1965 for this source]. Et Polybius alibi τῷ πραγματικῷ, alibi τῷ γενεαλογικῷ primas defert. Ego de posteriore assentiri ausim: Est enim haec, quae reliquas omnes illustret, et sine qua illae ferme fructum nullum praebeant ... Quem enim fugit, in historiis potissimum de personis, quae res gessere, agi, has autem rursus familiis discerni oportere? Et certe quidem cum secundum coelestis doctrinae veritatem et Ecclesiae conservationem, sint habeanturque bona, quibus mortalium felicitas comprehenditur atque constat, praecipua, Imperia et artes, etiam familias, quae utraque condiderunt, illustrarunt, propagarunt, non negligendas, sed summo honoris cultu afficiendas, non potest non apertum omnibus esse. Fit autem istud eo pacto rectissime, si earum obsequio et memoriae studeamus, hoc est ortum, incrementum, interitum investigemus: aut investigata cognoscamus. Habent enim semper ut ipsa imperia, ita et familiae, suas quasi periodos fatalesque vices, seu ut Quintiliani verbis utar, initium, incrementum, summam. Nec potest non talis cognitio ut principibus, quique alii reip. clavum

History, accordingly, should take the form of tables – long genealogical tables that laid out the history of rulers, family by family.

Reineck's precepts derived directly from his practice. Early in the 1570s, he had published a massive, 1,300-page account of the families of the first three monarchies – a work that largely consisted of genealogical tables, which his publishers found very difficult to reproduce, with detailed commentaries.[41] After he completed his work on method, he set about revising this compendium into its final form – the staggering 2,070 pages of the *Historia Iulia sive Syntagma Heroicum* of 1584. When Reineck praised the pleasure and usefulness of genealogical research, he did so from first-hand knowledge. In the sixteenth and seventeenth centuries, to be sure, everyone in a position of political or cultural power knew the stud book as well as one of Jessica Mitford's Hons and Rebels. Joseph Scaliger learned this to his cost, when astute genealogical research by his enemies in Italy proved that he was not, as his father had convinced him, a descendant of the della Scala of Verona, worthy to wear the purple robes of a prince when examining doctoral candidates at Leiden, but the grandson of a painter and illuminator, Benedetto Bordon.[42] But why argue that history should consist in a vast adumbration of the *Almanach de Gotha*? What put this particular bee in Reineck's bonnet?

tenent, iucundissima, ita omnibus utilissima esse. Sane si recte rem aestimemus, etiam ipsum Nobilitatis decus hoc quasi fundamento nititur. Est enim illa, si Aristoteli credimus (nam ad amussim ista hic disceptari nec debebant, nec poterant) vetustas et integritas generis seu parta maiorum in rempub. meritis ac propagata dignitas."
[41] Reineck 1574. [42] Billanovich 1968.

To some extent, the wider development of historical practice shaped Reineccius's narrow, tabular vision of the past. Fantastic genealogies blossomed across mid-sixteenth-century Europe as never before, and influential scholars competed to draw them up. Nanni included with his fakes long genealogical tables that traced the peoples of northern Europe and Iberia back to noble ancestors, boldly inventing where the blank spots appeared in the record: hence Dryius, founder of the Druids, and Longo and Bardus, ancestors of the Longobards. Many others followed his lead. Wolfgang Lazius, the immensely learned medical man whose inky spoor marks hundreds of manuscripts in the Austrian National Library, was a genuinely erudite collector and antiquary, and he desperately sought solid information about such burning questions as the exact size of the Roman foot. But when he set out to trace the origins of the German peoples, he too felt the hot, intoxicating breath of the spirit of invention on his cheek, and succumbed. Lazius claimed to have found a Hebrew inscription that recorded the death of "Mordechai the great warrior" in the Vienna suburb of Gumpendorf, and used it to prove that the modern Viennese descended directly from, of all people, the Jews who settled the country after the Flood.[43] Immensely erudite Italian scholars like Onofrio Panvinio, as Roberto Bizzocchi has shown in a magnificent, picaresque book, not only reconstructed the families of ancient Rome, but gratified the taste of modern Italian nobles for proof that their families had Roman origins.[44]

[43] Lazius 1557, 20–3. Characteristically, Lazius also did quite sober work on Roman epigraphy; see Stenhouse 2005, esp. 118–24.
[44] Bizzocchi 1995.

Genealogical fantasies flourished even more mightily in the Gormenghast-like courts of the Holy Roman Empire, where Joannes Trithemius cut imaginary Carolingian historians out of whole cloth in order to fill the Germans' centuries of wandering between the fall of Troy and their arrival in the west. The emperor Maximilian, ever conscious that the Habsburgs had come recently to power, had a special taste for evidence that their roots stretched back to the past. He made multiple efforts to gain access to Hunibald, Trithemius's chief authority – efforts that embarrassed the learned abbot, who found himself reduced to claiming that wicked monks at his former monastery of Sponheim had sold this non-existent text.[45] Yet Maximilian's credulity had limits. The historian Johannes Cuspinian heard him put sharp questions to another of his court scholars, Joannes Stabius: "Are you tracing my descent back to Noah's Ark? And claiming that the creator of my family tree was Japhet, the third son of Noah, who exposed his father's genitals? If a bad tree never yields good fruit, how can a good and fertile stock come from a root that is not good?" In the discussion that followed, Maximilian made clear his real anxiety: he did not want to become a credulous laughing stock in an age of criticism.[46] Controversies raged.

---

[45] For the full story and the texts see Chmel 1840–1.

[46] Reineck 1580a, 25: "Nec dissimilem in Austria sua de Stabii Austriacae familiae originem a Iapheto, Nohae F. deducentis, refutatis ineptiis a Maximiliano I. Caes. retulit historiam Cuspinianus: Quae etsi stylo et orationis genere negligentiore exposita, per se tamen memorabilis sit, hic eam de verbo ad verbum ascribo: Audivi coram, inquit, Divum Maximilianum saepius loquentem cum Stabio: Tu me ex arca Nohae ducis? et stemmatis originisque meae auctorem tribuis Iaphet, tertium

Reineck envisioned his chronology as a buttress for the historical legitimacy of the Empire. But he also set out, like a good, critical humanist, to shred some of the fantastic lineages that busy scholarly spiders had spun for their noble patrons. Vanity, he pointed out, had always fostered genealogical invention. Like Baudouin, he examined ancient precedents for modern ways of studying the past. After the Gauls burnt Rome, early records were lost. When Caesar traced his ancestry to Venus or Galba, more mysteriously, to Pasiphe, they used genealogies drawn up "to gratify certain men by inserting their kin into very distinguished and prominent families which had nothing to do with them."[47] The genealogist must not allow his art to be distorted by such pressures. Reineck, moreover, built on precedents set by other north German scholars as he attempted his critical sorting of ancient and modern family trees. As early as 1567 his friend Georg Fabricius, an expert

scilicet Nohae F. qui pudenda patris detexit? quasi ex radice non bona, possit produci stipes bona et fertilis, cum tamen mala arbor nunquam bonum producat fructum? Et licet Stabius acute Divo Caesari multis aulicis astantibus respondisset (nam haud vulgariter amabatur a Caesare, quod omnibus constat et compertum est) tamen Caesar postea dixit: Caveas hanc ignominiam mihi et posteris meis inurere, qui mihi irascentur, et alii exerta lingua subsannabunt. Hactenus Cuspinianus."

[47] Reineck 1580a, 25: "De historicis id genus notetur locus Plutarchi e Clodii cuiusdam temporum indice: Clodius, inquit, antiquos illos temporum commentarios ostendit in Gallica urbis calamitate periisse: eos autem, qui nunc extant, compositos esse ab aliis, qui in gratiam certorum virorum genera eorum in praecipuas familias, maximeque insignes, nulla omnino ratione ad eos pertinentes, ingesserint. Hactenus Plutarchus." According to Reineck, Caesar traced his ancestry to Venus and Galba his to Pasiphe "haud dubie nulla alia de causa, quam ut saltem vetustatis opinione plus sibi familiaeque dignitatis conciliaret."

antiquary, sent him genealogies of Macedonian and Spartan kings compiled by the Rostock humanist David Chytraeus – himself the author of an often-reprinted *ars historica*, and a believer in a critical approach to family histories.

Critical remarks and procedures for sifting evidence gratify the modern reader. But Reineck saw his work as more than a bulwark against the fantasies of crooked scholars and deluded heralds.[48] He claimed it was the vital center of history. In fact, he went so far as to distort Polybius – who admitted that as some readers liked pragmatic history, others enjoyed genealogy – to support this view. And his zeal matters. Many pre-modern societies, as the medievalists Patrick Geary and Michel Pastoureau and the Indian historians Bernard Cohn and Romila Thapar have taught us, see genealogy as a profound form of historical thought – one that offers vital charters for modern rulers and institutions.[49]

In pre-modern Europe, everyone knew how hard royal families could find it to preserve an unbroken line of male rulers, and how catastrophic it could prove when royal powers of generation and conception failed. In particular, as Paula Sutter Fichtner has shown, the princely families of the Holy Roman Empire worried continually not only about the earliest stages in their family trees, but about the present and future ones as well. Lutheran princes knew that divine command obliged them to have intercourse as often as possible with their consorts. Many of them produced six, eight, or ten

---

[48] On the fascinating case of Britain, where heralds and antiquaries fought bitterly over who had the authority to determine genealogical questions, see Kendrick 1950 and Woolf 2003.

[49] Pastoureau 1979; Geary 1994 and 2006; Cohn 1961; Thapar 2000.

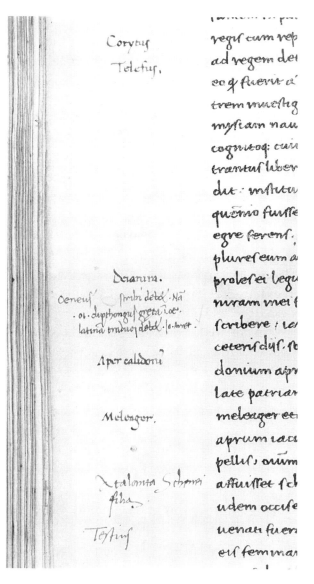

FIGURE 7. Diodorus Siculus, as translated by Poggio Bracciolini. The Latin translations of the Greek historians Diodorus Siculus and Dionysius of Halicarnassus, carried out by humanists like Poggio in the mid-fifteenth century, did much to stimulate historical thought. In the marginal note reproduced here, the humanist and antiquary Giovanni Tortelli grumbles about a diphthong missing from the name Oeneus in Poggio's work.

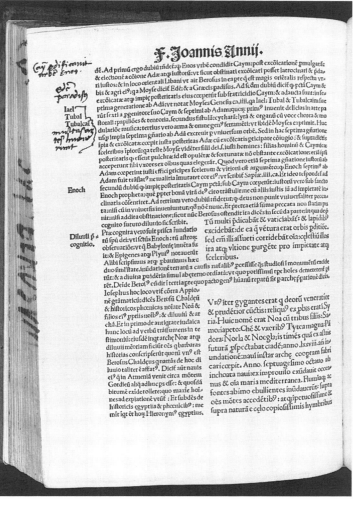

FIGURE 8. Annius of Viterbo recreates ancient history. No one did more to stimulate the development of historical criticism than the ingenius forger Giovanni Nanni, or Annius, who swathed the texts of Berosus, Manetho, and other authors which he composed with commentaries that demonstrated their reliability. In this copy of the Paris, 1512, edition, heavily annotated by a Florentine reader, Berosus describes how Noah used his knowledge of astrology to predict the Flood.

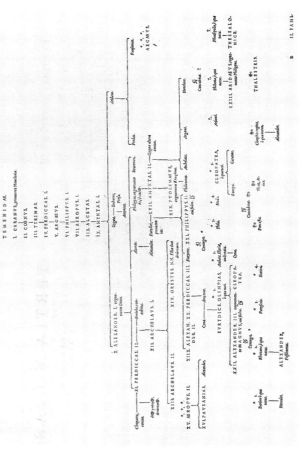

FIGURE 9. Reiner Reineck recreates history as genealogy. A genealogy of the kings of Macedonia, as reconstructed in his work on the rulers of the Four Monarchies and many others (Basle, 1574).

pitolino traditur, lorica eos aureâ uti solitos: & meminit Florus, ita
Ptolemei Dionysij submersi in Nilo corpus postea cognitū. Sepulcra
in parte regie prope Alexandri delubrū habuêre: ad quæ inspicienda
cùm Alexandri uiso corpore ambitiosè ab Alexandrinis inuitaret Au
gustus Cæsar, Regem se, non mortuos uidere uoluisse, respondit.

NVMMVS PTOLEMÆI.

Quis nam Ptolemæus hic fuerit, quæ doceant argumenta nulla sunt. Si quid tamen coniecturis dandum,
rectè Ptolemæus Lagi accipitur. Nam quod facies ceu repræsentat ingenium placidum & moderatum, id de eo
prodidêre omnes. Communicauit autem hunc nobiscum nummum uir nobilis, & antiquitatis studiosiss. Iulius Commeristadius. Cui ea parte debitam â nobis memoris obseruantiæ gratiam cùm referre
minus liceret, non habere quidem non debuimus.

ii   FAMI.

FIGURE 10. Reineck reproduces what he takes as a coin of
Ptolemy Lagi, noting that the face represented on it matches the
account of the king's temperament given in historical sources.

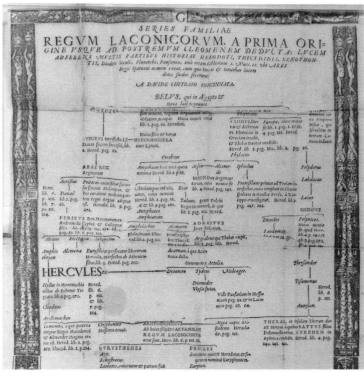

FIGURE 11. Genealogy in the teaching of history. This broadside genealogy of the kings of Sparta was drawn up by the influential teacher and historian David Chytraeus. It illustrates that Reineck was by no means unusual in believing that genealogy formed the core – or at least part of the core – of history and that the student of history must master the generations of great families, ancient and modern.

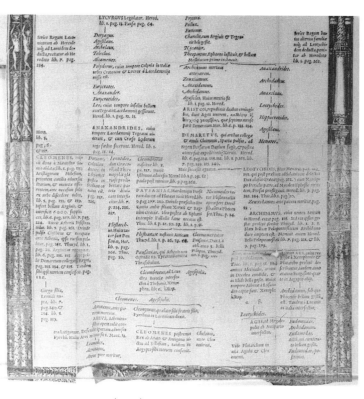

FIGURE 11. (cont.)

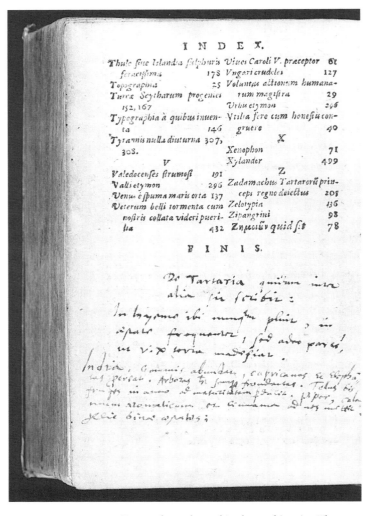

FIGURE 12. Geography and travel in the *ars historica*. The owner of a copy of the 1591 edition of Bodin's *Methodus* followed the author's lead in turning the end papers of his copy into a small but fascinating notebook on Tartary, Constantinople, Hagia Sophia, and the Hyperboreans.

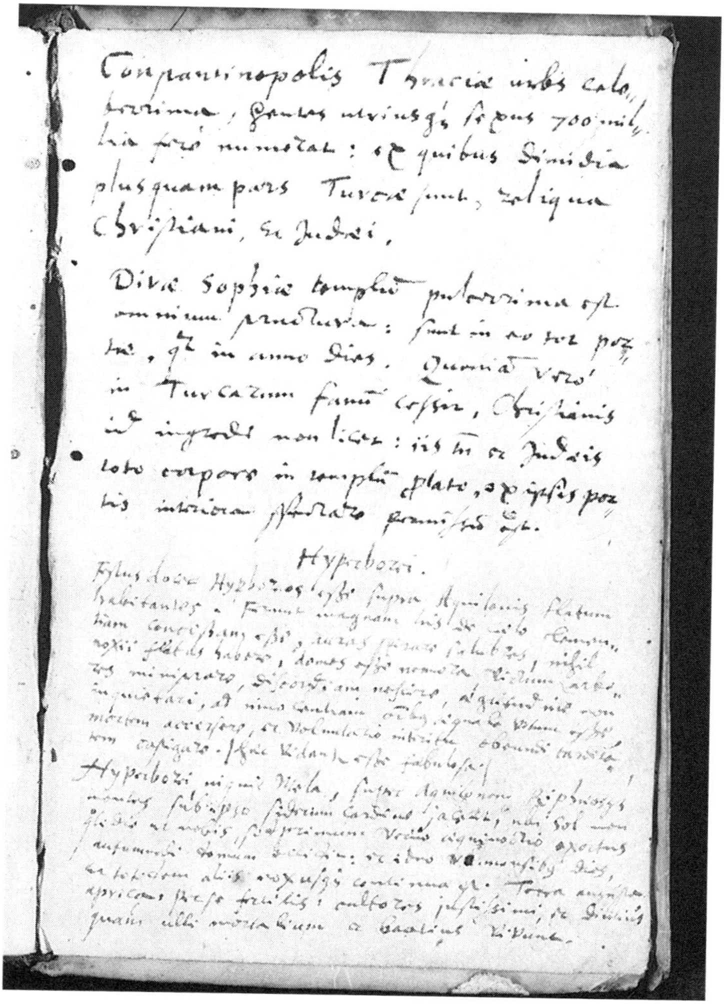

Conpantinopolis Thraciae urbs cele-
berrima, ... utriusque sexus 700 mil.
... fere numerat: ex quibus dimidia
plusquam pars Turcae sunt, reliqui
Christiani, et Judaei.

Divae Sophiae templum pulcherrimum est.
omnium pulcherrima: ... in ... po-
... in anno dies. Quoniam vero
in Turcarum fanum cessit, Christianis
id ingredi non licet: iis tamen et Judaeis
toto corpore in templum plate, ... ipsis potius interiora ... est.

Hyperborei.

Fertur docere Hyperboreos ... super Aquilonis flatum
habitantes a ... magnam his ... ...
... ...
... ... domos ... nomine ... ...
... ...
... ...
... ...

Hyperborei ... ... super Aquilonem Hyperboreos
... subiecto septem ... ...
... ...
... ...
... ...
apricas ... fertilis; cultores justissimi; ...
quam illi ... ...

FIGURE 12. (cont.)

live male children. Inheritance, however, was normally partible. Fragmentation inevitably followed – fragmentation of territory and resources.[50] No one knew this better than Reineck's masters in Braunschweig-Lüneburg. The territories of Lüneburg, split among three lines, came back together in the 1560s only because two branches of the family died out; Braunschweig remained split until the family annexed it and joined it to Lüneburg in 1584.

When Reineck practised and preached the vital importance of "the genealogical part of history," then, he expressed a vision of time shaped by his own period and place. In his world of well-ordered police states, charters rested on birth, orders emanated from the top, and birth order often determined the destiny of individuals and of states. To that extent, genealogy could become a critical method, a key to all mythologies and many truths – or at least a rigorous introduction to the complex ways in which providence had blessed or withheld favors from great kin groups, and their states in turn had survived or failed. Unlike us, Reineck's contemporaries and immediate successors were not genealogical innocents, and they appreciated this enterprise. David Chytraeus turned out genealogical charts, which he had printed as broadsides, like his announcements of his lectures on the ancient historians, to serve the needs of his students. Even Keckermann, who had his doubts about the vogue for genealogical research – the Dukes of Lorraine, he complained, could not possibly be the descendants of the Trojan Antenor, especially if his funeral inscription in Padua should be genuine – cited Reineck

[50] Fichtner 1989.

as a diligent worker and primary authority in this contested field.[51] Seventeenth- and eighteenth-century German historians from Conring to Gatterer continued to emphasize the vital importance of genealogy and heraldry – which formed central parts of the new Kameralwissenschaft of the eighteenth century and central methods of the new historiography practised in Göttingen.

Reineck embellished his genealogies, now and then, with reproductions of ancient coins that bore profile portraits of important rulers, from Priam to the redoubtable queen Artemisia. Every time he did so, he thanked the friends who had sent him the originals. These genteel tips of the old fedora revealed more than Reineck's courtesy. They also declared that his work represented more than an individual achievement. A far-flung community of German antiquaries – Sambucus and Crato von Kraftheim in Vienna, Giphanius in Strasbourg, Chytraeus in Rostock, Rantzau in his country estate at Segenberg and Neander at the Paedagogium in Ilfeld – sat like Balzacian collectors in their Kunst- und Wunderkammern, delicately examining coins and other relics of the ancient world. They commented on drafts of Reineck's work, reported others' favorable opinions, sent him maps and tables, encouraged him to treat Lazius's *Migrations* as a labyrinth into which one wandered at one's peril, and gently corrected slips of his pen.[52] A number of these men eagerly exchanged coins and expert opinions about their authenticity with Reineck. Handsome, if approximate, woodcut images of the coins they approved gave what he had to say a more than individual authority.[53]

---

[51] Keckermann 1610, 19–22.   [52] Reineck 1583.   [53] Ibid.

But the coins also served another purpose. When Reineck printed the effigy of one of the Ptolemies, he remarked that he could not identify the ruler for certain. But he also noted that "If there is any place for conjecture, this can properly be taken as Ptolemy the son of Lagus. For the countenance reveals a placid, mild spirit, and all agree that he had these qualities."[54] Reineck, like so many of his contemporaries, believed that he could read the mind's construction from the face. Physiognomics offered the keys to this kingdom of interpretation, and many scholars applied them – as Francis Haskell suggested some time ago – as deftly to ancient portraits as to modern bodies.[55] Some experts nourished doubts. Baudouin, for example, admitted that that the "bodily image" of Justinian "which we have seen in his coins, had something Gothic and unintelligent about it." But he immediately pointed out that Justinian's deeds, "which would have been impossible to conceive or to command without the aid of a heroic mind and judgement, show that physiognomy deceives us in this case."[56] Nonetheless, here too Reineck did what came naturally: his practices

---

[54] Reineck 1574, I, 145: "Quisnam Ptolemaeus hic fuerit, quae doceant argumenta nulla sunt. Si quid tamen coniecturis dandum, recte Ptolemaeus Lagi accipitur. Nam quod facies ceu repraesentat ingenium placidum et moderatum, id de eo prodidere omnes."

[55] Haskell 1993.

[56] Baudouin 1545, 75: "Sed videamus reliqua. Quidam aiunt Iustinianum prorsus illiteratum fuisse atque adeo ἀναλφαβητὸν. Sed nescio an id satis probari possit. Certe aliter iudicat Platina in vita Bonifacii secundi. Vt ut tamen fuerit, siquid literarum in eo desideratum est, abunde pensatum fuit consilio et subsidio prudentum. Indicat quidem corporalis eius effigies (quam in antiquis numismatibus vidimus) quiddam Gothicum ac stupidum: sed physiognomiam hic fallere, ostendunt eius gesta, quae nec cogitari nec imperari potuerunt, sine

164

represented a plausible period way to give his readers insight into the characters of the great men and women who, by his account, made history happen. That helps to explain why his correspondents treated him as a model historian, whose opinion on the date when the Olympiads began was very much worth having, whose willingness to make a personal inspection of the tomb of Widukind deserved emulation, and who might even know whether ancient precedents existed to help interpret the comet of 1580.[57] Even a generation later, when Bartholomäus Keckermann sharply criticized the authors in Wolf's collection for their "often strange and contradictory judgments on history, which miss their mark by a great distance, and throw the minds of students into disorder and confusion," he treated Reineck as a foeman worthier of his bent nib.[58]

Jean Bodin enraged scholars across the Holy Roman Empire as effectively as Reineck, a few years later, would

magna quadam heroici animi et iudicii praestantia. Privata opera non commemoro, nec res scrutor domesticas, in quibus fortassis multa sunt quae vituperes. Iaceant illa, quae nec Deus extare, nec autor ipse voluit edi, Procopii *anekdota*, quibus continebantur graves in Iustinianum notae et acerba privatae eius vitae reprehensio. Nos solum publicam huius principis vitam laudamus … "

[57] Reineck 1583, 17 vo (Giphanius on the Olympics); 39 ro (Chytraeus on Widukind); 31 ro (Rungius on the comet).

[58] Keckermann 1614, II, 1310: "Sunt enim, ut dicam quod res est, in illa Penu Historica, saepe mira et tortuosa iudicia de Historia, quae longe aberrant a scopo, et discentium ingenia turbant atque intricant, nisi Logicum et Methodicum et dextrum iudicium ad eorum lectionem offeratur: Vt non dicam quam varia et inter se pugnantia sint iudicia nonnullorum, qui de Historia et eius studio scripserunt, ita ut Lectores minus instructi nesciant, quid probare, quid reprobare debeant." For Reineck see the criticisms on 1314, 1341, 1350.

engage them in discussion. Unlike Reineck, however, he became not only a local, but an international celebrity – one whose *ars historica* sparked debate all the way across Europe. In its time, Bodin's *Method for the Easy Comprehension of History* (1566) dominated the field – so much so that Wolf entitled the first edition of his collection "Jean Bodin's Method of History and other texts." George Sandys called Bodin "the Censurer of all histories." To this day he commands a level of attention denied to innovative scholars and dazzling writers like Patrizi and Baudouin – to say nothing of Reineck or Chytraeus. Yet the *Methodus* frustrates and appalls its dizzy modern reader. Bodin tried to embrace the whole encyclopedia, arguing that divine, natural, and human history should be parallel enterprises. He made his "method" – which claimed to show how each people's constitution fitted its character, as shaped by its original locale and climate – into a vast Watts Tower of found objects drawn from every imaginable source, ancient and modern.[59]

Bodin devised a formalized art of historical criticism, one that offered precise rules for the selection and evaluation of past historians and that has impressed more than one modern student with its radical modernity – its acceptance of the historian's need to use secondary accounts as well as primary ones. But he took these rules, which emphasized the honesty and credibility of ancient priests, directly from Annius, sometimes word for word, and thus showed that he had not grasped one of his colleague Baudouin's simplest, clearest lessons.[60] Every time Bodin formulated a crisp new principle, moreover,

[59] See esp. Moreau-Reibel 1936; Brown 1939; Tooley 1953; Couzinet 1996.
[60] Grafton 1991.

166

it turned in application, as steadily as the needle to the pole, to bizarre and astonishing conclusions. Bodin made clear, in passages that adumbrate the historical detective work of Marc Bloch, that a people's language contains vital clues to its past. To prove it, in perhaps the most famous passage in his work, he instanced the Walloons or, in Latin, Ouallones – those French-speakers who had wandered northwards to Belgium, centuries before his time, through the primeval forest, plaintively asking "Où allons-nous?" as they went.[61] No wonder that even the young John Pocock turned away in horror from this endlessly maddening text when he composed his brilliant sketch of "the French prelude to modern historiography." Not for him a tangle with what he called the "strange, semi-ruinous mass" of Bodin's *Methodus*.[62] Yet most of Bodin's contemporaries, and many later readers, considered him *the* authority on the *ars historica*. His work received signal honors: warm appreciation and sharp criticism from Keckermann, a reprint in 1650, and prominent mention in every bibliography of the *ars historica*, down to that of Nicolas Lenglet Dufresnoy in 1713. Even in sceptical Cambridge – as Bodin discovered during his visit in 1580 – copies of Bodin's *Republic*, which extended and qualified the arguments of the *Methodus*, lay open on every don's desk. What did these well-informed readers see in Bodin?

Bodin devoted one pregnant chapter to refuting what he described as two connected errors: the theory of the Four

---

[61] Wolf (ed.) 1579, I, 357: "Ouallones enim a Belgis appellamur, quod Gallis veteribus contigit, quum orbem terrarum peragrarent, ac mutuo interrogantes quaererent, *où allons nous*, id est, quonam proficiscimur?"

[62] Pocock 1957.

Empires and the myth of the Golden Age. In chapter 2 of the book of Daniel, the prophet interprets for Nebuchadnezzar a statue that the Great King saw in a vision. Its head consists of gold, its shoulders of silver, its loins of brass, its legs and feet partly of stone and partly of mud. In the king's dream, a great stone smashes the statue. Daniel not only told the king what he has dreamed, but also identifies it as a true vision of history. A series of four empires would rule in turn, and then divine action would bring history to an end. Many sixteenth-century world historians, especially Protestants, took this vision as the most authoritative guide to past and future alike. They identified the four empires: Assyrians and Babylonian, Medes and Persians, Macedonians and Romans. And they took the Holy Roman Empire of their own time as the last of all.[63] Daniel's vision – as Arnaldo Momigliano pointed out long ago – followed Greek models, both in structuring history as a series of coherent periods and in treating each as worse than the one before. It was relatively easy, accordingly, to accommodate it to the Greek and Roman myths that portrayed the earliest period of human history as a Golden Age – a pastoral paradise without private property, weapons, or the spirit of heroism that, in the words of Otto Neugebauer, "must often have made life in Greece hell on earth."[64]

Bodin scathingly rejected both views. Many learned men accepted the theory of the Four Empires, he admitted: "It has won over countless interpreters of the Bible; it includes among modern writers Martin Luther, Melanchthon, Sleidan,

[63] Seifert 1990 offers the best account.
[64] Neugebauer 1969, 71.

168

Lucidus, Funck and Panvinio – men well read in ancient history and things divine."[65] Every one of them agreed: the vision indicated that there would be four world empires, and that the Holy Roman Empire that still existed would be the last of them. Like Baudouin, he knew he was living in a very large and diverse world. Like Baudouin, he agilely surfed the high-breaking waves of information that poured in from all corners of the globe and scoffed at the parochialism of those who refused to see them beat and overwhelm Europe's shores. Only a wilful refusal to look up from one's desk and examine the world as it was, Bodin argued, could possibly explain the notion that four empires had dominated world history. "What," he asked, "has Germany to oppose to the sultan of the Turks? Or which state can more aptly be called a monarchy? This fact is obvious to everyone – if there is anywhere in the world any majesty of empire and true monarchy, it must radiate from the sultan."[66] The theory also omitted such prominent exceptions as the Goths, the Arab caliphates, and the Tartars. History, properly studied, revealed "almost an infinitude" of great empires, and refuted all efforts to stuff the entire past into Daniel's prophetic corset.

[65] Wolf (ed.) 1579, I, 298: "Inveteratus error de quatuor imperiis ac magnorum virorum opinione pervulgatus tam alte radices egit, ut vix evelli posse videatur. Habet enim prope infinitos bibliorum interpretes, habet e iunioribus Martinum, Melanchthonem, Sleidanum, Lucidum, Funccium, Onuphrium: rerum divinarum et antiquitatis homines valde peritos"; Bodin 1945, 291.

[66] Wolf (ed.) 1579, I, 299–300: "Sed ad exteros veniamus. Quid habet Germania quod principi Turcarum opponat? aut quis merito maiore monarcha dici potest? patet hoc quidem omnium oculis. si enim est usquam terrarum ulla maiestas imperii ac verae monarchiae, in eo profecto elucet"; Bodin 1945, 292.

As to the Golden Age, Bodin railed, this was in fact the age of Ham, who grasped the genitals of his father Noah, murmured an incantation, and rendered him sterile; the age of the Romans, who sacrificed humans at their gladiatorial shows; and of primitive laws, which had failed to punish crimes as they should and, if unchanged, would have allowed wickedness to flourish unchecked. By contrast, a salient legal instance proved the "refinement" of modern customs: "Thievery, which once incurred only a civil judgment, not only according to the laws of the Hebrews but also to those of the Greeks and the Latins, now everywhere in the world is repaid by capital punishment."[67] History, for Bodin, was not a long slow funeral march from light to darkness, but if anything the reverse.

Predictably, Bodin's views proved incendiary – especially in the Holy Roman Empire. The universal chronicle of the astronomer Joachim Carion, which, after Philipp Melanchthon reworked it, became the standard text for teaching world history in Lutheran universities, treated the theory of the Four Empires as the framework through which one should learn to read all histories. "Anyone who wants to profit by reading history must fold all of chronology since the Creation into a fixed order."[68] From the start, this chronicle highlighted the central role of Germany in the final drama of world history:

[67] Wolf (ed.) 1579, 1, 306: "nam furta quae olim civili tantum iudicio, non modo Hebraeorum sed etiam Graecorum et Latinorum legibus, nunc ubique gentium capite puniuntur"; Bodin 1945, 298.
[68] Carion and Melanchthon 1557, 12: "Qui igitur cum fructu aliquo historias vult legere, is omnia tempora a mundo condito complecti debet in certum ordinem."

But this is the true history of the world, in which the most powerful kingdoms and monarchies have succeeded one another in a certain order, and the world has never declared their power as it has in this age. Therefore we shall divide this period into four monarchies. For God seems to have wanted to keep the world in operation with a certain fixed form of control, so that a sense of shame and honor would be conserved, and the evil punished, and to that end he created monarchies. But monarchies exist where one man has the highest power, to conserve peace and make law. But monarchies of this kind were so powerful that other kings – even when they lived outside them – could not resist or oppose them. And there were only four of these monarchies in a certain fixed succession. First the Kingdom of the Assyrians, after them the Persians ruled, then the Greeks, and finally the Romans. And God has raised Germany to the peak of this empire in these last times, before all the other nations.[69]

---

[69] Carion and Melanchthon 1557, 14: "Caeterum haec aetas vera et propia est mundi, in qua potentissima regna et Monarchiae ordine quodam sibi mutuo successerunt, neque unquam perinde potentiam suam et virtutes declaravit mundus quam in hac aetate. Igitur separabimus hoc tempus in quatuor Monarchias. Nam videtur voluisse Deus certa quadam gubernatione mundum in officio contineri, ut pudoris et honestatis ratio conservaretur, et mali punirentur, ideoque Monarchias instituit. Sunt autem Monarchiae huiusmodi regna, ubi summa rerum omnium potestas penes unum est, publicae pacis et iuris conservandi causa. Fuit autem huiusmodi Monarchiae tanta potentia, cui alii reges, quanquam extra eius imperium constituti, non potuerunt se opponere vel opprimere. Et extiterunt tales Monarchiae successione quadam ordinaria tantum quatuor. Primum regnum Assyriorum fuit. Post hos Persae imperarunt, deinde Graeci, postremo Romani. Et ad huius imperii honorem ac fastigium evexit his postremis temporibus Germanos Deus

German scholar after scholar leapt to defend the theory of the Four Empires from the attack of one who – as the theologian Quenstedt put it – "vomited slanders on the German nation." Matthias Dresser, for example, argued at length that one must not apply human categories to a divine prophecy. The empires symbolized by Nebuchadnezzar's image were not the greatest in geographical or human terms. In any event, no human empire had ever ruled the world as a whole. The four empires were those that God, for His own purposes, made stronger and more glorious than the rest.[70] So much, he argued, for the Ethiopians, the Tartars, the Spanish, the French, and any other claimants to world empire that Bodin might wish

prae nationibus reliquis." For German theories on the meaning of world history in this period see esp. Klempt 1960, Seifert 1990, and Brosseder 2004.

[70] Dresser 1606, II, 6–7: "Cui respondeo: Monarchiam non regionum spaciis aut populorum numero, nec ulla Principis origine illustri metiendam esse, sed ex nativo fonte, hoc est, Prophetae ipsius verbis et sententia [ed. -ae] aestimandam. Non enim in vaticiniis divinis humanum adhibendum est iudicium, neque consulenda ratio, sed solius verbi divini ductum sequi oportet. Quod nisi fecerimus, labefactare facile poterimus Danielis prophetiam, et omnia eius regna evertere. Age enim si locorum aut regionum multitudine atque amplitudine metiri voluerimus Monarchiam: ecquid stabit Assyriorum, Persarum, aut Graecorum Monarchia? quippe qui neque Europae neque Africae, neque Orientis omnes partes complexi sunt. Quotus enim quisque eorum populis Septentrionalibus? quis Africanis? quis Indianis omnibus imperavit? Ergo nihil efficies, si hoc modo argumentari voles: Monarchia dominatum totius terrarum orbis continet. Talem vero nemo ab initio mundi consecutus est aut tenuit ... " 7: "Quid igitur nominat Propheta Monarchiam? Vocat regnum κατ᾽ ἐξοχὴν quod Deus potentia, fortitudine, et gloria praeter caetera regna armavit, et in omnes dominari vult."

to cite. Their size and power did not make them world monarchies in the prophetic sense.[71] Bodin's attack on histories based on Daniel proved, in the end, a sort of theological own goal: he provoked many who might never have thought of doing so to defend prophetic history, and to do so with fierce tenacity.

Bodin's counterhistory – like everything in Bodin's work – fused the brilliant with the bizarre. To sustain his argument that the ancient world was primitive, he cited Thucydides's brilliant, sophistic argument "that a little before his time such was the barbarity and ferocity of men in Greece itself that by land and by sea piracy was openly practised . . . Yet since fortifications did not exist at that time and there were no defenses, justice resided in force, and the old colonists were continually driven from possession by new ones."[72] When he went on to

---

[71] Dresser 1606, 11, 38–9: "Absit etiam, ut vel levitate vel petulantia ingenii, aut plures Monarchias fingamus, quam expresse ponit Daniel aut propter infirmitatem Imperio Romano titulum 4. regni aut Monarchiae denegemus: ne et Deo, autori istius vaticinii, et experientiae ipsi reclamare videamur. Sit potentior Princeps Aethiopum, sit Rex Regum et dominus dominantium Geog magnus Tartarus Cham, teneat Rex Hispaniae Imperium maius aut amplius Romano sive Germanico: non tamen propterea est Imperator seu Monarcha Romanus a Daniele praedictus. Desinat ergo obiicere nobis Ioannes Bodinus, vel Tartari, vel Aethiopis, vel Arabum, vel Galli etiam imperium, nec tam spectet quid amplum sit aut magnificum in mundo, quam quid cum vaticinio Prophetico congruat." For an interesting Catholic critique of Bodin see Possevino 1597, 12 ro–15 ro.

[72] Wolf (ed.) 1579, 1: 305–6: "Sed ne videantur haec fabulis similia, Thucydidi verissimo historiae parenti assentiamur: is enim testatum reliquit paulo ante sua tempora tantam fuisse hominum in ipsa Graecia barbariem ac feritatem, ut terra marique latrocinia palam exercerentur, et sine ulla contumelia quaeri a praetereuntibus consueverit, utrum latrones, utrum piratae essent necne [1.5.2]?" Bodin 1945, 298.

argue that modern inventions like printing could "vie with anything of the ancients," by contrast, he drew on arguments that cutting-edge humanists had been developing for generations – ever since Lorenzo Valla showed, in a brilliant diatribe, that the ancients had not known the modern clock, bell, or compass, and Polydore Vergil devoted a whole book to praising ancient and modern inventors.[73] Unlike Patrizi, who shared his belief that historians should take an interest in technology and weigh modern resources against ancient ones, Bodin here took the side of modernity in what, as Hans Baron rightly pointed out, was really the first Quarrel of the Ancients and the Moderns – one fought out by humanists in fifteenth-century Italy and continued in the sixteenth-century north.[74] Bodin's contemporary Loys le Roy – another lawyer and humanist who wrote on the interpretation of history, ten years after Bodin – argued as early as 1542 that nature had not exhausted her strength, and that men could still bring forth genuine innovations. In 1577 he would pursue this theme even more energetically than Bodin, citing printing, gunpowder, and the compass as clear evidence of the legitimacy of the modern age.[75] But when Bodin described the deeds of Ham, he took the side of what had become

---

[73] See Valla 1973, Vergil 2002, and the classic article by Copenhaver 1978.

[74] Baron 1959.

[75] Le Roy 1559, 24 vo: "NON omnis flos eruditionis siti veteris ubertatis exaruit: non antiquis solis aditus ad summam doctrinam patuit. Non est natura, quod plerique falso queruntur, ita superiorum seculorum foecunditate exhausta, ut nihil amplius pariat et procreet heroicis simile temporibus. Eadem nimirum est semper et ubique sui similis, nec minus potens quam olim, neque minus ad gignenda et alenda praeclara ingenia efficax. Quin valentiorem hodie credi par est, robore adiutam et confirmatam: quod sensim per tot secula accrevit." See also Le Roy 1577.

tradition, and drew with equal confidence on Cato's *Origins* – a text forged by Annius.[76] It was from the Annian Berosus, not the Bible, that Bodin learned how Ham had sterilized his father.

Bodin, in other words, composed his book not as a beaver builds a dam, but as a magpie makes a nest. Still, the reasons why his work had such explosive impact are clear. In his debate with the Germans, two radically different visions of the past and its lessons confronted one another. Bodin's opponents – like the older historians he attacked – saw the past as a text inscribed by God's hand. The study of history and chronology existed, in their view, only to make these larger meanings plain, and the past, rightly interpreted, was a dynamic hieroglyph of the divine purpose. The great nineteenth-century statistician Charles Minard plotted the attrition of Napoleon's army against the spaces and temperatures it encountered in Russia. Centuries before, the Christian chronologer Eusebius, whose work circulated in dozens of manuscripts and, after 1470, printed editions, had laid out all of history from Abraham's time to his own in nineteen parallel columns. The reader saw states rise and fall until all of them funneled down into a single two-page spread, as God unified the world under Rome so that the ministry of Jesus could be universal. Eusebius rejected

---

[76] Wolf (ed.) 1579, 1, 304–05: "quae autem innocentia fuit in Camese, qui parentis optimi pudorem nova quadam et insigni contumelia violavit?" Cf. Berosus, book 3, in Nanni 1545, 25 recto: "Is patrem Noam odio habebat, quia alios ultimo genitos ardentius amabat, se vero despici videbat. Potissime vero idem infensus erat patri ob vitia. Itaque nactus opportunitatem cum Noa pater madidus iaceret, illius virilia comprehendens taciteque submurmurans, carmine magico patri illusit, simul et illum sterilem perinde atque castratum effecit, neque deinceps Noa foemellam aliquam foecundare potuit."

millenarianism; but many sixteenth-century millenarians plotted the past just as he did. They used Daniel's statue or the Hebrew prophecy known as the Tanna debe Eliyahu to create sharp, vivid timelines that gave events their larger meaning. No one embodied this vision of the past in more crystalline form than the painter Albrecht Altdorfer, in whose painting of Alexander at the Issus, history reaches halftime, as the third empire of the Macedonians smashes the second one of the Persians. And no one repeated this vision more often or more emphatically than the Reformation world historians, Sleidan and Melanchthon, on whose works Bodin depended – no one, that is, except the radical Huguenots and their Catholic opponents in the League, both of whom, as Denys Roche has shown, saw themselves as living in the last days.

Provoked by what he read, terrified by what he witnessed, Bodin deconstructed these alluring visions of the vast canvas on which history unrolled. Time, in his view as in Le Roy's, revealed on inspection no obvious signs of the divine hand at work, but second-order rules, numerological and astrological, and endless change – change in languages, in the characters of the people who spoke them. In 1543, Copernicus had used the experience of passengers on a ship to relativize rest and motion: "As a ship floats peacefully along, the sailors see everything outside it move, reflecting the image of its motion, and think that they and everything on board are at rest. By the same token, it could also happen that the earth's motion makes the whole universe seem to move around it."[77] By showing that

---

[77] Copernicus *De revolutionibus* 1.8; 1975, 16: "Quoniam fluitante sub tranquillitate navigio, cuncta quae extrinsecus sunt, ad motus illius

passengers on a ship could take the port as receding from them, he supported his bold theory that the apparent motions of the heavens could in fact be those of a revolving, traveling earth. With similar boldness, Bodin used the same image to relativize the qualities of historical periods. Old men, he suggested, idealized their youth because of the sufferings inflicted by age, and saw their own times as faithless and wicked. The same illusions darkened their views of the deeper past: "like travelers who have been on a long voyage, they tell the young of golden times and a golden age. But what is happening to them is the same thing that happens to those who, as they are carried out to sea from a port, think that the houses and town are moving away from them. So they believe that pleasure, humanity, and justice have taken flight to the heavens and deserted the earth."[78] Bodin's wording – *qui cum a portu evehuntur in altum, domos urbesque a se discedere existimant* – may well represent an allusion to the line from Virgil that Copernicus cited, *Aeneid* 3.72: *Provehimur portu terraeque urbesque recedunt.* But even if Bodin did not have Copernicus directly in mind, he carried out something like a Copernican revolution in thinking about the nature of past time. Gabriel Harvey, who grasped this part of Bodin's message, summed it up neatly in the margin of his copy of another summary of world history, where he called attention

imaginem moveri cernuntur a navigantibus ac vicissim se quiescere putant cum omnibus quae secum sunt. Ita nimirum in motu terrae potest contingere, ut totus circuire mundus existimetur."

[78] Wolf (ed.) 1579, I, 310–11: "ac velut ex longinqua navigatione profecti aurea saecula, auream aetatem adolescentibus narrant: sed perinde illis accidit, ut iis qui cum a portu evehuntur in altum, domos urbesque a se discedere existimant: sic illi oblectationem, humanitatem, iusticiam in caelum evolare ac terras deserere opinantur."

to Bodin's "notable passage", "laws, customs, words, deeds, all human things are varied, labile, fragile, to put it in a nutshell – mortal." [79] No wonder that some readers, like Harvey, used Bodin's book as a cosmographical compendium, a collection of evidence on many parts of the world, and added their own excerpts to his. The connections between the *ars historica* and the arts of travel and travel writing showed their explosive potential vividly in the *Methodus*.

As the logic and order of time became harder to decipher, the central importance and larger meaning of space became clearer and clearer. Like Baudouin, Bodin saw the new history he called for as part of a revolution in information of many complementary kinds. He himself used new information about space – especially the spaces outside Europe – to rebuke his fellow Christians for their narrowmindedness about the past. He traced in space, as is well known, the seeds of modern national characters, formed by climate and geography. When he suggested that cosmopolitan knowledge of this kind must now supplant traditional schemata about the past, he sketched

[79] Harvey, marginal notes in British Library C.60.f.4, Freigius (1583) 109: "Notabilis Locus Bodini, de Linguaru[m] alterationibus, et innovationibus"; "Vt hominu[m], sic Linguaru[m] sua infantia, pueritia, adolescentia, juventus, maturitas, senectus est, etiam mors deniq[ue]. Eccè Leges, mores, verba, facta, humana omnia, varia, fluxa, caduca, postremo mortalia." Freigius summarizes what Bodin has to say on the change of languages: "Vna [sc. causa] est in ipso decursu temporis, quo non modo linguae, sed etiam res omnes immutantur, ac tota rerum natura senescit" (108–09); "Altera causa est in coloniarum ac populorum inter ipsos confusione" (109); "Tertia linguae mutandae causa in ipsa regionis natura versatur" (109). Note also Harvey's note on 111: "Vt Locoru[m], et Linguaru[m], ita etia[m] Religionum mira alteratio, et variatio."

a process that would take almost a century after his time – until at least 1650, when Georg Horn finally produced the *Arca Noae*, the first Latin textbook of world history that found room for the Aztecs, the Incas, and the Chinese.[80]

The *ars historica*, as Bodin conceived it, offered nothing less than a reevaluation and reconfiguration of time itself – one that rejected predictions, of the sort that Patrizi saw as history's business, in favor of interpretation; that effaced the traditional "time maps" with which so many historians had laid out the future as well as the past; and that opened up the possibility that human enterprise was changing and improving the world – the same lesson taught by the *Kunst- und Wunderkammern* which displayed natural objects like stones and plants, natural objects like shells that seemed to cross the boundaries between nature and art, and works of human craft that improved on nature's endowments.[81] It was hard, as one read the Germans and heard the preachers calling for Armageddon, to maintain this belief in history as made by men – so hard that Bodin soon abandoned it, in favor of a strange form of Judaism and a hunt for witches, all inspired by a personal spirit that instructed him with taps on the shoulder to pursue some enterprises and abandon others. Yet some artists of history took his point. No one did so more crisply than Isaac Dorislaus, Brooke's Reader in History at Cambridge. As he worked his way admiringly through Bacon's *Advancement of Learning*, he came upon the passage – now famous – where the Lord Chancellor connected recent improvements in human knowledge with the apocalyptic promise of Daniel 12:4:

[80] Horn 1650; cf. Grafton, Siraisi, and Shelford, 1992.
[81] Zerubavel 2003; Bredekamp 1995.

And this Proficience in Nauigation, and discoueries, may plant also an expectation of the furder proficience, and augmentation of all Scyences, because it may seeme they are ordained by God to be *Coevalls*, that is, to meete in one Age. For so the Prophet *Daniel* speaking of the latter times foretelleth: *Plurimi pertransibunt, & Multiplex erit Scientia,* as if the opennesse and through passage of the world, and the encrease of knowledge were appointed to be in the same ages, as we see it is already performed in great part, the learning of these later times not much giuing place to the former two Periods or Returnes of learning, the one of the Graecians, the other of the Romanes.[82]

Dorislaus condemned Bacon's millenarianism with one lapidary Greek word, a humanist's way to express total rejection of the connection Bacon had drawn between the growth of human knowledge and divine intervention in history: "ἀπροσδιόνυσον," "nothing to do with Dionysus."[83] In his response to Bacon as in his later political career, Dorislaus stood for an ideal of time and politics as realms ruled and shaped by human action.

Any history of the *ars historica* must reveal continuities across space and time. All three of these men worried about Annius of Viterbo and Berosus the Chaldean; all of them thought about what the new antiquarianism and political philosophy meant for the study of history; all of them admired the same canon of good historians, ancient and modern. Yet each found substantial room in the tradition to employ his own sharp tools, to speak to his own defined readership, and to address pressing,

[82] Bacon 1605, II, 15 vo.
[83] Cambridge University Library LE 7.45.

180

local problems. One reason that the *ars historica* survived so long was that it provided a shell, a portable house and carapace, which any hermit crab of a humanist could inhabit and move about in, safely, as he explored strange and dangerous intellectual spaces. The tradition offered more room than now seems possible: room within which individual talents could explore, and display, the riches of local scholarship, philosophy, and science. No wonder that it had to be invented. No wonder either that, in the 1570s and after, some of Europe's most innovative and distinctive writers were engaged in productive dialogue with the *artes historicae*.

The natural philosopher, medical man and astrologer Girolamo Cardano, was a practising historian who overturned the conventions of both historical writing and historical interpretation with his brilliant, polemical *Encomium of Nero*.[84] Cardano also developed a number of astrological theories of history, which received rough handling in the *Methodus*, and he repaid his critic in a brilliant chapter of his *Proxeneta (On Political Prudence)*, on which he was still working on in 1570.[85] Like Baudouin, Bodin thought it vital to be able to "see" history happening. "What is more delightful," he asked, "than to contemplate through history the deeds of our ancestors as in a picture placed before our eyes?"[86] His instructions for students

---

[84] See Siraisi forthcoming for Cardano's work, set in a broad and brilliantly reconstructed context.

[85] For Bodin's critique of Cardano see 1945, 148–49, 232–34; Wolf (ed.) 1579, I: 145–46, 235–36. For the date of the *Proxeneta* see Grafton 2001b, xxiv.

[86] Bodin 1945, 12; Wolf (ed.) 1579, I: 5: "quid autem suavius quam in historia velut in proposita subiectaque tabula res intueri maiorum?" For a different view cf. Brendecke 2004.

reflected this view. Bodin laid special emphasis on the general works that could lay out all or part of history in a vivid way. The new student should begin by "choosing for himself a common, so to speak, painting of all of time, bare and simple, to look at" – a chronological table, in other words, which literally showed the course of history.[87] The advanced student should savor the works of Leandro Alberti and Sebastian Münster, "one of whom placed all Italy, the other Germany, as in a picture before the eyes and combined the history of these peoples with their geography."[88]

Cardano dedicated chapter 70 of the *Proxeneta* to a swinging attack on Bodin, whom he did not name. "Do not," he warned, "prefer a history that covers a long period and many reigns. For the more it includes, the less accurately written it must be. As when one man paints a wall, and another a panel: the one who paints the wall cannot apply the same diligence to every detail."[89] So much for Bodin's beloved universal historians – mere fresco painters, in Cardano's view, vague and careless, far inferior to the panel painters who worked in the

---

[87] Bodin 1945, 21; Wolf (ed.) 1579, I, 15: "Primum igitur communem velut omnium temporum tabulam, nudam illam ac simplicem nobis ad intuendum proponamus."

[88] Bodin 1945, 80; Wolf (ed.) 1579, I: 74: "His coniungo F. Leandrum et Munsterum, quorum alter universam Italiam, alter Germaniam in tabula veluti sub aspectum collocarunt et populorum historiam cum geographia coniunxerunt."

[89] Cardano 2001, 621: "Quamobrem historiam ne praetuleris longum tempus et plurima regna complectentem, nam, quanto plus amplectitur, eo minus accurate scriptam esse necesse est. Velut si quis parietem totum depingat, alius tabellam; non eandem singulis partibus qui parietem depingit poterit adhibere diligentiam."

hallucinatory detail of oils. Bodin called Thucydides "the truest parent of history" and drew from him, as we have seen, his belief that antiquity had been an iron age.[90] "Thucydides has nothing to offer," Cardano insisted. "He wrote of ancient affairs that are very distant from our customs, and was a member of the popular faction writing for a republic; finally, he strove for display, not the sinews of history."[91] Never blindly committed to consistency, Cardano followed his attack on Thucydides and general histories with a recommendation to read Thucydides nonetheless, as well as Leo the African's work on his native continent – a sprawling book in which African and European conventions of description combined, to fascinating and bewildering effect – exactly the sort of effect he seemed to think good historians should not produce.[92]

But the most striking part of Cardano's chapter comes between the two references to Thucydides. "It is very hard," Cardano tells the reader, "to write history, and it is therefore rare. First of all, because of the need for skill and style and practice; second, because of that for diligence and effort in chasing down the smallest points; third, because of that for judgment."[93] By including too much detail, the historian would bore his

---

[90] Bodin 1945, 298; Wolf (ed.) 1579, I: 305.

[91] Cardano 2001, 621: "Thucydidi omnia desunt: antiqua, moribus a nostris longe aliena, Reipublicae scripsit et popularis fuit, demum qui ostentationi servivit, non historiae nervis."

[92] Cardano 2001, 621. On Leo's work see the brilliant analysis in Davis 2006.

[93] Cardano 2001, 621: "Difficillimum enim est historiam scribere et ob id rara. Primum ob peritiam et stylum atque exercitationem, secundum ob diligentiam et laborem in minimis persequendis, tertium ob iudicium. Nam, si parva quaeque describat, ridiculum opus faciet et legentes afficiet taedio; sin magna solum vel etiam mediocria tradat, optimam

readers. By including too little, an even worse error, he would leave them in ignorance. In the end, indeed, Cardano found it almost impossible to write a history that would yield "the effective truth of things." Bodin, following Tacitus, had hoped that a historian who worked well after the events he described could write with some objectivity.[94] Cardano ruled this – or pretty much any other – form of objective history impossible: "For all great and middle-sized things have their causes in small things, but those causes are hidden. The betrayals, solicitations, secret conversations, corruption of servants, friends, counselors, and commanders, hatreds, rivalries, slanders, and vain hopes which cause everything can hardly be known. Those who know do not set themselves to write history, and even if they wanted at first to reveal these things, it would perhaps not be prudent, and long afterwards much falls into oblivion."[95] As we now know, Cardano drew the sceptical arguments he used against Bodin not from his mother wit but from another of the *artes historicae* – the skeptical dialogues of Patrizi, like himself a speculative Italian philosopher, but like Bodin someone who thought hard about history. It was not only Bodin's

partem ad cultum vitae et ad instruendum lectorem praetermittat necesse est; ita ut legendo nihil ex eo discas."

[94] This point is made most forcefully by Franklin 1963.

[95] Cardano 2001, 621: "Siquidem magna omnia et mediocria ex minimis ortum habent, sed causae illae occultae, proditiones, sollicitationes, colloquia secreta, corruptio ministrorum, intimorum, consiliariorum, ducum, veteres inimicitiae, odia, aemulationes, obtrectationes, spes inanes, a quibus omnia pendent, vix sciri possunt; et qui norunt historiae scribendae animum non adhibent et, si etiam vellent tum primum patefacere haec, non bene forsan consultum esset, multo post pleraque in oblivionem transeunt."

criticism that interested Cardano, in short, but the genre as a whole.

Michel de Montaigne was – as he would have been the first to insist – less erudite than Cardano. But like Bodin, he had studied the law, and he read the *Methodus* with interest around 1578. Montaigne found support there for his own long-established practice of writing judgments of historians in his copies of their books.[96] Bodin, he noted, "had given an adequate treatment, and one in accord with my own opinions," of the difficult problems involved in deciding which historians deserved credence.[97] When it came to the practical assessment of individual historians, however, Montaigne followed Bodin in spirit by disagreeing with him. "Jean Bodin," he declared, "is a good author of our time, and much better endowed with judgment than the rabble of scribblers of his period. He deserves to be judged and reflected on."[98] In the *Methodus*, however, Bodin both praised and criticized Plutarch:

> He narrated often unbelievable and clearly preposterous things about Pericles, who used to sell for his own convenience the annual harvest which he received from the farms and buy the necessities of life. But he used the phrase "they say," lest anyone should incautiously agree with the tale. For another instance, in the life of Lycurgus he wrote

---

[96] Montaigne *Essais* 2.10, 1999, II: 418–20. For a full analysis and the larger context see the superb study of Quint 1998.

[97] Montaigne *Essais* 2.10, 1999, II: 418: "Mais cecy a esté suffisamment traicté par Bodin, et selon ma conception."

[98] Montaigne *Essais* 2.32, 1999, II: 722: "Jean Bodin est un bon autheur de nostre temps, et accompagné de beaucoup plus de jugement que la tourbe des escrivailleurs de son siecle, et merite qu'on le juge et considere."

that a Spartan boy had borne unto death the cruelest tearing and mangling of his vitals to conceal the theft of a fox.[99]

Montaigne demurred: "I find him a little bold in the passage of his *Method for History* where he accuses Plutarch not only of ignorance (there I would have let him say it, for this is not my prey) but also because this author often writes things that are incredible and wholly fabulous (these are his words)."[100] In an elaborate essay he went on to argue that Bodin went wrong here by failing to consider the powers of the soul. He noted that Plutarch had not qualified his account with the phrase "as they say" – true enough, but irrelevant to Bodin, who did not in fact state that Plutarch had done so.[101] More characteristic and more effective was the mass of examples, modern as well as ancient, that Montaigne retold to prove that the story of the Spartan boy was credible. The courage with which simple peasants had undergone torture during the French Wars of

---

[99] Bodin 1945, 64; Wolf (ed.) 1579, I, 58: "ac de Pericle qui fructus annuos, quos ex praediis percipiebat, suo commodo vendere ac victui necessaria emere consuevisset, saepe incredibilia et plane fabulosa narrat, sed utitur verbo φασὶ, ne quis temere assentiatur. ut in Lycurgo scribit puerum Lacedaemonium crudelissimam lacerationem et iliorum distractionem ad necem usque pertulisse, ne vulpis furtum detegeretur." On Plutarch and the traditions of Spartan heroism in early modern thought see Rawson 1969.

[100] Montaigne *Essais* 2.32, 1999, II, 722: "Je le trouve un peu hardy en ce passage de sa Methode de l'Histoire, où il accuse Plutarque non seulement d'ignorance (surquoy je l'eusse laissé dire, car cela n'est pas de mon gibier), mais aussi en ce que cet autheur escrit souvent des choses incroyables et entierement fabuleuses (ce sont ses mots)."

[101] Montaigne *Essais* 2.32, 1999, II, 723: "... et que ce mot: Comme on dit, il ne l'employe pas en ce lieu pour cet effect ..."

Religion – and even the wonderful "conte" of the woman who claimed her husband had lice, and, when thrown into water, drowned "still making the gesture, above her head, of one who kills lice" – these and other cases of everyday heroism and obstinacy disproved Plutarch – and made clear that Montaigne found in Bodin stimulation to rethink some of his own favorite questions.[102] It seemed only natural to him that, as soon as he wrote "Venons à Plutarque," he began to discuss Bodin. Any cultivated reader of history, he suggests, would have done the same – and he himself was clearly as engaged with the modern theorist whom he criticized as with the ancient historian whom he defended.[103]

Reineck, of course, received less attention than Bodin or Patrizi from the good and the great. Yet he too stimulated sophisticated historical research and argument at the University of Helmstedt, where he served for some years as a research historian without formal teaching duties.[104] Heinrich Meibom the elder, who became professor of poetry in Helmstedt in 1583, continued Reineck's work as an editor of medieval historical texts, and restrained himself more successfully than Reineck had from correcting their Latin. And Henning Arnisaeus, who studied and taught in Helmstedt, managed to accept, as Reineck and Meibom had not, Bodin's powerful argument that the prophecy of Daniel did not foretell the entire course of world history.[105]

---

[102] Montaigne *Essais* 2.32, 1999, II, 722–27.
[103] See Blair 1997b and Smith 2001.
[104] For a good discussion of the university in this period see Kauertz 2001, 54–68.
[105] Dreitzel 1970, 36–37, 314–15. See also Henze 1990.

The *artes historicae*, in other words, struck many sparks – some of them in highly unexpected places. The genre not only offered space for many kinds of reflection, but also stimulated it. It served as a useful tool for teachers, a valued preparation for statesmen, a helpful source for courtiers, and much else. At the height of the mid-sixteenth-century vogue for powerful ways of ordering and assessing information about the world, the *ars historica* was, and seemed to be, on the cutting edge of humanist thought. It was precisely the sort of discipline to whose practitioners students flock, hoping to receive pearls of wisdom and listening for the buzzing of bees in bonnets.

4

Death of a genre

How does a tradition end? Sometimes, like a language, a tradition dies with the last person who embodies it. After Samuel Johnson read James Boswell's Latin thesis for the Faculty of Advocates in Edinburgh, he remarked with characteristic bluntness, "Ruddiman is dead." Thomas Ruddiman, printer, publisher, Latinist, and librarian of the Faculty, had corrected the Latin of the young advocates' works before they were formally submitted. Now he was gone – and with him the tradition of precise Latin scholarship that had inspired Ruddiman's edition of the works of George Buchanan. Scottish Neo-Latin died with Ruddiman.[1]

The crowd-pleasing death scene of the *ars historica*, by contrast, seems impossible to identify with that of a single individual or even the publication of a single deadly critical book. It is not hard to provide a *terminus ante quem*. On 22 December 1766, the Prorector and Senate of the University of Göttingen celebrated the opening of a Historical Institute, under the directorship of Johann Christian Gatterer, *professor ordinarius* of history. This institute promised the young scholars and aristocrats who flocked to the university the most up-to-date historical training in Europe – a training that Friedrich August Wolf applied to the creation of *Altertumswissenschaft*, and Wilhelm von Humboldt to the invention of that sublime

---

[1] Duncan 1965.

product of German administrative ingenuity, the research-centred University of Berlin.[2] The great classical scholar Christian Gottlob Heyne celebrated the institute's creation in a powerful address.

For twelve years, Gatterer had run a historical "academy." In this informal but formidable setting he taught his pupils to envision history as a broad-gauged inquiry into past societies as a whole: "the spirits of peoples (*ingenia populorum*), their customs, their rites, their institutions, laws, arts, crafts, and all the products of the human intellect." More important still, he portrayed history not as a set subject but as an object of research. Students of history must not merely con their texts, but survey the past as one would survey unknown lands, forcing their way through difficult passages and cultivating the parts of Clio's territory that remained wild. Gatterer provided them with all the tools they needed: samples of different scripts, seals, heraldic symbols, coins, medals, "and all the other forms of monument that bolster the credibility of historical arguments."[3] The university, Heyne concluded, appropriately recognized Gatterer's achievement by endowing what amounted to a historical seminar with a formal, public status.

In this short speech, Heyne formulated the creed of a new school – the Göttingen school of history, whose history has been traced by Carlo Antoni, Herbert Butterfield, Peter Hanns Reill, and most recently Michael Carhart, and which laid the foundations on which Ranke and other somewhat

[2] See Butterfield 1955; Marino 1975 and 1995; Leventhal 1994; Clark 2006.
[3] Heyne 1785–1823, I, 286–87.

ungrateful heirs built in the nineteenth century.[4] Though Heyne couched his thoughts in Latin, moreover, he clearly thought in the German of his own time. The "ingenium populi" that Heyne identified as the primary object of historical research was the same evanescent, glittering being that Herder, whom Heyne admired, would call the *Volksgeist*. Yet the forms of historical research that Gatterer taught seem strikingly familiar to any reader of Baudouin or Bodin. Heyne admired Gatterer because he insisted on an interdisciplinary approach to historical research and traced connections between the geography and climate of each people's home and its character – rather as Heyne's friend Winckelmann traced connections between the beauty of Greek art and the beauty of the Greeks themselves, the latter achieved by constant exercise in the perfect sunlight of their homeland. Bodin by himself adumbrated almost every element of Gatterer's new method, including the theory that each nation had a character originally formed by soil and climate and later carved into new forms by human effort. The bright new tools that Heyne celebrated, the levers and wrenches that enabled him and other *Aufklärer* to make a radical break with scholarly tradition, had already gleamed in the workshops of the sixteenth-century theorists who called for the creation of a perfect history.

Heyne knew all the traditions of learning. Not only a professor of Greek, he also managed Göttingen's unique library, the best organized in Europe – and the only one in its day to rejoice in a firm yearly budget for acquisitions.[5] In the

---

[4] Butterfield 1955; Antoni 1951 and 1968; Reill 1975; Carhart 1999. For the wider context see Bödeker *et al.* (eds.) 1986.

[5] Clark 2006.

heart-stoppingly laborious manner of the German professors of the time, he somehow found time to read everything that came in, and wrote some 8,000 reviews of these new books for the Göttingen *Gelehrte Anzeigen.* For all Heyne's enthusiasm for such cutting-edge work as Robert Wood's *Essay on the Original Genius of Homer*, he also made a point of tracing the development of older scholarship, the so-called *historia litteraria,* in the prefaces to his own editions of the classics.[6] Why then did he see no connection at all between the new historical scholarship that Gatterer taught, and that he himself practised in such ground-breaking essays as his study of Hellenistic culture, "On the Genius of the Age of the Ptolemies," and the tradition of the *artes historicae*?[7] How had Bodin and his companions come to be so firmly dead that Heyne did not even see them off with an obituary? The slow end of this tradition, it seems, came about for two sets of reasons – some internal to it, the others external – that gradually sucked the life from it, leaving its practitioners to worship what even they may eventually have seen was a dead god.

In its heyday, the new art of history seemed to carry all before it. In the decades just before and after 1600, the *ars historica* glowed with all the prestige and charm that can invest a fashionable genre. Those who read *Les mots et les choses* in the 1960s or 1970s will know what it felt like to read Bodin in the 1570s and 1580s. Bliss was it, at least for Bodin, to be alive in 1580 in Cambridge, where every desktop sported a copy of his *Republic* – a work that he saw, for all its theoretical departures

[6] Grafton 1991.
[7] Heyne 1785–1823, I, 76–85. On Heyne's historical scholarship see Mettler 1955, Menze 1966, Leventhal 1986, and Polke 1999.

from the *Method*, as a formal continuation of the earlier book. Baudouin, Bodin, and the rest convinced the erudite patricians who managed universities and learned gymnasia across Europe to see history, as they did, as a formal discipline, one comparable to law in utility and status. Curators and ministers, Jesuits and *Politiques* agreed that they must appoint lecturers and professors in history. Leiden, the most thrusting and innovative of universities, put history at the center of the curriculum that attracted, within a quarter of a century, the largest student body in Europe.[8] Justus Lipsius, the great Tacitean who promised to recite the text of his favorite ancient historian from memory with a knife poised at his throat, to be plunged in if he made a single error, came to teach history and antiquities and stayed to lecture on Roman history and the ancient art of war. He became an academic star – his presence fought over by universities from Italy to Flanders, and his work appropriated and reconfigured by scholars from north Britain to the Holy Roman Empire.[9] Joseph Scaliger succeeded him, and received for doing so the highest salary, not only in the university, but in the city of Leiden itself, as well as permission to do no lecturing at all – though he did offer advanced historical and philological training to individuals whom he thought gifted, like the young geographer Philip Cluverius and the young jurist Hugo Grotius.[10] The university library devoted more presses to history than to any other field except theology, and equipped its readers with such tools of the new critical history as globes, atlases, and views of cities.

[8] See in general Wansink 1981.
[9] See e.g. Kühlmann 1982; Soll 2000; Soll 2005.
[10] Grafton 1983–93, II.

193

The new professors of history worked in differently mysterious ways, their wonders to perform. Take Isaac Dorislaus, the first Brooke's Reader in history at Cambridge, and Degory Wheare, the first Camden praelector in history at Oxford. Dorislaus, a Dutchman, came to England in 1627 at the recommendation of his internationally renowned teacher, G. J. Vossius, who had turned down the position when it was offered to him but did not mind suggesting that a pupil take his place.[11] Wheare, a Briton, enjoyed family connections to the Dorsetshire gentry, an Oxford education at Broadgates Hall, now Pembroke College, and close ties to the English antiquarian community: no damned nonsense about merit was needed to justify his appointment in 1623.[12] Dorislaus lectured on Tacitus, Wheare on Florus – a historian of the imperial age, the tone of whose four short books on the rise and decline of Rome Sir Ronald Syme described as "pious and ecstatic, condensed Livy."[13] Dorislaus electrified his hearers, only to suffer the fate of so many exciting teachers. After two lectures the authorities closed down his course. Forced to leave Cambridge, he spent his time doing research rather than disturbing the undergraduates. Wheare did not. In his 154th lecture, which he held in October 1631, he denied accusations of laziness, even though, as he had to admit, he had so far covered only one book of Florus in eight years of teaching. Wheare left no doubt why he had progressed so slowly through his text. His audience had discouraged him: "Your own eyes," he chided his auditors,

[11] On Dorislaus see the rich studies of Maccioni and Mostert 1984 and Mellor 2004–05.
[12] On Wheare see the superb study by Salmon 1997.
[13] Syme 1958, II, 503.

can serve as witnesses [note the appeal to autopsy] as to
how slowly, how lazily my audience assembles, how
infrequently and sluggishly it comes to listen here. And
when they arrive, they all loll about and look at us in a
posture of supreme idleness, they hear us with insolence
and prejudice. No one comes freely, or stays to the end, but
all complain that they have lost their half-hour by not
losing it. My fellow academics, my hearers lack diligence,
they lack attentiveness, their professors are despised and
neglected, as is their learning. Letters lie in the mud.[14]

No danger of subversion here, as Wheare pioneered Oxford's
long tradition of unheard professorial lectures.

Yet Dorislaus and Wheare, for all their differences in
style and delivery, attacked their tasks in the same way, as the
artes historicae had taught them too. Both made clear, in their
different ways, that one read history to understand past states
and constitutions. "I cannot find anywhere," Dorislaus told his
auditors in Cambridge, "that even in the time of the emperors
who usurped sovereignty in the free republic, the democracy
was ever abrogated by *ius* or *lex*."[15] The rise of early Rome,

[14] Bodleian MS Auct. F. 2. 21, 13: "Vestri ipsorum oculi testes esse possunt,
quam lente, quam pigre ad audiendum coeatur: quam infrequenter et
cunctanter, huc ad audiendum accedant: et quum accesserint,
quotusquisque non supine et oscitanter nos inspicit? aut supersiliose et
cum praejudicio nos audit? quotusquisque libenter adsidet, ac ad finem
usque perdurat? nec queritur se suam semihorulam quia non perdiderit,
perdidisse? certe (Academici) deficit auditorum diligentia, deficit
observantia: dispreti negliguntur Professores, eorum contemnitur
disciplina. Literae ipsae jacent."

[15] PRO SP 16 86 No. 87 1: "Principum ipsorum tempore, qui in Libera Rep.
Regium imperium usurparunt, δημοκρατίαν jure vel lege abrogatam
nusquam comperio." Cf. now Mellor 2004–05, 192–93.

Wheare explained in Oxford, could be understood only if one followed the division of the people into orders, the development of the Roman constitution and the rise of the Roman art of war, all of which he treated systematically. By doing so, of course, he further slowed his progress through Florus.[16] Both drew general axioms, of different kinds, from the events they described, and made clear that they meant these to apply to action in the present as well as the study of the past. "Anyone who has part of the *imperium summum*," Dorislaus explained, "must have the right to defend that part" – a thesis he then buttressed with a sharp contemporary reference: "The Belgians debated this point with the king of Spain, using arms."[17] "It is an axiom of politics," Wheare stated as he described the campaign that Regulus waged against the Carthaginians in Africa, "to push wars so far as possible into hostile territory, for the enemy is naturally terrifed and must recall his forces to defend himself" –

---

[16] Bodleian MS Auct. F. 2. 21,12: "Huc accedebat Reipublicae ratio ab ipso Romulo urbis conditore ordinata, a nobis itidem suo loco, non paucis, aut obiter explicata: ubi Populi distributio, Senatus, Equites, et Plebis ordines; Tribus, Curiae, Sacra Legesque latae sese considerandas obtulerunt. Neque mihi temperare potui, quin Sacra, et Ceremonias, omnemque cultum divinum a Numa Pompilio institutum diligenter exponerem: dierum etiam et temporum distinctionem minutatim observarem: Pontifices, Augures, Flamines, Salios, Vestales, exquisite (prout quivi) describerem: omnem denique Plebem, per Collegia distributam, particulatim notarem. Quid militarem disciplinam, artemque bellandi dicam, a Tullo Hostilio conditam? quid urbem aedificiis ampliatam ab Anco?"

[17] PRO SP 16 86 No. 87 1: "Nam quiquis imperii summi partem habet, non potest non jus habere eam partem tuendi: Hanc quaestionem Belgae cum Hispaniarum Rege armis disceptarunt." Cf. now Mellor 2004–05, 190–91.

a point he supported with meticulous, apposite references to Machiavelli, Ammirato, and Bodin.[18]

Both men's hearers understood exactly what they had in mind as the proper way to draw lessons from history. Matthew Wren described Dorislaus's second lecture as "stored with such dangerous passages (as they might be taken) and so appliable to the exasperations of these villanous times, that I could not abstayne before the Heads there present to take such offense, that such a Subject should be handled here, and such lessons published, and at these times, and E Cathedra Theologica before all the University."[19] Wheare, for his part, prefaced his lectures with a formal treatment of the *ars historica* as a whole, in which he discussed at length both the work of historians and the preparation of a skilled reader. This part of his course became in turn the core of his printed work on the subject, a modest but successful book that went through a number of editions in both the original Latin and Edmund Bohun's English translation.[20] The *ars historica*, in other words, flourished

---

[18] Bodleian MS Auct. F. 2. 21,54: "Politicum enim axioma est, Bellum in hostile solum quantum possumus transferre debemus, nam ex ratione magis terretur hostis, et ad sua tutanda revocatur. Atque hinc Poeni non jam de Sicilia solum de salute sua agrisque propriis decertare cogantur. Non me latet quaestionem hanc [Vtrum praestet in hostili, an in proprio solo cum hoste dimicare] in utramque partem a politicis disputari: at mihi quidem videntur ea longe praeponderare argumenta, quae quoties invasurus hostis timetur, bellum potius extra fines praeveniri, et in hostico solo melius praeoccupari probant, quam domi et intra fines expectari. videre potest Nicholaum Machi. disput. l. 2. c. 12. et Scipionem Ammir. l. 8. disp. 2. Bodinus quidem experte loquitur [mg. sin.: De Rep. l. 5 c. 8]…"

[19] Maccioni and Mostert 1984, 425.   [20] Salmon 1997.

in the late sixteenth and early seventeenth centuries. Its precepts found prominent and dramatic illustration not only in English lecture-halls, but also in Gomarist Leiden, Remonstrant Amsterdam, Lutheran Heidelberg, and the Jesuit citadel, the Collegio Romano, where Agostino Mascardi lectured with equal relish on spurious Chaldean texts cooked up long before by Annius of Viterbo and on genuine Chinese histories newly imported by his fellow Jesuits.[21]

They found application too, as statesmen trained in the disciplines of late humanism applied the lessons of history to their own day. Some contemporaries attributed Essex's revolt to the impact that his reader of history and politics, Henry Cuffe, had on him.[22] A more obvious pupil of the artists of history was the great French lawyer and parlementaire, Jacques Auguste de Thou, who spent his last years researching and composing a great history of his own time. He set out systematically to avoid every one of the pitfalls that Patrizi and Bodin had mapped. To give accurate accounts of decisions in high places, he drew on his own experience of the French court and others that he had visited on diplomatic missions. To avoid the prejudices natural in one who had participated in events, he sent his accounts of contentious issues to fellow citizens of the Republic of Letters whose political allegiances were not French. De Thou persisted even when the Augsburg patrician Marx Welser, himself both scholar and politician, warned him that Frenchmen and Germans would never agree about the dealings of Francis

---

[21] For contrasting views of Mascardi 1662, more accessible as Mascardi 1859, cf. Spini 1948 and 1970 with Doni Garfagnini 2002, 325–70 and Bellini 2002.

[22] Jardine and Grafton 1990.

I and Charles V – and, even more scathingly, that even engaged scholars like de Thou and Welser could only scoop their
information from the surface of the sources, not penetrate to
the real essence of affairs. De Thou's magnificent preface to his
Histories, addressed to Henri IV, cited the example of the early
church, as movingly evoked by Sulpicius Severus, to prove that
exile and execution could not put an end to heresy in modern
times any more than they had in antiquity. Not surprisingly,
de Thou mentioned only one modern scholar: François Baudouin, who had conjured his *ars historica* out of the ongoing
business of church history.[23] This tradition of critical history-
writing, moreover, did not die out in France with the Gallican
movement spearheaded by de Thou. Work in progress by
Jacob Soll and Caroline Sherman makes clear that Colbert and
other agents of the French monarchy built the information-
gathering machines of absolutism from the components that
the artists of history forged and polished.[24]

[23] For de Thou's own account of his experience and working methods see
de Thou 1733, I, 17: "Cumque in castris et in aula assiduus essem,
plerisque magnis negotiis a te praepositus sum, ex quorum tractatione
magnam mihi multarum rerum, quae ad id, quod prae manibus est,
requirebantur, notitiam comparavi; idque consecutus sum illustrium
virorum, qui in aula consenuerunt, familiaritate, ut quae de rebus nostris
per libros [al. libellos] sparsim et incertis auctoribus vulgata fuerant, ad
veritatis normam exigerem: in eoque studium meum, quamdiu in tuo
comitatu fui, inter publica negotia exercui, donec in hoc ergastulum
forense me necessitas muneris compulit." For Baudouin see ibid., 9. For
his network of correspondents and his occasional disagreements with
them see Grafton 1997c.

[24] See esp. Soll forthcoming. Caroline Sherman is currently writing a
doctoral dissertation at Princeton on the Godefroy, a dynasty of jurists,
historians, and antiquaries that served the French crown.

And yet, even as the eyes of students across Europe glazed under the hail of bibliography, parallels, and axioms, and the arteries of academic dignitaries snapped like pipestems when history men drew too radical analogies with their own times, the sands were running out of the *ars historica*'s own hourglass. The *ars historica*, as I have tried to argue, formed part of a much larger effort to master and use the floods of information pouring into Europe from travelers, navigators, and missionaries – a parallel, in many ways, to the *ars peregrinandi*, or learned art of travel, so well studied by Justin Stagl and Joan-Pau Rubiés.[25] The most prominent and original writers in the field, Patrizi, Baudouin, and Bodin, all insisted that the critical reader of history must embrace the known world in all its immense variety. Doing so, however, put unbearable strain on traditional theories of history. Consider Wheare. Unlike Bodin, with whom he politely disagreed, Wheare was a Four Monarchy man. Patristic authority, he argued, clearly supported the theory: Sulpicius Severus, that favorite of erudite humanists, argued that Nebuchadnezzar's image "bore the figure of the world," and that the prophet's interpretation of it "was precisely fulfilled." Four empires really had dominated all of history, two Asian and two European.[26]

---

[25] Stagl 1983, 1995; Rubiés 1996, 2000a, 2000b; see also Elsner and Rubiés (ed.) 1999. For the ancient precedents see above all the fine studies collected in Alcock, Cherry, and Elsner (eds.) 2001.

[26] Wheare 1684, sec. iii, 20–21, esp. 20: "Haec aliquanto longius produximus, a quibus tamen supersedisse poteramus, nisi hanc opellam a nobis expressisset *Johannis Bodini* viri impense docti argutatio; qua decantatam illam regnorum antiquioris mundi divisionem in quatuor *Monarchias, nupera auctoritate et insulsa Neotericorum quorundam opinione niti*

Wheare knew perfectly well, as he told his students, that dozens of historians had traced the histories of the world and its individual nations since the Fall of Rome. Some of them even challenged comparison with the ancients. Guicciardini, for example, had won the precisely chosen epithets "prudens" and "peritus" from no less an authority than Lipsius, who praised his Tacitean ability to conceal all his emotions – except his hatred for the Duke of Urbino.[27] Steeped in the English antiquarian tradition, Wheare also insisted with special force that "we should not, in our zeal to study foreign histories, be thought wholly ignorant of or uninterested in our own," and he recommended the corpus of medieval texts carefully assembled by Henry Savile and the *Theatre of Britain* that John Speed had constructed by "careful study of our native writers and others, and examination of archives, rolls, public monuments and ancient documents."[28]

astruit. Nobis vero ex supradictis, contra liquido paret: *Summa* quatuor *imperia*, antiquitus observata et designata fuisse. Quorum priora duo, in *Asia* successive floruerunt, ideoque *Asiatica* dicta: duo reliqua, suo ordine in *Europa*, eademque ratione *Europaea* nuncupata."

[27] Wheare 1684, sec. xxvi, 79–80.

[28] Wheare 1684, sec. xxvii, 81: "Ne tamen exoticas dum scrutamur *Historias*, nostratium rudes prorsus aut negligentes existimemur: lubet superiori *Catalogo*, mantissae loco, attexere Rerum *Britannicarum* Scriptores nonnullos; atque una ordinem, quo eos arbitramur legendos, quasi digito commonstrare"; sec. xxxi, 91–92: "Is peragrata *Magna Britannia*, scriptoribus patriis aliisque curiose pervolutatis, Archivis, Tabulariis, Monumentis publicis, veteribusque schedis excussis, *Theatrum* struxit *Imperii Britannici*, splendidum mehercule, et merito suspiciendum ... " For the scholarly traditions on which Wheare reflected here see Kendrick 1950; Fox (ed.) 1956; McKisack 1971; Levine 1987; Parry 1995.

So far as he could, Wheare concealed the strains caused by his simultaneous recognition that history had run a long, independent course and insistence on the doctrine of the four monarchies. After his death, however, Nicholas Horseman added a long *Mantissa* to Wheare's book. This covered in depth the modern histories that Wheare himself had passed over too lightly. Horseman listed dozens of historians of states and cities around the world, emphasizing the vital importance of the polyglot series of travel accounts that provided information on the Indies, China, and Japan. He even included such Jesuits as Acosta and Martini, who had described the Americas and Asia.[29] John Hayes, who published the later editions of Wheare, also added Gabriel Naudé's *Bibliographia politica* of 1648. Here Naudé advised the student simply to buy "those writers that are available, as a collection, in the elegant typography of the Elzevirs, and are organized so cleverly in their places and their volumes, that those who have written on ancient and modern Italy, on the kingdoms of England, France, Spain, Sweden and Denmark, or about the Eastern and Western Empires, or about the constitutions of the Venetians, and the Swiss Republic, and other peoples, can all be found there in so many pocket-sized books – something of the greatest utility to men engaged in politics."[30] Naudé's appeal to the thirty-five Elzevir Republics –

---

[29] Horseman, in Wheare 1684, *Mantissa*, sec. xiv, 121.

[30] Naudé, *Bibliographia politica*, in Wheare 1684, 284: "Verum ne tibi forte coronam in mustaceo ambire videar, aut gloriam potius ex ingenti auctorum nomenclatura desiderare; parco illos omnes sigillatim referre, qui *nitidissimis Elzeviriorum Typis simul collecti habentur*, ac suis quique locis ac voluminibus tam ingeniosa serie dispositi, ut qui de *Italia* antiqua et nova, qui de Regnis *Angliae, Galliae, Hispaniae, Sueciae*, et

the publishing world's first true subscription series, which eschewed any form of systematic organization of history in order to accommodate a range of kingdoms and empires, ancient and modern, eastern and western, that no theoretical watchmaker was deft enough to fit into the traditional schemes – flew in the face of Wheare's traditionalism, and even in the face of the whole notion that history offered a uniquely effective breeding ground for prudence.[31] If Wheare's words still taught a traditionally neat, providential view of history, the material text that students actually bought when they asked for a copy of the *Relectiones hyemales* gave them a very different lesson: all coherence gone.

Whatever their differences, all practitioners of the *ars historica* agreed that the expert reader – the figure that Degory Wheare called the "Lector idoneus" – faced two tasks. He must set every member of the vast throng of historians who waited inside his library, eager to converse with him, back into his time and place. Yet many readers could never have mastered the ever-growing array of histories – as Christopher Colerus already acknowledged, a generation before Wheare, in a passage in which the desire and pursuit of the whole warred with the subversive frankness of the experienced teacher:

> In reading history you will take care to work in an orderly way. I summon you to each period, in order. The path is

Daniae, qui de Imperio Orientali Occidentalique, aut de *Venetorum Helvetiorumque Republica*, ac reliquarum Gentium administratione scripserunt, totidem velut Enchiridiis et manualibus libris includantur, maxima certe politicorum hominum utilitate, et doctrinae ipsius accessione haud prorsus futili vel poenitenda."

[31] On the Elzevir republics see Davies 1954 and Klempt 1960.

very straight. Let Jewish, Egyptian, Persian and Median affairs, those of the Greeks, Athenians, Lacedaemonians and Romans all have their authors. In the same way you will set out the more recent writers, who have written of the affairs of the Goths, Lombards, French, Spanish, Germans, Turks, Poles, Hungarians, Britons and other peoples. Even if you cannot actually read all of these, you should buy them, so they will be handy if you need to look something up.[32]

Once the trained reader had established this immense corpus, moreover, he must identify within it those writers who could still offer him practical advice, because they had lived and worked in a world recognizably like his own.[33] And finding historians who met these criteria proved harder than many expected. Justus Lipsius did more than praise Tacitus's grim frescos of the Empire in the throes of corruption, thronged with monstrous Mussolinian rulers, their foreheads engorged with choleric humor and their eyes glaring at the virtuous aristocrats and rebels who would die for challenging them. He claimed that they represented his own day, the era of the Dutch revolt, as well, and far better than the virtuous women and providential interventions that Livy portrayed. Tacitus, he told

[32] Colerus in Grotius *et al.* 1645, 186: "In *historia* legenda ordinem diligenter observabis. Ad seriem aevi cujusque te voco. Rectissima illa via. Res Judaicae, Aegyptiacae, Persicae, Medicae, Graecorum, Atheniensium, Lacedaemoniorum, Romanorum suos auctores habeant. Isto modo et recentiores constitues, qui Gotthorum, Longobardorum, Francorum, Hispanorum, Germanorum, Turcarum, Polonorum, Ungarorum, Britannorum, aliorumque populorum res scripsere. Hi omnes si legi non possunt, comparandi tamen sunt, ut si qua inquirenda, in promtu sint."
[33] Wheare 1684, *De ratione et methodo legendi historias*, sec. 1, 170–75.

204

readers in a famous preface, "does not go over the victories of
Hannibal which were such disasters to the Romans, the showy
death of Lucretia, the prodigies of the prophets or the Etruscan
prodigies, and all those other things that do more to delight
than to instruct the reader. Here, let me urge anyone to consider
the courts of princes, the inner lives, counsels, commands and
actions of princes, and he will find that he can use the evident
similarities that link our ages in so many ways, to show how the
same causes yield the same effects."[34] Thanks to the Tacitean
principle of "similar periods" (*similitudo temporum*), Lipsius
and his throngs of students could find in Tacitus both the history of the Roman empire and "a theater of modern life." The
fabric of the *Annals* and *Histories*, moreover, positively glit-
tered with the gemlike aphorisms and *sententiae* that learned
readers looked for most eagerly: "As those who embroider garments cleverly attach gems without mixing up or harming the
design, so he everywhere attaches *sententiae*, without omitting

[34] Lipsius, dedicatory letters to Tacitus, quoted in Wheare 1684, sec. xxi, 67:
"Utilem magnumque scriptorem (Deus bone!) et quem in manibus
eorum esse expediat, in quorum manu gubernaculum et reipublicae
clavus . . . Acer Scriptor (dii boni!) et prudens: et quem si unquam in
manibus hominum versari utile fuit, his certe temporibus, et hac scena
rerum expediat. Non ille Annibalis funestas Romanis victorias, non
speciosam Lucretiae necem, non vatum prodigia, aut Etrusca portenta
recenset, et quae alia sunt oblectandi magis quam instruendi Lectoris: hic
mihi quisque principum Aulas, principum interiorem vitam, consilia,
jussa, facta consideret, et obvia in plerisque nostrorum temporum
similitudine, ab iisdem causis pares exitus animo praecipiat. Invenies sub
tyrannide adulationes, delationes, non ignota huic seculo mala; nihil
sincerum, nihil simplex, et nec apud amicos tutam fidem; frequentatas
accusationes majestatis, unicum crimen eorum qui crimine vacabant;
cumulatas illustrium virorum neces, et pacem quovis bello saeviorem."

anything or doing any damage to his narrative." No historian could offer richer lessons in wisdom or prudence to the young man who aspired to counsel a king.[35]

Yet Lipsius himself admitted that he could not find everything he needed in Tacitus. As he set out to teach Prince Maurice of Orange and his followers the principles of Roman warfare – the complex set of principles about uniforms, standards, drill and codes of command that they would apply so successfully against the Spanish – he lectured, and then wrote, on the detailed treatment of the Roman military in book 6 of Polybius, and supplemented this with material from later Roman and Byzantine writers on armaments and tactics.[36] Others criticized even the notion that one could or should rely on Tacitus. Isaac Casaubon admitted that Tacitus had described the world he himself knew: "the lot of his birth bound him to this hard condition: he either had to keep silence or to write as he did." Modern statesmen and counselors, however, should inquire about him only as Bertie Wooster's friends, according to Jeeves, inquired about the young man's tailor: in order to avoid him. Even to suggest that modern princes resembled Tacitus's emperors amounted to a fantastic accusation, in Casaubon's view. And putting such terrible examples of behavior on display to the young and malleable prince amounted to a

[35] Lipsius 2004, 733: "Ut ii qui vestes acu pingunt, ingeniose gemmas inserunt, sine confusione aut noxa formarum: sic iste passim Sententias, serie narrationis nihil omissa aut laesa. Scaber tamen quibusdam et obscurus videtur, suone vitio, an ipsorum? Nam acute arguteque scripsisse fateor: et tales esse debere, qui eum legent. Ideo Consiliariis magis Principum, quam ipsis commendo: qui habeant hunc Sapientiae simul et Prudentiae verum ducem."

[36] See most recently de Landtsheer 2001.

recipe for perversion. Casaubon, like most humanists, ancient and modern, admitted that if all examples are more attractive than precepts, bad examples are more attractive than good ones.[37] Such later entrants in the *ars historica* stakes as Vossius and Wheare had to struggle to work out which authority they could safely, prudently, and critically follow.

More serious still was the basic hermeneutical question: how to read the history one finally selected. The *ars historica* promised to give the young reader the equipment to carry out this textual alchemy: to process the historians he read into sure guides to virtuous and effective action. It must persuade the young man bound for academic or for public life that the vital facts of history did not, in Carr's words, resemble fish laid out on a fishmonger's slab, but fish swimming in the ocean. Then it must teach him how to catch, gut, and cook the ones

[37] Casaubon 1609, o ii vo–o iii ro: "quarum rerum non tam cognitio potest esse fructuosa, quam exemplum perniciosum. verissime enim de talibus Plinio dictum, parum abesse a docente eum qui narret. Sed Tacitum nascendi sors huic durae conditioni alligaverat (qua de re saepius ipse gravissime queritur), ut vel silendum ei esset, vel ista scribenda. Tacitum igitur facile nos quidem excusamus: illos excusari non posse iudicamus, qui unicum hunc historicum omnibus aliis anteponunt: unum Tacitum, politicis hominibus assidue terendum pronuntiant: unum esse unde Principes et principum consiliarii documenta regendae Reip. petere debeant. cuius absurditatem sententiae si vellemus exagitare, facile probaremus, qui ita sentiunt, eos tyrannidis principes hodiernos tacite accusare; vel palam tyrannidis instituta videri velle eos docere. Quid enim Principi, praesertim iuveni, lectione illorum Annalium esse queat pernitiosius? Vt bona exempla, si saepe ob oculos versentur, proficiunt, etiam non sentientibus nobis; sic mala nocent: paullatim namque descendunt in animos, et vim praeceptorum obtinet frequenter legere aut frequenter audire."

he needed. We have already looked at the multiple canons and protocols developed as the artists of history assessed ancient and modern writers. But in this great age of rhetorical ped-agogy, what really appealed to their readers was their offer of a literary technology, a pragmatic method for processing the catch. But this method – as we shall see – had not only a natural and immediate appeal, but also less visible long-term weaknesses, which fairly soon undermined its status and that of the texts that taught it.

Fifty years ago, Robert Bolgar showed, in a classic page of his *The Classical Heritage and its Beneficiaries*, that the note-book was the humanist's key to all mythologies.[38] By compil-ing notebooks of examples and phrases, Guarino of Verona promised, his pupils – including Leonello d'Este – could mas-ter both the content and the style of the ancients. Whenever they needed to write, Guarino explained. the notebook would appear on cue, quiet and efficient as "an obedient servant," and offer exactly the name, myth or device that they needed. And speaking of servants, if the young aristocrat found it too much trouble to keep his own notes, "some suitable and well-educated lad – many such can be found" could always be en-gaged to do it for him.[39] In the print-burdened and print-illuminated world of northern humanism, as Margaret Mann Phillips, Zachary Schiffman, Ann Moss, Ann Blair, Elisabeth Décultot, and many others have shown, the notebook played an even more prominent role.[40] Erasmus told readers of his uniquely influential textbook *On Copia of Words and Things*

---

[38] Bolgar 1954, 88, 270–75.   [39] Guarino 1915–19, II, 270.
[40] Margaret M. Phillips 1969; Schiffman 1984; Moss 1996; Blair 1992, 1996, 1997a, 2000a, 2000b, 2003, 2004a, 2004b, 2005; Décultot 2000. A

that they should work their way through all of classical literature at least once and note down the results, under suitable headings, for reuse. His *Adages* offered something like ready-made notebooks for the young Latinist, organized under catchy titles. The schoolboy could learn far more easily there than from the originals how to tell a friend who refused to finish his dissertation to take *Manum de tabula*, and how to tell a ruler bent on waging war that *Dulce bellum inexpertis*.[41]

A special form of notebook method aimed at historians formed one of the core tools of the *ars historica*. David Chytraeus, professor of rhetoric and theology at Rostock, published in 1562 his advice for young students, based on a private course on Melanchthon's rhetoric.[42] Following Melanchthon, who had adapted Erasmus's rhetorical method to theology, Chytraeus advised his students to work out a set of *Loci communes* for every art. The correct way to read a text, he explained, was

sampling of recent studies by Helmut Zedelmaier, Klaus Weimar, and others, which trace – as Décultot 2000 also does – the history of these practices over the very long term – appears in Décultot (ed.) 2003.

[41] Grafton 2003.

[42] Chytraeus 1562b, A2 ro–vo: "Ego itaque cum in studio doctrinae Theologicae verser, et munus proponendi elementa verae de Deo doctrinae in hac Schola sustineam, proposui auditoribus quibusdam privatis, quibus PHILIPPI Rhetoricam tradebam, exempla Praeceptorum, bona ut opinor, et illustria, quorum pleraque ex libris scripturae sanctae et materiis Theologicis deprompta sunt. Cepi etiam ex Prophetis et Apostolis, Figurarum, Troporum, schematum et amplificationum exempla colligere, quae spero aliquibus utilia et grata fore." The copy of this work in Wolfenbüttel, Herzog August Bibliothek, P. 1262 8° Helmst. (2). is in fact bound in a Sammelbändchen with Melanchthon, *Elementorum rhetorices libri duo, recens recogniti ab autore Philippo Melanchthone*. Leipzig: In officina Valentini Papae. 1556, P. 1262 8° Helmst. (1) and other rhetorical texts.

to dissect it into its useful parts, fillet it, and attach every bit of meat to the proper *locus*, literally a place, and by extension a heading. The reader should enter *sententiae* under the headings of ethics, such as the virtues and vices, or the headings of physics and medicine; arguments under the headings of dialectic; figures of speech under the headings of rhetoric. Examples, similitudes, apologues, proverbs, apophthegms, and the like must also be sorted into their proper pigeonholes.[43] Chytraeus

---

[43] Chytraeus 1562b, K 5 ro–vo: "Multae sunt et amplissimae utilitates Praecepti de LOCIS COMMVNIBVS, in omni genere Artium, et in omni oratione.

   Primum enim in docendis omnibus Artibus utilissimum est, proponere summam doctrinae distributam certo ordine, in Locos Communes, eosque adhibita Methodo, integre et perspicue explicare.

   Deinde, omnia scripta tum demum recte et intelliguntur et enarrantur, cum ad Locos Communes, qui summam continent eius Artis, ad quam scripta pertinent, apte referuntur. Ideo in enarratione Evangeliorum, vel aliarum partium Scripturae sacrae, praecipua Orationis membra ad Locos Theologicos revocanda [ed. revocandae] sunt. In enarratione Librorum Ethicorum, ut Officiorum Ciceronis, Hesiodi, Phocylidis, Theognidis, Catonis, Proverbiorum Salomonis, Ecclesiasticae, etc., praecipuae sententiae sunt referendae ad Locos Communes Ethicos, hoc est, Virtutum et Viciorum, et Prudentiae, qua Virtutum Actiones gubernantur: in Physicis scriptis, ad Physicos, in Medicis, ad Medicos Locos referri interpretationem prodest.

   Postea in dicendo fontes omnium Argumentorum et Confirmationum sunt Loci Communes, qui plerunque Maiorem in Principali Syllogismo et caeteris probationibus constituunt, ut in Oratione Pro Milone, Maior est Locus Communis, quod Ius Naturae concedat interfici insidiatorem.

   Praeterea etiam Amplificationum [ed. –em] et Ornamentorum fontes sunt. Omnes enim materiae fiunt uberiores et splendidiores, cum ad Theses transferuntur.

   Postremo valde illustria lumina Orationis sunt cum apte intertexuntur graves γνῶμαι seu Sententiae magnorum authorum, Item

offered students not only these instructions, but a splendid list of possible headings and *loci communes*, strongly reminiscent of the imaginary Chinese encyclopedia that Foucault borrowed from Borges.[44] Suggestively, these included "History" and "The origins, growth, change, defeat and destruction of nations and peoples," both neatly sandwiched between astrology and magic on the one side and medicine on the other.[45] Quintilian had explained long before that the young student of rhetoric should make notes on the historians, who would nourish his style and provide him with examples that he could use to defend his clients. He cautioned against too close imitation of the historians' showy styles – not for the orator the "creamy goodness" (*lactea ubertas*) of Livy. Yet he did suggest that this form of reading should take a special, double form, and Chytraeus took the hint.[46]

> Exempla, Similitudines, Apologi, Proverbia, χρεῖαι seu Apophthegmata, et si qua sunt similia. Quorum cum magna sit varietas et copia apud optimos scriptores, nec quisquam adeo felici memoria sit, ut omnia meminisse, et ad usum quocunque tempore prompta et parata habere possit: Valde prodest annotatos habere titulos Locorum Communium, certo ordine distributos, ad quos omnia, quaecunque legimus aut discimus, tanquam in certas Classes redigamus."

44 Chytraeus 1562b, L2 vo – [L4 vo].

45 Chytraeus 1562b, L3 ro: "Geographia.
    Astrologia. Magia.
    Historia.
    Nationum et populorum origines, Incrementa, mutationes, clades, excidia.
    Medicina, Medici.
    Anatomica. Partes Hominis."

46 Quintilian 10.1.31: "Historia quidem alere oratorem quodam uberi iucundoque suco potest"; 10.1.34: "Est et alius ex historiis usus, et is quidem maximus ... ex cognitione rerum exemplorumque, quibus in

Chytraeus, as we have seen, taught formal courses on Herodotus and Thucydides, and worked them up into an *ars historica* – the one that most precisely reflects classroom practice.[47] He found it only natural to recycle the rhetorician's notebook method in this new field. "In sacred or profane history," he counseled, "it is most useful to lay out axioms about the adminstration of counsel, and narratives of events and the punishment of crimes, in accordance with the *loci communes* of virtue and vice." But his effort to find a special way to read the historians foundered under the pressures of everyday teaching. Chytraeus tried to tailor his advice to history's special form and context: "one must," he counseled, "take careful account of circumstances, time, persons, and places" – a piece of advice he strikingly did not repeat when explaining how to study orations and letters.[48]

In practice, however, Chytraeus treated the process of reading history as a simple, monological one, part of their larger mastery of rhetoric – and he placed even more emphasis on the stylistic side of reading than Quintilian had. He advised

primis instructus esse debet orator, nec omnino testimonia expectet a litigatore, sed pleraque ex vetustate diligenter sibi cognita sumet ... "

[47] On Chytraeus as a teacher of history see Klatt 1909 and Völkel 2000.

[48] Chytraeus 1562c, C vo–C2 ro: "In HISTORIIS sacris seu ethnicis, utilissimum est ad locos communes Virtutum et Viciorum, et *gnomas* de gubernatione consiliorum, et de eventibus et scelerum poenis, narrationes referre, et circumstantiarum, temporis, personarum, locorum, etc. rationem diligentem habere.

In ORATIONIBVS et EPISTOLIS plerisque loci generis Deliberativi, ordinem enarrandi monstrant: ut primum Status causae, deinde principalia argumenta, et membra et singulorum partes, affectus, vis et pondera verborum, phrases, figurae, et ornamenta explicentur."

his students to slice and dice each book of Herodotus and
Thucydides into *sententiae*. These he encouraged them, much
as Quintilian might have, to rip from their original context and
store for use in wildly different circumstances. In preparing
students to read the Melian dialogue, for example, Chytraeus
told them that the text contained "many very sweet principles,
most worthy of being memorized, such as, 'The fairness of
the proposal that we shall peacefully instruct one another is
not open to question [5.86].' For these two virtues, justice and
peace, should shine out and appear with special brilliance in all
human disputations and colloquies."[49] Chytraeus did not quote
the second half of the sentence, in which the Melians, who were
speaking, noted that the Athenians' preparations to make war
on them had rendered this pious wish moot ("but these acts of
war, which are not in the future, but already here at hand, are
manifestly at variance with your suggestion"). He also deleted
from the phrase that he quoted the Greek particle *men*, the
presence of which would have alerted readers of the quotation
that it was the first of two linked and contrasting statements.
And he ignored the outcome of the dialogue, which ended with
a hideously one-sided war and the total destruction of Melos.
Chytraeus, in other words, envisaged the notebook as a system
that processed past texts for present use. Like a good sausage
machine, it rendered all texts, however dissimilar in origin or

---

[49] Chytraeus in Wolf (ed.) 1579, II, 554: "colloquium Meliorum et
Atheniensium, in quo multae dulcissimae γνῶμαι et dignissimae
memoria ponuntur, ut, ἡ ἐπιείκεια τοῦ διδάσκειν καθ' ἡσυχίαν
ἀλλήλους οὐ ψέγεται. Debebant enim hae duae virtutes, ἐπιείκεια καὶ
ἡσυχία, in omnibus disputationibus et colloquiis hominum, eruditorum
praesertim, praecipue lucere et conspici . . . "

style, into a uniform body of spicy links that could add flavor to any meal – and whose origins did not always bear thinking about when one consumed them. Chytraeus's art of reading history remained within the roomy confines of the rhetorical tradition.

Yet applying historical examples was a complex matter. Machiavelli, in the *Prince*, highlighted the troubling case of Agathocles – a low-born Syracusan who rose to power, but used such evil means that he did not deserve praise or emulation, in Machiavelli's own view, even in the context of a treatise that recommended that rulers adopt any means that were practical, however immoral they might be. He thus suggested that applying examples called for a subtle sense of judgement and discrimination, which should in turn become more acute as one applied it to a wider range of past examples.[50] Bodin confronted the same problem of assessment and judgement head on in the *Methodus*. He set out to transform the rudimentary text-processing systems of the rhetorical tradition into a distinctive method – an automatic interpretation machine that was sophisticated enough to deal constructively with texts that offered unappealing advice or examples. The reader of history, he advised, should make himself three notebooks, with the *loci* of divine, natural, and human history as their headings. He laid out sample categories for each, and advised the reader to lay them out at the front of the book, "in this order, or any other that one may find more convenient. The result will be that we insert everything worthy of recall that we encounter in reading history in its place. And in the margin of the book we can

[50] Kahn 1986, 1994.

add the notes for the different sorts of human affairs, counsels, sayings, and facts (for this is how the contents can handily be sorted out for action), and that with capital letters. Then we will have to see what is honorable, shameful, or indifferent in each case. And then we should write CH, that is, honorable counsel – or, if someone prefers to reject the Stoic doctrine, and separate the honorable from the useful, the shameful from the useless, I will not resist. Let him then set up four categories: shameful, honorable, useful, useless. Take then Themistocles's counsel about burning the ships [of the Athenians' allies], which he had shared with Aristides, at the people's command. Since this seemed useful to Aristides, but not honorable, we will put it under the heading *How to Take Counsel for the State*, and add in the margin the letters *CTV*, that is, *consilium turpe utile* – a shameful, but a useful, plan."[51] For Bodin, in other words, the proper sorting of examples required their scrutiny and classification, and their use required a further moral self-scrutiny.

---

[51] Bodin in Wolf (ed.) 1576, 30; 1579, I, 30: "His locis in capite cuiusque libri hoc ordine, aut ut cuique commodius videbitur, constitutis: consequens erit, ut quicquid in historiarum lectione memoratu dignum occurret, suo loco inseramus, et in margine libri rerum humanarum notas adiiciamus consiliorum, dictorum, ac factorum (sic enim res ipsae ad actiones commode referentur) idque literis maioribus. deinde videndum erit, quid in singulis honestum, turpe, aut adiaphorum sit. et eo modo notandum C.H. id est, consilium honestum. aut si quis malit repudiata Stoicorum disciplina, honestum ab utili, turpe ab inutili disiungere, non repugnabo. constituet igitur quatuor genera, turpe, honestum, utile, inutile. itaque consilium Themistoclis de navibus exurendis, quod pro Republica iubente populo Aristidi communicarat, quia utile visum est Aristidi, non tamen honestum: locum hunc ad caput de consiliis pro Republica capiendis referemus, adiectis in margine notis C.T.V. id est, consilium turpe utile."

He transformed the notebook from a sausage machine into something much more complex and puzzling, a Heath Robinson contraption designed to force the reader to think critically and dialectically about his texts, their contexts, and his own world.

Some contemporary and near-contemporary readers – like Johannes Wolf, who praised Bodin as offering the handiest of the *artes* in his collection – evidently agreed that these new devices for gathering, hunting, collecting, and processing information held much promise.[52] Even some of those who did not share Wolf's enthusiasm for Bodin admired his method. Philip Sidney, when advising his younger brother on how to study history, showed British disdain for Gallic wordiness when he remarked that "you may read Boden and gather out of many words some matter." But his advice on practices of reading showed that he had mastered and accepted Bodin's method: "But what I wish herein is this, that when yow reade any such thing yow straite bring it to his heade, not only of what art, but by your logicall subdivisions, to the next member and parcell of that art. And so as in a table be it wittie word of which Tacitus is full, sentences, of which Livy, or similitudes whereof Plutarch, straite to lay it upp in the right place of his storehouse, as either militarie, or more spetiallie defensive military, or more perticularlie, defensive by fortification, and so lay it upp. So likewise in politick matters."[53] It seems highly likely that Gabriel Harvey,

---

[52] On the title-page of Wolf's 1579 *Penus* the collection is described as "octodecim scriptorum tam veterum quam recentiorum monumentis et inter eos Io. praecipue Bodini libris methodi historicae sex instructa."
[53] Letter of 15 October 1580 in Sidney 1962, III, 131–32.

with whom Sidney had discussed both Livy and Bodin a few years before, called his attention to the *Methodus*.[54]

Others nourished sharper doubts. Keckermann, for example, noted that Bodin had paid too much attention to the judgment of his examples, far too little to the method for storing them. In fact, he argued, there was no point creating volumes of historical examples. Bodin resembled a mad gardener, who tried to cultivate a plot of land by sowing it with every sort of fruit, tree, herb, and vegetable, in a confused mass, with no fixed distances between them or beds set aside for individual flowers.[55] Examples, Keckermann explained, meant

---

[54] See Jardine and Grafton 1990.

[55] Keckermann 1614, I, 495: "Et eos qui ingentia illa et tricubitalia volumina et Tomos consuunt, quibus quicquid legunt vel indice alphabetario vel aliquo arbitrario et tumultuario ordine velut in Locos Communes conscribant, Herculeum quidem laborem sumere, sed inanem: sed talem, quo charta misere prodigatur, ingenio vero, et iudicio, et memoriae male eatur consultum. Vt enim hortulanus, qui spaciosum aliquem et amplum hortum culturus est, si omnis generis frutices, arbores, herbas, olera inter sese confuse conserit, nullis certis spatiis, nullis areis distinguit, ingentem quidem laborem sustinet, sed ita, ut nec fructuosum nec pulchrum aut amoenum hortum sit habiturus: ita etiam illi, qui promiscue omnem doctrinam Theologicam, Philosophicam, Politicam, Historicam sub unam Locorum Communium Methodum confuse congerunt, non prosunt ingenio et memoriae, qui esse debebat talis operae finis: sed vehementer nocent utrique. Qui enim dextrum et regulatum iudicium ibi esse possit, ubi est confusio doctrinarum? qui queat memoria iuvari et firmari, ubi nulla est antecedentium et consequentium connexio? ubi vel plane non sis reperturus, vel reperturus difficulter et aegre quod in memoriae subsidium connotaras. Vt enim omnis ordo bonum quid est, et constans, et certum, et utile: ita confusio malum quid, et incertum, et inutile, imo noxium." On Keckermann see now Freedman 1997 and Hotson 2002.

nothing unless they stood for general concepts, and history totally lacked these. And compiling notebooks as vast as the sources they digested – like Bodin's projected union of divine, natural, and human history, "enormous, vast, and totally unfit for everyday use" – made a task fit only for Sisyphus.

In fact, Bodin's practice was more supple and sophisticated than his own description of it or Keckermann's parody suggested. He himself made clear, in both his *Methodus* and *Six Books of the Republic*, that the most important questions one could ask in reading historians were constitutional and political. And he showed, in a central passage in the *Method*, exactly how systematic analysis and collation of evidence had led him to envision the state in a new way – as an organism held together by a defined, sovereign authority, the attributes of which he laid out: "Therefore, after I compared the arguments of Aristotle, Polybius, Dionysius, and the jurisconsults, with the whole history of states, I saw that the sovereign part of the state consists in five parts: the first and most important, in creating the highest magistrates and defining their tasks; the second in making or abrogating laws; the third in declaring and concluding wars; the fourth in the last appeal from all other magistrates; and the last in the power of life and death."[56] Just collect your cases, Bodin seemed to imply, and you would arrive at a radically

---

[56] Wolf (ed.) 1576, 170; 1579, I, 170: "Itaque Aristotel[i]s, Polybii, Dionysii, ac Iurisconsultorum rationibus inter se, et cum universa Rerumpublicarum historia collatis: video summam Reipublicae in quinque partibus versari. una est ac praecipua, in summis magistratibus creandis, et officio cuiusque definiendo: altera in legibus iubendis aut abrogandis: tertia in bello indicendo ac finiendo: quarta in extrema provocatione ab omnibus magistratibus: postrema in potestate vitae et necis . . ."

new way to conceptualize the constitution – one without clear precedent in earlier traditions, and that evidently did not require the moralizing annotation of excerpts from historians that he had called for. Evidently, Bodin – unlike Chytraeus – did not confine himself to the use of conventional rhetorical or moral concepts as he worked through the excerpts in his notebooks.

But Bodin's conclusions proved unstable – and revealed the instability of his method. In the *Methodus*, he suggested that different bodies in a state could retain some authority even if they did not have sovereignty – as the Romans, for example, had done. In the *Republic*, desperate to find some resolution for France after ten more years of civil war, he laid out a new and radical doctrine about the indivisibility of sovereignty in chapter 1.8. Here too, he used examples ancient and modern, famous and obscure to prove that a magistrate who had a temporary grant of absolute power was not sovereign.[57] But though Bodin boasted of the novelty of his conclusions, he never made clear how his system of collecting and annotating texts had yielded them – nor why it yielded different results in his two books, including, as Julian Franklin rightly notes, a very odd treatment of the Roman constitution, which, he now claimed, had not been mixed at all. A central feature of

---

[57] Bodin 1593, 123: "Ces maximes ainsi posees, comme les fondements de la souveraineté, nous conclurrons que le Dictateur Rommain, ny l'Harmoste de Lacedemone, ny l'Esymnote de Salonique, ny celuy qu'on appelloit Archus à Malte, ny la Bailie ancienne de Florence, qui avoyent mesme charge, ny les Regents des Royaumes, ny autre Commissaire ou Magistrat, qui eust puissance absolue à certain temps, pour disposer de la Republique, n'ont point eu la souveraineté..."

the notebook method, as Blair and others have noted, is that it reduces much of the information it stores to tiny pill-like summaries of information, stripped of their local and temporal bearings.[58] It was only natural, then, that Bodin's method eventually allowed him to move his facts like counters into different places on the game board, and that Bodin's conceptual needs and decisions, rather than his research, determined his conclusions. The notebook could not determine the results of the analysis.

In some ways, then, Keckermann was right to insert his bent nib into the weak point in Bodin's methodological armor. It took a methodological move to politics – a field in which the notebook method played an important, but subsidiary, role, and Bodin addressed himself to questions long established in the tradition – for Bodin to arrive at coherent results. Keckermann himself drew this moral. The intelligent reader, he argued, must abandon hope of finding instruction in history and master the true discipline of Politics. Its "certain and flexible method" would enable him both to put order into his historical examples and to draw the right conclusions from them. Under the headings one should not copy but summarize the passages in question, giving references to the originals. And one should concentrate not on examples but on the counsels that the historian included – both those that historians explicitly mentioned and those that had to be teased out of their work.[59] Other histories – histories of nature, for example, or histories of marriage and childbirth – should be stored not in

[58] See Bodin 1992, Blair 1992, and Blair 1997a.
[59] Keckermann 1614, 1, 500: "Neque vero ea tantum consilia a Politices Studioso notanda fuerint, quae disertis verbis ab Historico narrantur,

an amorphous historical notebook but in shapely smaller ones devoted to the true disciplines of physics and law. For only such "systems ordered to deal with universal matters" could provide a rational system for storing and finding excerpts. A historical commonplace book must, in Keckermann's view, end up as inchoate as Philip Sparrow's fictional lecture on Literature and Death and Sex and War: "a theosophic, pneumatic, physical, architectonic, theological, ethical, oeconomical, political, juridical, medical volume."[60] History, he insisted, provided not

sed utile omnino et salutare fuerit exercitium ingenii et iudicii Politici, si ex ipsis Historiarum eventis ingeniosa resolutione facta excogitentur et inquirantur ipsa consilia, unde tales eventus, quales exponuntur, extiterint: quae ipsa quoque consilia in Locis Communibus notentur, ut si forte similes eventus aliquando in Republ. vel optentur, vel metuantur, similia consilia aut promi possint aut caveri."

[60] Keckermann 1609, II, 86–7: "Atque ita plane statuant Auditores, errare Bodinum et alios, qui peculiaria volumina historica, sive, quod idem est, singularium exemplificantium volunt constitui, cum tamen impossibile sit singularia notari methodice, nisi quatenus sunt imagines universalium, atque adeo quatenus possunt referri ad titulos Systematum de rebus universalibus dispositorum. Ita ut volumen Locorum communium historicorum sit volumen tuum Theosophicum, Pneumaticum, Physicum, Architectonicum, Theologicum, Ethicum, Oeconomicum, Politicum, Iuridicum, Medicum.

Ad istorum autem voluminum titulos oportet referri omne id quod in historiis legis, E.g. legis historiam aliquam de spectris, prout multae tales leguntur, non debes alibi notare quam in volumine Pneumatico. Leges historiam miram de cane vel equo, non debes alibi notare quam in volumine Physico. Legis historiam quae acciderit circa aedificia vel arces vel castra, notabis in Architectonico. Legis historiam aliquam sacram de martyribus et eorum constantia, notabis in Theologico. Legis historiam et exemplum singularis temperantiae vel fortitudinis, notabis in volumine Ethico. Legis historiam de amore coniugali, de fausto vel infausto coniugio, de filio male educato, de

principles but raw materials. This was, in fact, very much how Botero, Althusius, Grotius, and other authorities would, in the late sixteenth and seventeenth centuries, use history: not as an independent discipline but as the empirical handmaiden of politics, a handy and endless cornucopia of examples to fit any theoretical need, all inconvenient details planed away. The only point Keckermann omitted was that he was in fact recommending Bodin's own later practice. The fate of Bodin's method, in his own hand as in those of others, suggested that treating history as an art of directed reading might not yield the results that the artists of history had hoped for.

Bodin was not the only one who tried to devise a foolproof historian's notebook. Lipsius agreed that Chytraeus's simple rhetorical categories did not provide enough guidance to the reader. He worked up a third device: one stripped down to the Roman essentials. Make four notebooks, he told Nicholas Hauqeville, in an often-reprinted set-piece letter of 1600, for *memorabilia, ritualia, civilia,* and *moralia* respectively. As

divitiis mire acquisitis, etc., notabis in Oeconomicis. Legis historiam de principis inauguratione, coronatione, de tributis et exactionibus, de mutata Reip. forma, de tyrannide, de bello, etc., notabis in volumine Politico. Legis speciales casus de haereditatibus, de testamentis, de actionibus in iudicio et foro, notabis in volumine Iuridico. Legis denique historiam et exemplum de mirabilibus morbis, aut mirabili cura, notabis in volumine Medico.

Et nihil etiam est quod Bodinus dicit, *esse peculiariter notanda consilia, dicta, et facta.* Nam dicta proprie ad universalia pertinebunt, si sunt sententiae notabiles, ut et consilia: haec enim vel erunt canon, vel dabunt canonem novum in disciplina universali. Et si forte dicta vel consilia sint singularia, pertinebunt tamen ad universalia praecepta, perinde ut facta, sic ut penitus supervacaneum futurum sit peculiaribus voluminibus ista distinguere."

memorabilia he designated "great things, of the sort one reads or hears about with wonder or emotion: the remarkable power of some king or people, their creations, their wealth, prodigies, and new or unusual events."[61] *Ritualia* comprehended ancient rites and institutions.[62] *Civilia* took in everything "relevant to life and the common government," and *moralia* "everything that goes towards forming us and our lives privately."[63] The reader should then divide each of the four books into its proper titles, ideally in alphabetical order, and then fill them with sentences and examples. Lipsius pointed out that he himself had provided, in his *Politica* (1589), a readymade notebook of *civilia*, in the form of a cento of aphorisms drawn from Tacitus and other authorities, carefully laid out in categories and ready for use by those "whose family or fate calls them to the state."[64] Where Bodin's notebook held

---

[61] Letter to Hauqueville in Vossius *et al.* 1658, 166 = Wheare 1684, [A6 vo]: "Quid *Memorabilia*? res designo magnas et cum admiratione aut motu legendas sive audiendas. ut est notabilis *potentia* alicuius regis aut populi, *opera*, vel *opes*, *prodigia*, et novi aut insoliti *eventus*. uno verbo quidquid non obvium et magnitudine vel raritate se commendat."

[62] Vossius *et al.* 1658, 166 = Wheare 1684, [A6 vo]: "*Ritualia* autem, quae pertinent ad instituta ritusque veteres, sive quos in publico sive in privato usurpabant. Alios enim istos Orientales, Graeci, Romanique habuerunt."

[63] Vossius *et al.* 1658, 166 = Wheare 1684, [A 7 ro]: "At *Civilia* appello, quae ad vitam et regimen commune faciunt, et hanc hominum iure et legibus devinctam societatem. *Moralia* denique, ea quae privatim ad nos et vitam formandam, virtutibus amicam, vitiis alienam."

[64] Vossius *et al.* 1658, 168 = Wheare 1684, [A7 vo]: "Sequuntur et excipiunt *Civilia*: utilissima pars iis, quos genus aut destinatio ad rempublicam vocant. Is liber tres partes habeat, antiqua et verissima divisione: status *regum, optimatum, populi*. In quaque parte notes et eo referas, quae *firmanda* sunt aut *vertenda*: et haec ipsa subtilius divinas, ut a me in

food for abstract analysis, Lipsius's provided fuel for concrete action.

Keckermann insisted that Lipsius too made fatal category errors. Both *memorabilia* and *ritualia* were ragbag categories, which lacked the methodological foundation that could have given them a reason for being: "I do not approve of Lipsius's opinion on the volume of matters to do with ritual. It would cause a great confusion of titles and disciplines. There are spiritual rituals, such as those used in exorcism. There are architectural rituals. There are theological rituals . . . To set out all the headings for these in one volume is not a proper way to make systematic headings for notes."[65] The reader should simply use red or green ink to set a pointing hand, or a sun or moon, by the *memorabilia* in all his notebooks; as to *ritualia*, they too belonged in the notebooks that covered

Politicis factum." On this letter and Lipsius's own practices see Waszink 1997, Moss 1998, Laureys 2001, and Lipsius 2004.

[65] Keckermann 1609, II, 87: "Nec probo sententiam Lipsii de rituali volumine, propter eandem causam; quia oriretur magna titulorum confusio et disciplinarum, si omnia ritualia peculiari volumine notanda forent. Sunt enim ritualia, pneumatica; ut ritus et ceremoniae, quae observantur in adiuratione Daemonum, etc. Sunt multa ritualia Architectonica quae ad aedificia pertinent. Sunt multa ritualia Theologica, ut ritus sacrificiorum, expiationis peccatorum, etc. et omnes ceremoniae. Sunt ceremonialia Ethica, e.g. ritualia civilitatis morum, ritualia liberalitatis et hospitalitatis in conviviis. Sunt ritualia Oeconomica, ut nuptiae, vestes; item suppellectilis domesticae, et plura alia. Sunt etiam ritualia multa politica, ut ritualia regum et inaugurationis eorum, spectacula, triumphi, funera. Sicut ergo omnium istarum disciplinarum titulos in unum volumen velle digerere, non est methodicos locos scribere: ita etiam ritualia ista omnia uno volumine methodico comprehendi non possunt."

their different forms. Ceremonies of hospitality, for example, belonged with ethics, and ceremonies of kingship with politics.[66]

For all the energy Keckermann brought to bear on dismantling the *ars historica*, he seems to have missed a second fundamental conflict within the artists' historical method. When Lipsius recommended that the reader keep a notebook of *ritualia*, he did not claim that such matters would help the reader cope with public life. Rather, he argued, "all profound understanding of ancient writers depends on this."[67] With this brief and passing reference Lipsius admitted that in effect he taught two ways to read history. On the one hand, he instructed his reader to collect examples and counsels for public and private life, and promised that these would prove directly relevant to action. On the other hand, he told the same reader to collect examples of rites and ceremonies in order to read the ancient texts with deeper understanding of the complex states and societies that had produced them. The one form of reading was

---

[66] Keckermann 1609. II, 87: "Si quis dicat, Lipsium per *memorabilia* intellexisse *summe memorabilia* et *admiranda* imprimis, ut quidem se etiam explicat, respondeo, talibus peculiare volumen methodicum posse nec tribui, nec esse necesse. Non potest tribui, quia memorabilia sunt in omnibus supra enumeratis disciplinis; quale autem illud methodicum volumen est futurum, in quo decem ad minimum disciplinarum tituli sunt disponendi? Nec necesse est memorabilia peculiari volumine (loquor de methodico, non de adversario) notari, sed possunt ista memorabilia et summe admiranda aliqua nota in volumine insigniri, ut nempe tinctura rubella aut viridi, manum cum indice appingas, aut etiam solem et lunam, et ita facile poteris summe admiranda a minus admirandis distinguere, sub quolibet methodico titulo."

[67] Vossius *et al.* 1658, 166 = Wheare 1684, [A6 vo–A7 ro]: "et ab ea notitia, seria omnis intelligentia dependet veterum scriptorum."

finite, crisp, directed outwards; the other was infinite, slow, and endlessly dialectical. For as the reader collected more *ritualia*, he would understand his texts more profoundly – and they would give him deeper knowledge of rites and ceremonies, which would in turn foster still deeper readings. The notebooks for *civilia* and *moralia* still belonged to the *normal* category of machines for living and writing. That for *ritualia*, by contrast, adumbrated something like that famous, mythical beast, the hermeneutic circle supposedly studied in eighteenth- and nineteenth-century German hermeneutics.

On the whole, the *artes* written after Bodin, Lipsius, and Keckermann pretended that all was right with the reading of the world. Lipsius, suffused with confidence by his discovery of the supreme relevance of Tacitus, boasted that he had made philology into philosophy. Wheare, by contrast, taking his cure from Seneca, urged the reader of history to work both as a philologist and a philosopher, making separate notebooks to support him in the two tasks. He thus tacitly abandoned the whole idea, basic to the *ars historica*, that critical study of historians past was necessarily and directly connected to active use of historical examples in the present.[68] Vossius, similarly, urged a young Englishman to read Livy as preparation for public life, making notes of all powerful expressions, all great examples, and all the subcategories of both civil and military prudence. At the same time, he advised the boy's father to have him read "all the passages in Livy and other writers that touch on Roman customs with the handbooks by Joannes Rosinus at hand, since these include that people's antiquities,

[68] Wheare, *Historicae lectionis usus*, in Wheare 1684, secs. ii–v, 180–203.

226

the site of the city, the gods, the priesthoods, the Comitia, the magistracies, the laws, and so on. Anyone totally ignorant of these things will draw little profit from reading the ancients."[69] Up to this point philology served philosophy. But Vossius also noted that when the boy was older he should read "the writers from whom Rosinus gathered his material, and the others whom he never had the chance to see" – should move from using antiquities to support his purposeful procession through the text to making them, rather than action, his central concern.[70]

---

[69] Vossius to Edward Misselden, in Vossius 1691, 183: "Quia igitur non male apud nos coepit, velim in patriam redux pede eodem pergat: ac cum Cicerone Livium iungat. In Historico hoc primum attendat quae ad elegantiam sermonis pertinent. Codicem habeat in quo annotet verba et formulas ex Livio a se excerptas, ac subiiciat singulis quomodo ea hoc tempore transferre possit in usum suum. Altera cura esto Historiae. Quemcumque Livianum leget Librum, eius sibi compendium concinnet, minimum duplo auctius epitome veteri, quae cuique Libro praemitti solet. Tertium esto, ut ea consideret quae mores majorum virorum vel prudentiam tangunt civilem. Praeceptaque et exempla singula ad locum referat communem. Hoc fine codicem habeat in quo chartae distinguantur titulis virtutum moralium et capitum prudentiae tum togatae, tum militaris. In ordine istorum titulorum, utrum Aristotelem an alium sequatur, non multum arbitror referre. Velim etiam quia passim et in hoc scriptore et in aliis occurrunt quae tangant mores ususque Romanos, ad manum ei semper sint collectanea Rosini, quibus complectitur gentis eius antiquitates, de urbis situ, diis, sacerdotiis, Comitiis, Magistratibus, legibus, et alias. Nunc si quis in istis plane fuerit hospes, is exiguo fructu veteres leget. Ac hac quidem aetate Rosinus ad ista suffecerit." Vossius goes on to emphasize the close reading of Livy's "luculentae orationes." See Wichenden 1993.
[70] Vossius 1691, 183: "Postea satius fuerit ipsos legere ex quibus sua Rosinus collegit, et alios quos Rosinus videre non potuit."

Writers and practitioners of the *ars historica* claimed that they knew how to walk the tightrope that stretched between practical application and pure historicism. In fact, however, they could not explain even to themselves how the modern reader was supposed to go about both setting his texts back into their own times, with all the skill of a philologist, and making them relevant to his own day, with the bravura of a rhetorician. Though Keckermann did not see it quite this way, he put his finger on a fatal structural weakness in the *ars*, a fissure in its beating heart. For when challenged, Lipsius himself had to admit that his practice as an interpreter was inconsistent. In his *Politica*, he told the reader how to deal with the sort of heretics who insisted on disturbing the public peace. "*Ure*," he said, and "*seca*": burn and cut. Dirck Coornhert and others, enraged by what they saw as encouragement of the worst cruelties of the Duke of Alba, protested fiercely. How could Lipsius – who professed that he wished to make no windows into souls – support the torture and burning of heretics? He had not done so, Lipsius protested: he had simply quoted Cicero's *Philippics*. And anyone knew that in its original context, the expression "*ure et seca*" did not literally call for fire and sword, but simply recommended strong measures. Coornhert had criticized the text from ignorance. The old man should go back to school and polish up his notebooks. This was an elegant excuse: in this case, historicism gave Lipsius intellectual wiggle room. But it was also deeply confusing. How was any reader of Lipsius's ideal notebook to know whether he should read a given passage from an ancient text in its literal or in his historical – in its philosophical or in its philological – sense? Here the notebook method offered no guidance, and the incoherence at the heart of the *ars historica* matched the incoherence in historians' practice.[71]

In part, then, the *ars historica* collapsed from within almost before it took on canonical form, as the strains placed upon it by readers trying to make texts do work became too strong for the rough and ready tools, methods, and frameworks that its authors had improvised, mostly from existing pedagogical stores, as they constructed the genre. At the same time, a second set of challenges, external to the *ars historica*, weakened it from the outside. The artists of history, as we have seen, recognized travel – properly conducted – as a powerful source of information. But if information acquired by modern, trained observers through direct experience mattered so much, and if all information looked more or less the same once it had been salted away in notebooks and then pulled out again to spice a modern treatise, why should past experience that happened to be found in books trump it? Keckermann wrote his own manual of the *ars historica*. But he also argued as early as 1609 that travel could provide richly detailed information about the way men spoke and lived – so richly detailed, in fact, that it could not be drawn from texts:

> As in gathering precepts, so in gathering examples or histories, we make progress not only by reading, but also by observing, that is, either by hearing or by seeing. Whatever you hear or see in your travels or at home of counsels, sayings, and facts, you should immediately work out to which discipline that history or example belongs, and note it down under the headings of that discipline.

[71] Güldner 1968; Bonger 1978; Grafton 2001a, 97–137, 227–43.

229

This practice is immensely useful, and often proves more profitable than the reading of history. For one cannot read all the histories that one hears, and not everything that we hear or see is written down, especially in the affairs of private men. These can be quite memorable, and very useful for us to imitate: yet no historian considers it worthwhile to write a history about them.[72]

From Keckermann to Descartes, who would argue that travel and history yielded exactly equivalent levels of insight, was a short step. More seriously still, Keckermann's reader could find it hard to understand why he should concentrate on history at all, when he could study the other sharp new subject, politics, and apply the lessons of travel to it. It is hard not to think that Keckermann was busily sawing off the branch on which he sat – or at least, once again, contributing to the vogue for politics that dwarfed that for history in the universities and the public sphere of the seventeenth century. It is no

[72] Keckermann 1609, I, 116: "Porro sicut in praeceptis, ita quoque in exemplis sive historiis non tantum proficimus legendo, sed etiam observando, id est, vel audiendo, vel videndo. Quare quicquid in peregrinatione, vel etiam domi auditis, aut videbitis in consiliis, dictis, et factis, statim cogitabis ad quamnam disciplinam ista historia, sive exemplum pertineat, et sub istius disciplinae titulis notabitis. Quae res mirificam utilitatem habet, et saepe plus prodest quam lectio historiarum; cum non omnes historiae legi possint, quae audiuntur, nec omnia scribantur, quae audimus aut videmus, praesertim in rebus privatorum hominum, quae etsi sint saepe valde memorabiles, et nobis ad imitandum utilissimae, tamen nullus historicus eas dignas iudicat, de quibus historiam scribat." Keckermann was an expert on geography as well as history, and devised an innovative program for the study of the field. See Büttner 1978, and for another, rather different version of this tale of decline see Blanke 1991.

accident that the founding myth of seventeenth-century political thought – the state of nature – emerged from accounts of
travel rather than study of history and historians.

History itself, moreover, changed in the late sixteenth
and seventeenth centuries. The politic history that displaced
the traditional chronicle was a genre practised by statesmen,
former statesmen, and professional crown historians dictating
periodic sentences.[73] These man knew the arts of history, and
many of them – like Jacques-Auguste de Thou and William
Camden – at least professed that their works rested on critical
study of the sources and systematic efforts to eliminate the
biases that could easily infect a historian of the contemporary
world. To that extent, the theorists seemed to have conquered
the contemporary world of historical practice. Yet none of the
politic historians, even de Thou, escaped attacks – some of
them justified – for partisanship. More serious, none of them
found a way to indicate, explicitly and in the body of his text,
how he had sifted and assessed the evidence.[74]

Baudouin, as we saw, called for a union of what had
been the largely separate practices of historians and antiquaries, and Bodin envisioned something similar. But few readers
accepted these demands when they set out to write or criticize
contemporary histories in their turn. Antonio Agustín, for example, was one of the most skillful of the sixteenth-century
antiquaries, as William Stenhouse has recently confirmed: a
critical student of inscriptions who did his best to set precise
rules for transcription. He should have been ideally qualified

[73] See the important treatment of the British case in Woolf 2000.
[74] Grafton 1997c.

to read and edit the history of Aragon written by his friend and fellow antiquary Jerónimo Zurita. But as the two men corresponded, Zurita found himself put more and more on the defensive. Agustín complained that Zurita's work lacked "the direct and oblique speeches that so greatly adorn the histories of Thucydides, and Livy, and Sallust," as well as exemplary moderns like Guicciardini and Giovio.[75] Though Zurita admitted that Pompeius Trogus had been wrong to condemn speeches in history, he insisted that they would amount to little more than empty rhetoric here, especially as the records had often been made many years after the events: "It seemed to me that I lacked enough material for this, and when I did have it, if I had tried to write it in imitation [of the ancients], I would have had to omit infinite things, and it would be better not to leave them out, than to go on rhetoricizing, and in this way detracting from my main subject."[76] This answer left Agustín

---

[75] Agustìn to Zurita, 5 December 1578, in Andrés de Uztarroz and Dormer 1878, 475: "La historia de v.m. comparada con los Historiadores Españoles que hasta agora han salido a luz es muy buena, y aventajada, pero no tiene todas las partes que tienen los Griegos, y Latinos buenos, y lo que mas se echa de ver es la falta de las oraciones diretas, y obliquas que en Tucidides, y Livio, y Salustio dan gran ornamento a su historia. En los comentarios de Cesar estàn mas dissimuladas, pero hailas, y Cornelio Tacito el idolo de v.m. ahunque es duro, y baxo de lengua, tiene buenas oraciones, y breves. Las del Guichardino tengo yo en mucho, y algunas de Paulo Iovio: de las de Hernando del Pulgar no me acuerdo; ofendeme tanto el acabar las clausulas con el verbo a la postre, y otras cosas dèl, que ahunque se levanta mas que otros, lo tengo por escritor Barbaro, como a Garibay, y a Fray Gauberto."

[76] Zurita to Agustìn, 12 December 1578, in Andrés de Uztarroz and Dormer 1878, 476–7: "Conforme a esto yo veo bien lo de las oraciones obliquas, y rectas, y no me parece bien del todo la opinion de Trogo que las condena,

unsatisfied. Worse still, he wanted to update the language of original documents that Zurita inserted into his work, simply because they contained words that had become obsolete.[77]

pues los mas excelentes Griegos, y Latinos los vsaron tan acordadamente. A mi me pareciò faltarme mucho caudal para esto, y quando le tuviera, si avia de procurar que fuesse con aquella imitacion, se avian de dexar infinitas cosas, que es menos inconveniente que no se ayan perdido, que andar rhetoriçando, y perdiendo el credito en lo principal. Mayormente que en la historia del Rey Catholico van algunas que estàn ordenadas muchos años antes que yo tuviesse el aviso, y parecer de V.S. y aquella no se pusieran sino con fundamento de aver passado en realidad de verdad, sino todo, mucha parte dello, pues sobre lo cierto, y sabido se puede poner alguna joya en lugar que no pareciesse falsa."

[77] Zurita to Agustín, 13 January 1579, in Andrés de Uztarroz and Dormer 1878, 481–82: "Hazer esto V.S. con el passatiempo que aqui digo, se declara por la mas nueva cosa, y estraña que yo he visto, ni oydo jamàs en este genero de letras, que de la misma manera se pone a corregir la Carta del Rey Don Iuan de Castilla que yo pongo a la letra en estos anales, que ha mas de CLX. años que se escriviò, como a Zurita, *maguera*, aunque, *abondamiento*, abundancia: y no solo el lenguaje del Rey, pero la referendata del Secretario, la fize escrivir, *fiz*; V.S. que sabe con quanto respeto, y religion se tratan las cosas antiguas se pone a corregir el lenguaje del Rey Don Iuan? Que puede ser esto sino llevarse V.S. desta aficion que tiene a ser, no digo muy riguroso censor, pues està claro que no se nota por hazer beneficio a los vivos, ni a los muertos en emendar aquello, sino que sepamos que V.S. no quiere que en ningun tiempo se aya hablado de aquella manera: veamos si tiene V.S. razon, ò le di yo causa para ello en dezirme que me acuerde de lo que dize Horacio del precepto de Quintilio, *si quid recitares, etc.*, pues aquel merecia aquella reprehension, y castigo porque recitava sus obras, que era pidir ser advertido, y corregido antes de publicarlas; y yo ni he recitado a V.S. ni embiadole quadernos antes de imprimir para que vsasse de su censura, sino que V.S. vsa de su oficio, y assi verèmos qual ternà mas razon, V.S. en hazer la riza que piensa hazer en essos libros sin averme yo sometido a su censura, ò advertir yo a V.S. de muchas cosas della, que para mi ha sido

Agustín, one of the most skillful antiquaries, included in his notebook on historical and other matters, the *Alveolus*, precise instructions on how to use ink and paper to make direct, exact copies of inscriptions – copies that would reproduce "a text with the same letter forms and points" – a method that, as Stenhouse has shown, he devised and used in the 1550s.[78] Yet writing in the late 1570s, he clearly did not grasp the artists' bold idea that history could appropriate the methods and practices of antiquarian scholarship. As so often, Francis Bacon summed up a widely held view when he remarked, in *The Advancement of Learning*, that by collating multiple sources, material and

maravilla grande que V.S. no las considerasse. Quiero poner exemplo en vna; yo llamo Don Alonso al hijo primogenito del Infante Don Hernando, que fue Rey de Aragon, y V.S. de su autoridad añade Infante, que si yo lo dixera, merecia ser mas justamente reprehendido, porque en aquel tiempo ninguno se llamava Infante, ni lo fue hasta que su padre fue Rey, y entonces fue Infante de Aragon, y despues Principe de Girona. Que esto sea assi, dexado aparte, que los hijos de los Infantes en España no se llamavan Infantes, sino en los tiempos muy antiguos, que se diò este nombre no solo a los hijos de los Reyes, pero a los de la Casa Real como a los de Carrion, y Lara, deste Don Alonso que V.S. quiere que llame Infante, verà el testamento del Rey Don Enrique su tio, que le llama Don Alonso, y yo tengo el instrumento original de la dote de la Infante Doña Maria su muger, en que se declara, que siendo su padre Infante se llamò D. Alonso, y despues de Rey, Infante, y despues Principe."

[78] Agustín 1982, 91–92, at 91: "Per cauar di una tauola di rame o di pietra bene una scrittura con le medesime figure di lettere et punti . . . " For his and others' practices see the lucid account in Stenhouse 2005, 50–54. The *Alveolus*, with its fascinating mxture of cutting-edge philology and traditional anecdotes and exempla of the sort normally found in a historical commonplace book, nicely illustrates the paradoxes of Agustín's view of history.

verbal, one could produce only "Antiquities, or remnants of History."[79]

Politic history, moreover, metamorphosed fairly rapidly into a vast array of narrative practices, each radically different from the others. Marmoreal narratives produced by courtiers under royal sponsorship, as smooth and empty as modern university brochures, brushed covers with exposés written by radical clerics like Paolo Sarpi, bent on revealing the machinations that had brought about the compromises of the Council of Trent, the Massacre of St. Bartholomew, and the Venetian interdict. Some of these books – like José de Acosta's magnificent *Natural and Moral History of the Indies,* first published in Spanish in 1590 and soon translated into Italian, French, English, Dutch, and Latin – marked radical breaks with historiographical tradition. Acosta's book represented something like the realization of Bodin's program at its most ambitious: a history that rested, indirectly at least, on native sources, embedded human history in a rich geographical context, and attended at least as much to the histories of God and nature as to that of men and women. But Horseman, in his *Mantissa* to Wheare's *Relectiones,* managed only to warn readers that they should read Jesuits like Acosta and Martino Martini, the pioneering historian of China, "cautiously, since they are often excessive in their praise of their miracles and martyrs."[80] Yet even Acosta's history abridged and altered what

---

[79] Bacon 1605, II.2.3, II, 11 ro.

[80] Wheare 1684, 121: "Et universim, res utriusque Indiae, Orientalis et Occidentalis, Chinae, Japoniae, Magellanicae etc. ex Navigationibus et Peregrinationibus Lusitanorum, Belgarum, Anglorum, Hispanorum, cognosci possunt. Quibus Jesuitae addendi, ut *Petr. Maffaeus, Joh. Acosta,*

his informants had to say about Chinese and Meso-American languages, which he thought inferior to European ones.[81] No wonder then that most of the more radical views that poured into Iberia and Rome, which became the centers of global information networks, and the rest of Europe found only the palest of reflections in the *ars historica*.[82]

Far less stately but far more readable texts competed with them: a lemming-like stream of pamphlets, corantoes, and broadsheets, some printed and many handwritten in commercial scriptoria that accompanied the larger, slower works into the public sphere.[83] These tiny creatures scampered like mice around the feet of the vast official and critical narratives, offering subversively entertaining accounts of battles, reports of monsters, and gossip about the private lives of the good and the great. Gradually governments learned to manipulate the nimble new media as well as the stately old ones, and waged pamphlet wars of their own. Anastasia Stouraiti has shown that Venetian propagandists during the war of Malta used pamphlets to put forward government views and then recycled these supposedly eyewitness accounts of events in larger, purportedly objective histories – which the informed read with all the wincing, minefield-exploring caution

Mart. Martinius, et alii: quos tamen caute legere oportet, cum plerumque nimii sint in miraculis suis et martyribus extollendis." Naudé, characteristically, showed more enthusiasm: ibid., 259.
[81] Grafton 2001a, 77–93, esp. 89–92.
[82] See most recently Gruzinski 2004, and cf. the classic synthesis of Elliott 1970; see also Davis 2006.
[83] See Woolf 2000; and, more generally, Love 1993; Raymond 1996; Raymond (ed.) 1993 and 2006; Dooley and Baron (ed.) 2001. For the French scene see esp. Jouhaud 1985 and Darnton 1995.

of a modern political junky examining rival bloggers on the web.[84]

As early as 1633, the great bibliographer Gabriel Naudé made clear that the modern student of politics found himself confronted by a range of genres that the critical techniques of the *ars historica* had not been devised to control:

> The political specialist must also become quite familiar with those historians who approach libel in their excessive freedom, not to say audacity. They bring into the open the secrets of princes and the hidden deceits and wicked deeds of their ministers, and everything that ought to be clothed in dark night, like the Eleusinian mysteries, in the functioning of any politic government. They bring Diana into the open, naked and unclothed, and put her on view for the profane. This category includes Procopius, Matthew Paris, Theodoric Vrie, Pierre d'Ailly, Machiavelli, and the anonymous authors of all those conclaves, the Histories of the Council of Trent ... and then there are all those *libelles* that tell the public immediately *What the King whispered in the Queen's Ear*, and *What Juno gossiped about with Jove*.[85]

---

[84] Stouraiti 2001.

[85] Naudé, *Bibliographia politica*, in Wheare 1684, 288: "Pertinet etiam ad Politicos, in isto genere Historiarum diligenter versari, quae nimia sua libertate, ne dicam audacia, proxime ad libellos famosos accedunt: dum secreta Principum, occultasque fraudes et nequitias Ministrorum, ac omnia, quae in politicis Regnorum administrationibus, velut sacra Eleusinia, nocte quadam obscura tegi debent, in apertum proferunt, nudamque et sine veste *Dianam* unicuique profano conspiciendam praebent: quemadmodum omnino fecisse existimandi sunt *Procopius, Matthaeus Paris, Theodoricus a Nihem., Petrus de Alliaco, Clemangis, Machiavellus,* et *Auctores Anonymi tot conclavium, Historiae Concilii*

The range of texts that amused and astounded Naudé as he worked in Mazarin's great library – and which, as he remarked, were prohibited reading by the church, so that the wise reader must take care to provide himself with a license to read them – widened in the decades that followed, as informal, disputatious salons and coffeehouses replaced the decorous library as the privileged place for reading and civil conversation. To write a history – as Pietro Garzoni saw when he set out to tell the story of the War of Morea for a Venetian public that had become accustomed to read historians skeptically – required the consultation of official archives, the creation of his own systematic collection of copies of documents, and the weaving of networks of correspondence – a project as political, in some ways, as the Venetian effort to stabilize its foothold in Greece.[86] By the time of the Glorious Revolution, the *artes historiae* seemed old-fashioned, far too traditional and earnest to convey the intense and wild scenes of contemporary historical production.

Even earlier, Casaubon himself had his doubts about whether scholars really could, or should, counsel men of affairs. "Note," he wrote in one of his collections of maxims,

Tridentini, Ephemeridis propudiosae Ludovici XI. compilationis rerum ad Historiam Caroli IX. et Sacram Rebellium Galliae unionem pertinentium; ac alii denique similes Libelli qui statim in vulgus effundunt, *Quid Rex in aurem Reginae dixerit, Quid Juno fabulata est cum Jove.* Hi autem omnes, quoniam facta plerumque atque infecta canunt; Nunciique tam ficti quam veri tenaces existunt; et Sacris Ecclesiae constitutionibus eorum lectione interdicitur; judicio propterea in omnibus opus erit, et accepta a Magistro Sacri Palatii aut ipsomet Summo Pontifice, si opus erit, Licentia."

[86] Stouraiti 2005.

that like the 'book-trained doctor,' as we noted in Galen and Aristotle, the 'book-trained ship's captain' is a very dangerous thing. The case of the 'book-trained politician' is absolutely the same. A tragic example of this is provided by the case of the Count of Essex. When this man, who in other respects had excellent qualities, was in doubt as to what he should do, a learned man, who was afterwards hanged, gave him some advice, using the words of Lucan. Lucan's words were more or less to this effect: He who as a private individual had not found friends, would find many more of them when he took up arms. That verse doomed Essex.[87]

Not even Casaubon, the staunch defender of Polybian history, could ignore the fate of the scholar Henry Cuffe – whom Essex actually blamed, in violation of all codes of honor, for seducing him to rebel by reading Aristotle with him. More generally, the *artes historicae* had always recommended that

[87] Bodleian Library MS Casaubon 28, fol. 127 ro: " 'Οτι sicut medicus e libro quod notabamus apud Galenum et Arist. item gubernator navis e libro res periculosiss. sic prorsus politicus e libro. Tristiss. Exemplum fuit in Com. Essexio: cui viro alioquin optimo ἀποροῦντι dedit consilium Lucani verbis, homo doctiss. qui postea suspensus. Verba Lucani erant in hanc sententiam: qui privatus amicos non invenit, armatus plurimos est inventurus. Ille Versus fatalis fuit Essexio." For Cuffe and Essex see Jardine and Grafton 1990. Interestingly, the Cambridge don Richard Thomson, who wished, but did not expect, that Casaubon's newly translated Polybius might decrease the appeal of Machiavelli, regarded Casaubon as more qualified than he to discuss history and high politics because, unlike Thomson, he was not a mere academic: "Sed quid ego scholasticus homo ad te de his rebus? Et quidem qui Parisiis florentissima Europae nostrae urbe, Politicorum nutricula degis?" (British Library MS Burney 366, fol. 260 ro).

their readers concentrate on histories written by statesmen. How then should artists of history without experience of public life claim the authority to advise?

The assessment of ancient historians had changed in the same period, moreover, and even more radically than the production of modern ones. As humanists devised new philological tools and honed their old ones to a higher polish, they began to read ancient historians in ways that offered little aid and comfort to the artists of history, with their firm belief that *historia* must serve as *magistra vitae*. In 1568, when the brilliant Paris Latinist Denys Lambin published his edition of Cornelius Nepos, he addressed the reader in a long letter that fell naturally into two rather disconnected halves. Lambin's meticulous argument, based on minute textual observation, that the work in question was by Nepos rather than Aemilius Probus, a product of Republican rather than Imperial Rome, did little to confirm or enrich his long account of the uses of history, elegant in style but conventional in content.[88] In winter 1601–2, Isaac Casaubon held a series of private lectures on Herodotus for his friends in Paris.[89] The learned flocked to hear him.[90] They had reason, for Casaubon used these lectures to develop the suggestive arguments that his father-in-law, Henri Estienne, had devoted to Ctesias and Herodotus, the chief Greek writers on

---

[88] Lambin, "ad lectorem," in Cornelius Nepos 1608, [* 5 ro] – ** 3 ro. For an appreciation of the part of this text that amounts to a brief *ars historica* see Possevino 1597, 8 ro–vo.

[89] Bodleian Library MS Casaubon 24, 99 ro–112 ro. Casaubon describes these lectures thus on a leaf that serves as a sort of title-page for them: "σχεδίασμα εἰς Ἡρόδοτον, cum amicis illum exponeremus, animi caussa" (97 ro).

[90] Pattison 1892, 167–78.

Persian affairs, long before.[91] Casaubon treated Herodotus as a very special sort of Greek author. He had drawn the anger of Plutarch and others because he cast his net so widely as a

[91] See for one example Estienne's brilliant and counter-intuitive arguments on the credibility of Ctesias's Indica, in Ctesias *et al.* 1557, π vi ro-vo: "Quod autem ad res Indicas attinet, profecto mendacii illum multis in locis nemo non facile suspectum habuerit: sed quotusquisque est qui convincere queat et coarguere? Nescio (respondebit quispiam) quis eo tempore potuerit: at nunc possunt mercatores nostri qui illuc et ipsi navigant. Ain' tu? at unde illis, ut, quum sint ἀναλφάβητοι, ideoque iudicio eo quod literis et doctrina quaeritur, omnino careant: observare et observata aliis postea commemorare eadem quae viri docti possint? Ne longe abeamus, unde homini omnium literarum rudi, ut ligni παρήβου dicti naturam ita animadvertisse et animadversam ita queat describere ut hoc in libello a Ctesia descriptam habemus? ut omittam illud quod pro artis suae (quum medicus esset) solertia, ut observavit, ita et observasse debuit: nimirum illud lignum διδόσθαι τοῖς κοιλιακοῖς βοήθημα. vel tale quid quale alio quodam loco narratur? nempe aut miram cuiusdam radicis ad corrigendum nimium lactis usum virtutem: aut, quod de asinorum sylvestrium cornu refert? qui e poculis ex eorum cornu confectis biberint, neque spasmo eos neque comitiali morbo corripi: sed neque, dummodo aut vinum aut aquam aut poculentum aliquid aliud ex huiusmodi poculis bibant, illos hausto aut ante aut post minime interire veneno? Nequaquam profecto ab imperitis istis mercatoribus expectanda haec narratio fuerit. quid igitur illi narrabunt? nimirum se vidisse sylvestres asinos cornu in fronte gestantes, quod cuius coloris esset discernere non potuerint, sed nec satis eius magnitudinem consideraverint. Hanc autem vim huic cornu esse insitam, tam sunt nescii, quam ii qui nunquam ne Indorum quidem nomen audiverunt. Haec autem a me idcirco hic dicuntur, lector, ut quoties in quosdam homines incides, qui plus fidei de illis rebus, mercatoribus etiam literarum imperitis, quam vel doctissimis antiquis scriptoribus adhibendum esse credunt, in promptu tibi quod illis nugatoribus nespondeas, esse possit." Cf. also the interesting defence of Herodotus in Baudouin 1561a, 47–48; Wolf (ed.) 1579, 1, 630.

researcher, refusing to let patriotism stand in the way of information gathering and drawing on Persian and Egyptian as well as Greek traditions:

> Plutarch grew angry at Herodotus because when he described the antiquities of the Greeks, he used the testimonies of the Persians, the Egyptians, and other barbarians, and he thought that the Greeks were insulted when others received more credence than they did. For while all nations love themselves, still the Greek people seems to have outdone all others in this vice. This, then, was what Plutarch objected to, and he interpreted the diligence of Herodotus, which he displayed in drawing the ancient history of early Greece and other peoples from the writings or oral accounts of barbarians, as the Greeks called them, as a monstrous slander of the Greeks.[92]

Chytraeus, Baudouin, and others hailed Herodotus as the first of a series of pagan historians, mature practitioners of

---

[92] Bodleian Library MS Casaubon 52, 105 ro: "Ferebat iniquo animo Plutarchus Herodotum in Graecorum antiquitatibus exponendis Persarum, Aegyptiorum, aliorumque Barbarorum testimoniis uti. Putavit iniuriam universae Graecorum genti fieri, cum aliis plus quam ipsis crederetur. Nam cum omnis natio sui amans, tamen videtur hoc vitio gentes omnes superasse gens Graeca. Hoc igitur Plutarchum male habebat, et diligentiam Herodoti, qua usus ille in repetenda antiquitate veteris Graeciae et caeterarum gentium e scriptis aut sermonibus barbarorum hominum, ut Graeci vocabant, putabat velut notam esse et maculam quae nomini Graeco inureretur." Casaubon also notes Plutarch's wounded Boeotian pride (105 vo). In his copy of the 1566 Estienne edition of Herodotus (Cambridge University Library Adv.a.3.2, 2) Casaubon carefully noted Herodotus's references to his conversations with Egyptian informants and the efforts he had made to gain accurate reports about Egypt.

a developed art, appointed by Providence to take up the story of humanity where the Old Testament left off.[93] Casaubon, by contrast, made clear that he saw Herodotus's work as character-ized by the "simplicity of the early times." That explained why he had entitled it simply "History," leaving the "Critics" of Hel-lenistic Alexandria to add the second title, "Muses," centuries later. After all, as Casaubon noted, even those "books writ-ten in oriental languages" in his own day still lacked elaborate titles – a clear hint that he saw Herodotus's book as reflect-ing, in its form and style, the pervading influence of more sophisticated Eastern cultures, which had already developed their narrative traditions.[94] And in passing Casaubon noted

[93] Chytraeus in Wolf (ed.) 1579, II, 471–72: "Miranda autem et ingenti bonitate Dei factum est, ut fere in eo ipso momento, ubi Prophetica historia desinit, Herodotus Halicarnassaeus . . . suam historiam ordiatur: Qui non modo Cyri ac Persicae Monarchiae, cuius initia sunt in Bibliis, res gestas usque ad bellum Xerxis, optima fide et lenissimo ac suavissimo orationis genere contexuit, verum etiam regni Lydorum et Medorum, ac in primis Aegyptiaci historiam amplissimam, et multis in locis cum Prophetica congruentem, et antiquissimae gentis Ionicae ac urbis Atticae, et Regum Laconicorum et Corinthiorum historias descripsit. Ac omnibus caeteris historiae scriptoribus Ethnicis, tum antiquitate rerum ac regnorum, tum exemplorum multitudine, tum vero inimitabili purissimae et dulcissimae orationis elegantia et suavitate antecellit"; Baudouin notes that Herodotus starts where the prophets leave off at 1561, 83; Wolf (ed.) 1579, I, 654. See also Possevino 1597, 35 vo–42 ro.

[94] Bodleian Library MS Casaubon 52, 99 ro: "Titulus operis huius duplex est, alter ab Herodoto profectus, alter a Criticis veteribus qui eius opera recensuerunt. Herodoteus titulus est prima periodus de qua postea dicemus. non est dubium Herodotum cum opus vulgavit alium titulum non adiecisse, primum quia non opus est, deinde quia ea fuit simplicitas primorum temporum, ut titulos in quib. posteriora saecula lascivierunt (vel teste Plinio in praefatione) ignorarent. cuius rei argumentum est

the existence of forms of Greek historiography attested only, in his time, by fragmentary quotations and passing remarks: "another form of history dealt with a single state, such as the *Atthis* of Philochorus. It was the ancient *horographoi* who wrote the annals of the Greek cities."[95] Yet Casaubon too, when he set out to jot down his thoughts on the proper method for reading history, cast them in a highly conventional form. He urged readers of history to concentrate on "the literal sense and the author's style and narrative," to work out the *loci communes* under which they should store "those things that frequently come up in the practical affairs of political and military life," and to look for analyses of events and striking axioms.[96] More

> quod libri orientalibus linguis scripti tales titulos etiam nunc ut plurimum nesciunt . . . " Cf. also 99 vo: "Herodoti pater Lyxa mater Dryo loco satis honesto apud suos quod vel ex eo intelligas, cum tantum operae in erudiendo filio posuerunt: illis enim temporibus tralatitia res non erat studium literarum, quarum pro seculo peritissimum fuisse Herodotum satis hi libri indicant."

[95] Bodleian Library MS Casaubon 52, 110 vo: "alia circa civitatem unam sicut Philochori Atthis. et hi sunt veterum ὡρογράφοι qui annales urbium Graeciae descripserunt. ὧρος annus est: unde ὡρογράφοι scriptores Annalium."

[96] Bodleian Library MS Casaubon 24, 135 ro–136 ro (also summarized in Casaubon 1710, 42–3), at 135 ro: "Primum id operam dare oportet, ut literalem quem vocant sensum recte capiamus, stylum auctoris observemus, et narrationem historicam attendamus . . . Vt ad usum nostrum quae legimus referre possimus, utile sit locos communes animo esse complexum rerum quae magis frequenter occurrunt in praxi vitae communis sive togatae sive militaris. quam ad rem bene instituendam incredibiliter iuverit serio versatum esse in libris Politicorum Arist. et eorum qui militarem scientiam ad artem revocarunt" – a program that recalls that of Lipsius, for which see Lipsius 2004 and Waszink's

and more, it seems, the philologist, with his critical way of reading the ancient historians, moved on paths and towards goals that had little to do with pragmatism or politics – even when the philologist himself wanted to offer political instruction.

These fissures widened when the texts at issue challenged, as some ancient histories did, basic Christian presuppositions about the past. In 1598 and 1606, Joseph Scaliger created tidal waves in the rock pools of philology when he published the fragments of the genuine Berosus and Manetho – not the texts forged by Annius of Viterbo, but accounts of mythical and historical time in Chaldea and Egypt, composed in Greek by real ancient priests. Berosus explained how a creature named Oannes, with the body of a man and the head of a fish, had climbed out of the Red Sea and created civilization. This was enough to set a dozen dominies to composing furious sermons. But Manetho was even worse. He traced the Egyptian dynasties back, in a continuous series, not only to before the Flood, but to before the Creation itself, so that Scaliger had to set the earliest Egyptian dates in an imaginary historical period, which he described as "proleptic time."[97] Few accepted Scaliger's views at first. Even his friend Casaubon remarked, in his copy of Scaliger's book, that "I don't feel that these inventions of foolish

introduction. For Casaubon's project to write an *ars historica* see also his letter to Joannes a Witten, 1 October 1610, in Casaubon 1709, 360, on the political and military analysis that he meant to provide as a companion to his 1609 edition of Polybius: "Imprimis illud operam dedimus, ut viam indicaremus et rationem legendi cum fructu Historicos omnis generis. Sed otio nobis est opus ad perficiendum, quod dudum inchoavimus."

[97] Grafton 1983–93, II, 681–728.

peoples are very useful for true history."[98] But debate spread, through the great folios on chronology and on, by a kind of intellectual capillary action, into textbooks, short polemical works in the vernacular, and periodicals. By the 1650s, the identities of Berosus and Manetho, and the ancient, solid belief in priestly annals, tottered – as Edward Gibbon recalled, more than a century later, when he noted that the dynasties of Egypt had been his top and cricket-ball, and his sleep had been disturbed by the necessity of reconciling the Hebrew chronology with that of the Septuagint.[99] Yet the artists of history continued to write as if they knew only the Annian forgeries. Agostino Mascardi thought that a fellow Jesuit could have seen a "libro istorico" written at the time of Abraham, older than any other work of history. Yet he made no effort to confront in detail Scaliger's texts about Chaldea and Egypt, which he knew.[100] Though Wheare offered a brief discussion of the fragmentary histories of the ancient Near East in Greek, he made no effort to cope with the problems they presented. He dismissed the fragments of Berosus as the work of "the Monk from Viterbo, that tricky huckster," and mentioned Manetho not at all. Vossius, who took more interest in chronology, devised what became a popular way to deal with Manetho's list of dynasties. In his work on the ancient myths, he argued that they had ruled

[98] Isaac Casaubon, note in his copy of the *Thesaurus temporum* (Scaliger 1606), Cambridge University Library Adv.a.3.4; *Isagogici chronologiae canones,* 309: "Ego non video quae magna utilitas sit ad historiam veram in istis stultarum gentium figmentis: nam de periodo Iuliana est aliud."
[99] Rossi 1984 remains the best study of this period. See also Allen 1949 and 1970, Klempt 1960, and Levine 1999.
[100] Mascardi 1859, 21–22; for Scaliger's *Thesaurus* see 17.

simultaneously rather than consecutively, like the duchies of the Netherlands.[101] But he did not discuss these problems, or the texts that posed them, in his *ars historica*. An indefatigable bibliographer, Vossius compiled systematic biographical works on the Greek and Latin historians, which remained standard for at least a century and a half. His readers would have looked in vain, however, for any clear effort on his part to explain how increased knowledge of ancient works like Manetho's should transform the art that taught how to read them.

Gradually debate about other, even more central ancient authorities also spread. Scholars assailed early Roman tradition as a tissue of fantasy. Doubts about the completeness and continuity of the Old Testament, long permissible in Catholic exegesis, as Noel Malcolm has shown, took on a sharp edge in the new Protestant world.[102] After 1600, philologists like Johann Buxtorf and theologians like Johann Andreas Quenstedt began to argue, more and more sharply, that every word, every accent, and every mark of punctuation in the Hebrew and the Greek Bible was divinely inspired. La Peyrère and Spinoza did to the Old Testament no more than Alfonso Tostado had done a century and a half before – but they caused European scandals by doing so in an age of biblical literalism. Fifty years before, after all, Scaliger himself had already found himself saying, to the students in his chimney corner: "There are more than fifty additions or changes to the New Testament and the Gospels. It's a strange thing, I don't dare to say this. If it was a pagan author I would speak of it differently."[103] Most shocking of all,

---

[101] Grafton 1975.   [102] Malcolm 2002.

[103] *Secunda* Scaligerana, s.v. Josephe, in Scaliger 1740, ii: 399: "Il y a plus de 50 additions ou mutations au Nouveau Testament et aux Evangiles; c'est

and hardest to explain away, were the Chinese annals studied and translated by Martino Martini in 1657. These showed that China had existed before the Flood – and buttressed their dates with astronomical observations that checked out. Martini felt able to publish them, moreover, because his teacher and fellow Jesuit, Athanasius Kircher, had taught him that Egypt also began before the Flood – clear evidence of Scaliger's remote impact.[104]

Ancient history, like modern, became a field of dubious battle, where immensely learned armies clashed by night. By the beginning of the eighteenth century, Giambattista Vico declared himself ready to abandon the whole effort to bring detailed order into the early history of the nations. He dismissed their long early histories as fantasies, woven to gratify national pride, no more worthy of belief than the fantasies of modern chronologers like Olof Rudbeck, who indulged in equally vain imaginings about Atlantis and the Earthly Paradise. Yet of all these clashes and their implications, even the latest and best-informed *artes historicae* did not speak.

When the Querelle des Anciens et des Modernes blazed up in France and the Battle of the Books in England, finally, interpreters of the classical tradition drew apart into two distinctive groups. One set, who favored the Ancients, insisted that the earliest books in any given field – for example, the letters of Phalaris – were also the best, and the most relevant to the needs and interests of modern gentlemen. The other set, who favored the moderns, made fun of the primitive world that Homer

chose estrange, je n'ose la dire; si c'estoit un Auteur profane, j'en parlerois autrement."
[104] Grafton 2004.

and his fellow poets described, with their princesses who did their own washing and their castles that fronted on dungheaps. Up-to-date scholars like Richard Bentley sided, on the whole, with the Moderns. They knew they could no longer plausibly maintain that any old text could completely fill modern needs.[105]

In the decades just before and after 1700, a series of German scholars debated the question that Descartes and other philosophers had posed in its most radical form, and that challenging scholars from Scaliger to Bayle had made both more precise and more urgent: did history have any *fides*, any credibility, whatever? To follow these discussions is to watch the arts of history gradually sink from view – even the view of very learned Germans. Johann Eisenhart, who attacked the problem in 1679, referred to many contemporary sources and issues. But he was still engaged, on almost every page, with the historical literature of the sixteenth century. Cano and Bodin supplied him again and again with principles and cases in point, as when he cited Bodin's remark that the Greek historian Dionysius of Halicarnassus, a foreigner, might offer more reliable testimony than native Romans on the Roman past. More important, Bodin and his fellow coryphaei of the *mos Gallicus* gave Eisenhart the core of his project – which he described, in terms that would have made Bodin and Baudouin rejoice, as a call to unite history with jurisprudence. Only a few decades later, the appealingly sceptical Friedrich Wilhelm Bierling spoke a very different language. Legal archives, he admitted, looked like objective records of the past. But what should the critical historian

[105] See Levine 1977, Levine 1987, and Levine 1991.

make of inquisition records or the trials, duly recorded and attested, of those falsely convicted and condemned for making
pacts with the devil? Like Eisenhart, Bierling often reconfigured
methods and principles stated long before by the the artists of
history – as when, for example, he urged the importance of
studying the historian before one tried to judge his history. But
he did not say – and very likely did not see – that he was doing
so. The language and concerns of Bodin must have seemed
very distant indeed to this ingenious, sharp-eyed proponent of
Enlightenment.[106] Throughout the later seventeenth and early
eighteenth centuries, moreover, sophisticated scholarly tools
multiplied. Elaborate formal manuals of diplomatics, palaeog-
raphy, numismatics, and other fields reached print, and though

---

[106] On the debates on *fides historica* see Gossman 1968, Borghero 1983 and
Völkel 1987, and for the German background see also Fasolt 2004. For
Eisenhart's use of Bodin see e.g. 1679, 78–79 (on Dionysius of
Halicarnassus; for Cano see e.g. 70, 79–80). Eisenhart's "De
coniungendis iurisprudentiae et historiarum studiis oratio" of 10 June
1667, in Eisenhart 1697, 143–59, is in part a paean to the *mos Gallicus*, and
Bodin comes in for an extended programmatic citation on 156.
Bierling's *Dissertatio de pyrrhonismo historico* appears in Bierling 1999,
with its own pagination, and ranges between the wonderfully
up-to-date and snarky (46: "Acta judicialia etiam in rebus historicis
magnam vim probandi habere, non nego. Verum, cum non omnes
Judices Samuelem imitentur, hic quoque occurrunt difficultates
Pyrrhonismum stabilientes. Saepe ex ipso procedendi modo studium
partium elucet ... Quis ignorat artes hodiernae Inquisitionis? Acta
Magica, multos homines innocentes, saltem nullius pacti cum Diabolo,
prout id vulgo definiri solet, convictos, ad ignem damnantia, sciens
praetereo") and points of method established long before in the *artes
historicae*, not presented as such (56: "Inclinationes et ingenium
Historici, item ex qua gente ortus, cui religioni addictus sit, aut quibus
partibus prae aliis faveat, probe consideranda sunt").

they hardly put an end to the religious controversies that called many of them into being or stamped out wild speculations, they marked a sea change in historical method. These new, or renewed, *Hilfswissenschaften* were central to Gatterer's historical enterprise – and their genuine novelty prevented him from seeing the equally genuine continuities between his project and the arts of history.[107]

As the pressures multiplied, the fissures in the *ars historica* gaped wide. True, some thinkers continued to write *artes historicae*. But they no longer tried to maintain the subtle, difficult balance called for and largely achieved by Patrizi, Baudouin, and Bodin. Impenitent classicists like Bolingbroke still inscribed the Ciceronian commonplaces on their banners. But they paid a price for the ability to do this. Bolingbroke called for a study of history that rejected erudition and all its claims, moral and intellectual. He admitted that he was taking an extreme position, but he stood his ground with exemplary firmness. "A man must be as indifferent as I am," he wrote, "to common censure or approbation, to avow a thorough contempt for the whole business of these learned lives."[108] Bolingbroke went on to do just that. He made clear that "all the systems of chronology and history, that we owe to the immense labours of a SCALIGER, a BOCHART, a PETAVIUS, an USHER, and even a MARSHAM" had brought historical learning into disrepute. And no wonder:

> The same materials are common to them all; but these materials are few, and there is a moral impossibility that

[107] See Schwaiger (ed.) 1980 and Grafton 2001a, ch. 10.
[108] Bolingbroke 1752b, 7.

they should ever have more. They have combined these into every form that can be given to them; they have supposed, they have guessed, they have joined disjointed passages of different authors, and broken traditions of uncertain origin, of various people, and of centuries remote from one another as well as from our own. In short, that they might leave no liberty untaken, even a wild fantastical similitude of sounds has served to prop up a system.[109]

Bolingbroke singled out Bodin, of all people, as a prime specimen of the hapless antiquary who studied the ancient world for all the wrong reasons:

> I doubt that this method of BODIN would conduct us in the same, or as bad, a way; would leave us no time for action, or would make us unfit for it. A huge common-place book, wherein all the remarkable sayings and facts that we find in history are to be registered, may enable a man to talk or write like BODIN, but will never make him a better man, nor enable him to promote, like an useful citizen, the security, the peace, the welfare, or the grandeur of the community to which he belongs.[110]

In Bolingbroke, the tired assertion that "history is philosophy teaching by examples" served to introduce not the troubled, dialectical hermeneutics of a Bodin, but the firm, univocal classicism that also inspired Pope.[111]

By contrast, the Erlangen professor Johann Martin Chladenius abandoned any invocation of "historia magistra

---

[109] Bolingbroke 1752b, 7.   [110] Bolingbroke 1752b, 57.
[111] Bolingbroke 1752b, 14.

vitae." He devoted his pioneering studies of hermeneutics and history to close reasoning about what he called the "Sehepunckt" – the individual standpoint, given by birth, culture, and nation, within which any historian ancient or modern had to write. Chladenius was a professional scholar, trained in philology, and cut his historicist teeth on studies of ancient Homeric exegesis and the fate of Augustine's library during and after the fall of Hippo. By catching the ancient critics "like craftsmen at work in their shops," he showed that they had read their Homer unhistorically, using allegories to defend the Bard's supposed errors rather than treating them as products of history in their own right.[112] Yet though Chladenius treated the learned tradition with respect and professed his own allegiance to it, he stood as far from Bodin or Baudouin as Bolingbroke did. His treatises showed that Moderns could never simply draw on ancient historians: they could only read them, if at all, by dint of massive hermeneutical efforts, exercises in empathy, and the slow penetration of foreign cultures, the nature of which he

---

[112] Chladenius 1732b, 17: "Quam enim multa ex Aristarchi, Zenodoti, aliorum, eorumque Criticorum institutis longe diversissimorum, quam multa ex recentiorum Graecorum Critica, proferuntur, ex quibus, et vitia illius, et virtutes, intelligere possis. Vti enim non melius de praestantia artificis iudicatur, quam si in sua officina, opereque aliquo conficiendo, conspiciatur, quod ibi ignorantia vel etiam negligentia in ipsum statim opus redundat, ita ut a quovis animadverti ac manibus velut palpari possit, sic praestantiam veterum Criticorum cognituris, adeundi sunt illorum Commentarii, sollicitéque animadvertendum, quae loca, quibus de caussis, qua ratione, emendarint. Sic enim, qua in re peccarint, quid laudabile fecerint, facile intelligetur. Et dabunt veteres exemplum Criticae magis pietati quam integritati Poetarum inservientis: cum nihil in iis tolerarent, nisi quod cum religione, vel potius superstitione sua, conveniebat."

sketched at frank and frightening length. For Chladenius, the point of reading history, as established by the scholarly tradition, was simply to encounter each historian in his absolute isolation and singularity: the lessons of history were no longer moral and political but purely intellectual.

In this context, I think, we can see why scholars as different as Le Clerc and Perizonius, with whom we began, and Christian Gottlob Heyne some decades later, all saw so little connection between their arguments and the *ars historica*. They lived in a world in which it would not have occurred to anyone to seek, in the *artes historicae*, for either the programs for using texts or the protocols for understanding them that had made their authors famous. Bodin and Baudouin and Patrizi were dead – as dead as Ruddiman, or mutton.

Bolingbroke remarks, in a characteristically happy phrase, that "to converse with historians is to keep good company; many of them were excellent men, and those who were not such, have taken care however to appear such in their writings."[113] For me – though not for Bolingbroke – the artists of history have also proved good company. And their story, for all the mysterious gaps and crannies that await exploration, has offered rewards: some enlightenment about the rich, complex, and compelling history of historical thought in the centuries before historicism.

---

[113] Bolingbroke 1752b, 28.

BIBLIOGRAPHY

Manuscripts and libri annotati

Cambridge University Library

Mm 1.47 (Baker MSS 36)

Statutes for Brooke's Lecturer, pp. 143–152

Acton d.45.12, an annotated copy of Keckermann (1610)

Adv.a.19.2, Joseph Scaliger's copy of Henri Estienne's edition of
Herodotus (1570)

Adv. a.3.2 1–2, Isaac Casaubon's copy of Henri Estienne's editions of
Herodotus (1570 and 1566)

Adv.a.3.4, Isaac Casaubon's copy of Joseph Scaliger's *Thesaurus temporum* (1606)

Adv.a.3.5, Isaac Casaubon's copy of his own edition of Polybius
(1609)

LE 7.45, Isaac Dorislaus's copy of Bacon's *Advancement of Learning*
(1605)

O.4.5 an annotated copy of Bodin's *Methodus* (1566), signatures
illegible

Peterborough C. 28, a copy of Wolf's *Penus* (1576) with one note

London, British Library

C.60.f.4, Gabriel Harvey's copy of Freigius's *Mosaicus* (1583)

580.c.6 (3), annotated copy of Freigius's *Historiae synopsis* (1580)

MS Burney 366

London, College of Physicians and Surgeons

20cD139/7, 9959, John Dee's copy of Dictys and Dares (1573)

New York, Pierpont Morgan Library

Sallust with notes on Pomponio Leto's lectures

Oxford, Bodleian Library

Auct. F. 2. 21, Degory Wheare's lectures on Florus
MS Casaubon 24, 135 ro – 137 vo Casaubon on the method of reading
    history
MS Casaubon 28
MS Casaubon 52, 99 ro ff. Casaubon on Herodotus

Princeton University Library

Garrett 105 Diodorus Siculus, tr. Poggio Bracciolini
Kane 22 Xenophon, *Cyri institutio*, tr. Poggio Bracciolini
(Ex) PA6452 .A2 1555q Gabriel Harvey's copy of Livy (1555)

Vatican City, Biblioteca Apostolica Vaticana

Vat. lat. 3453 Giovanni Lamola's Gellius
Vat. lat. 1801 Valla's Thucydides
Inc. II.111 Sallust, *Works*. Venice: Baptista de Tortis, 1481. Pomponio
    Leto's *ars historica*
Inc. Ross. 441 Sallust, *Works*. Rome: Silber, 1490. Pomponio Leto's *ars
    historica*

Vienna, Österreichische Nationalbibliothek

9737b correspondence of Flacius Illyricus

Wolfenbüttel, Herzog August Bibliothek

MS 11. 20 Aug. fol.

988 Helmst.

394.65 Quod. (1) Chytraeus, *Chronologia* 1573

A: 108.3 Rhet. [3]) *Selectae orationes*, ed. Nicodemus Frischlin, 1588

T 1.12° Helmst. Bodin, *Methodus*, 1591

T 68.8° Helmst. (1) Chytraeus, *Chronologia* 1569

Broadsides

Wolfenbüttel, Herzog August Bibliothek

Fd 29, David Chytraeus, folding table, *Series familiae regum Laconicorum*

IH 2, Marcus Heling, *Colossus vel statua regis Babylonici Nobogdonosoris, in qua depinguntur iiii monarchiae Dan. II*, ed. Joh. Paulus Felwinger, 1676, without commentary (picture of colossus only)

IH 3, Marcus Heling, *Colossus vel statua regis Babylonici Nobogdonosoris, in qua depinguntur iiii monarchiae Dan. II*, ed. Joh. Paulus Felwinger, 1676

Primary sources

Aconcio, Jacopo (1791). *Ad Ioannem Wolfium Tigurinum epistola de ratione edendorum librorum*. Chemnitz: Hofmann.

Aconcio, Jacopo (1944). *De methodo e opuscoli religiosi e filosofici*, ed. Giorgio Radetti. Florence: Vallecchi.

Acosta, Jose de (1590). *Historia natural y moral de las Indias*. Seville: Japan de Leon.

Aelian (1731). *Kl. Ailianou sophistou poikile historia, Cl. Aeliani sophistae varia historia, cum notis integris Conradi Gesneri, Johannis*

Schefferi, Tanaquilli Fabri, Joachimi Kuhnii, Jacobi Perizonii et interpretatione Latina Justi Vulpeii, ed. Abraham Gronovius. Leiden, Amsterdam, Rotterdam, Utrecht, and The Hague: Luchtmans.

Agustín, Antonio (1982). *Alveolus (Manuscrito Escurialense S-II-18)*, ed. Candido Flores Selles. Madrid: Fundación Universitaria Española.

Allen, P. S. *et al.* (ed.) 1906–58. *Opus epistolarum Des. Erasmi Roterodami.* Oxford: Clarendon. 12 vols.

Bacon, Francis (1605). *The Tvvoo Bookes of Francis Bacon of the Proficience and Aduancement of Learning, Diuine and Humane.* London: Henry Tomes.

Baudouin, François (ed.) (1542). *Iustiniani sacratissimi principis Leges de re rustica, interprete et scholiaste Francisco Balduino Atrebatio Iuriscons. Item, eiusdem Iustiniani novella constitutio prima de haeredibus, et lege Falcidia, cum Latina interpretatione et scholiis eiusdem Francisci Balduini, multis locis nunc primum per eundem restitutis.* Louvain: Rutgerus Rescius.

   (1545). *In suas annotationes in libros quatuor Institutionum Iustiniani Imp.* Prolegomena *sive praefata de iure civili. Quae continent novam et eruditam, plenamque de tota Legum Romanarum ratione Commentationem, nec vulgarem historiam: ac de solida puriorique Iurisprudentia sanum iudicium.* Paris: Ioan. Lodoicus Tiletanus.

   (1554). *Commentarii in libros quatuor institutionum iuris civilis: et eiusdem libri duo ad leges Romuli, et leges XII. Tab.* New edn. Paris: Jacque Dupuys.

   (1556a). *Constantinus Magnus, sive de Constantini Imp. legibus ecclesiasticis atque civilibus, commentariorum libri duo.* Basle: Oporinus.

(1556b). *Responsio Christianorum iurisconsultorum ad Fr. Duareni commentarios de ministeriis ecclesiae atque beneficiis, et alias eius declamationes.* Strasbourg: Christianus Mylius.

(1557a). *Ad edicta veterum principum Rom. de Christianis: ex commentariis Francisci Balduini I.C.* Basle: Oporinus.

(1557b). *Notae ad Lib. I. et II. Digest. seu Pandectarum.* Basle: Oporinus.

(1560a). *Iustinianus, sive de iure novo commentariorum libri IIII.* Basle: Oporinus.

(ed.) (1560b). *M. Minucii Felicis, Romani olim causidici, Octavius, in quo agitur veterum Christianorum causa, restitutus a Fr. Bald. I.C.* Heidelberg: Lucius.

(1561a). *De institutione historiae universae et eius cum iurisprudentia coniunctione* προλεγομένων *libri duo.* Paris: A. Wechel.

(1561b). *Disputationes duae de iure civili, ex Papiniano Fr. Balduini.* Heidelberg: Ludovicus Lucius.

(1562). *Responsio altera ad Ioan. Calvinum.* Paris: Guil. Morelius.

(ed.) (1563). *Optati Milevitani episcopi, libri sex de schismate Donatistarum, adversus Parmenianum, multo quam ante hac emendatiores. Cum praefatione Fr. Balduini.* Paris: Claude Fremy.

(1564). *Responsio ad Calvinum et Bezam, pro Francisco Balduino Iuriscons. Cum refutatione calumniarum de scriptura et traditione.* Cologne: Werner Richwinus.

(1569). *Delibatio Africanae historiae ecclesiasticae, sive Optati Milevitani libri VII. ad Parmenianum de schismate Donatistarum. Victoris Vticensis libri III. de persecutione Vandalica in Africa. Cum annotationibus ex Fr. Balduini I.C. Commentariis rerum Ecclesiasticarum.* Paris: Claude Fremy.

Bierling, Friedrich Wilhelm (1999). *Dissertationes selectae*, ed. Martin Mulsow. Lecce: Conte.

Biondo, Flavio (2005). *Italy Illuminated*, ed. and tr. Jeffrey White. Vol. I. Cambridge, Mass. and London: Harvard University Press.

Blanke, Horst Walter and Fleischer, Dirk (1990). *Theoretiker der deutschen Aufklärungshistorie*. 2 vols. Stuttgart and Bad Cannstatt: Frommann-Holzboog.

Bodin, Jean (1566). *Methodus ad facilem historiarum cognitionem*. Paris: Martinus Iuvenis.

(1572). *Methodus ad facilem historiarum cognitionem, ab ipso recognita, et multo quam antea locupletior. Cum indice rerum memorabilium copiosissimo.* Paris: Martinus Iuvenis.

(1583). *Methodus ad facilem historiarum cognitionem, accurate denuo recusa: subiecto rerum indice.* Lyons: Apud Ioann. Mareschallum.

(1591). *Methodus ad facilem historiarum cognitionem, accurate denuo recusa: subiecto rerum indice.* Heidelberg: Apud heredes Ioannis Mareschalli.

(1593). *Six livres de la Republique.* 2 vols. Lyons: Vincent.

(1945). *Method for the Easy Comprehension of History*, tr. Beatrice Reynolds. New York: Columbia University Press.

(1951). *Oeuvres philosophiques*, ed. and tr. Pierre Mesnard. Paris: Presses Universitaires de France.

(1992). *On Sovereignty: Four Chapters from the Six Books of the Commonwealth*, ed. and tr. Julian Franklin. Cambridge: Cambridge University Press.

Bolingbroke, Henry St John, Lord Viscount (1752a). *Letters on the Study and Use of History.* 2 vols. Dublin: John Smith.

(1752b). *Letters on the Study and Use of History.* New edn. London: Millar.

Boussardus, Gauffridus (ed.) (n.d.). *[Eusebii Pamphili] Hystoria ecclesiastica.* Paris: François Regnault.

Bruno, Conrad (1549). *Libri sex de haereticis in genere. D. Optati epis-copi quondam Milevitani libri sex de Donatistis in specie, nomina-tim in Parmenianum. Ex bibliotheca Cusana.* Apud S. Victorem prope Moguntiam: Franciscus Behem.

Campanella, Tommaso (1954). "Rationalis philosophiae pars quinta, videlicet: Historiographiae liber unus, iuxta propria principia." In *Tutte le opere di Tommaso Campanella*, ed. Luigi Firpo, i: 1222–55. Milan: Mondadori.

Cano, Melchior (1776). *Opera*, ed. Hyacinth Serry, Bassano: n.p.; Venice: Remondini.

(1973). *L'autorità della storia profana (De humanae historiae auc-toritate)*, ed. and tr. Albano Biondi, Turin: Giappichelli.

Cardano, Girolamo (2001). *Il Prosseneta, ovvero Della prudenza polit-ica*, ed. and tr. Piero Cigada, ann. Luigi Guerrini. Milan: Berlus-coni.

Carion, Joachim and Melanchthon, Philipp (1557). *Chronicorum libri tres.* Paris: Cavellat.

Casaubon, Isaac (ed.) (1609). *Polybii Lycortae F. Megalopolitani His-toriarum libri qui supersunt.* Paris: Drouart.

(1710). *Casauboniana*, ed. Johann Christoph Wolf. Hamburg: Leibezeit.

(1999). *Polibio,* ed. and tr. Guerrino Brussich, with a note by Lu-ciano Cafora. Palermo: Sellerio.

Chladenius, Johann Martin (1732a). *De praestantia et usu scholiorum graecorum in poetas diatribe prima.* Wittenberg: Eichsfeld.

(1732b). *De praestantia et usu scholiorum graecorum in poetas dia-tribe secunda.* Wittenberg: Eichsfeld.

(1742a). *De fortuna bibliothecae D. Augustini in excidio Hipponensi disserit simulque orationem inauguralem qua professionem antiquitatum ecclesiasticarum extraordinariam clementissime sibi demandatam auspicabitur d. xix. Decemb.*

MDCCXLII habendam indicit M. Io. Mart. Chladenius. Leipzig: Langenheim.

(1742b [1969]). *Einleitung zur richtigen Auslegung vernünftiger Reden und Schriften.* Leipzig: Friedrich Lanckischens Erben. Repr. ed. Lutz Geldsetzer; Düsseldorf: Stern-Verlag Janssen & Co.

(1752 [1985]). *Allgemeine Geschichtswissenschaft.* Leipzig: Friedrich Lanckischens Erben. Repr. ed. Christoph Friedrich; Vienna, Cologne, and Graz: Böhlau.

Chytraeus, David (1556). *Oratio continens historiam Henrici Leonis Ducis Saxoniae et Bavariae, recitata Rostochii a Davide Chytraeo.* Wittenberg: Iohannes Crato.

(1562a). *Chronologia historiae Herodoti et Thucydidis.* Rostock: Stephanus Mylander.

(1562b). *Praecepta rhetoricae inventionis, illustrata multis et utilibus exemplis, ex sacra scriptura et Cicerone sumptis a David Chytraeo. Addita est eiusdem oratio, in funere illustrissimi principis Henrici, Ducis Megapolensis etc. recitata Sverini.* Leipzig: n.p.

(1562c). *De ratione discendi et ordine studiorum recte instituendo commonefactiones aliquot et regulae utiles, traditae a Davide Chytraeo.* Wittenberg: Iohannes Crato.

(1563). *De lectione historiarum recte instituenda. Et historicorum fere omnium series et argumenta, breviter et perspicue exposita a Davide Chytraeo. Addita est chronologia historiae Herodoti, Thucydidis, Xenophontis, Diodori Siculi, Cornelii Taciti, Procopii, etc.* Wittenberg: Iohannes Crato.

(1564). *De ratione discendi et ordine studiorum in singulis artibus recte instituendo.* Wittenberg: Schwenck.

(1569). *Chronologia historiae Herodoti et Thucydidis, recognita, et additis ecclesiae Christi ac imperii Romani rebus praecipuis, ab initio mundi usque ad nostram aetatem contexta.* Rostock: Iacobus Transylvanus.

(1573). *Chronologia historiae Herodoti et Thucydidis, recognita, et additis ecclesiae Christi ac imperii Romani rebus praecipuis, ab initio mundi usque ad nostram aetatem contexta.* Rostock: Iacobus Lucius.

(1575). "Pio et candido lectori," 28 August 1574. In Schubert 1575, A ro–Aiii vo.

Copernicus, Nicolaus (1975). *De revolutionibus libri sex*, ed. Ryszard Gansiniec *et al.* Warsaw and Cracow: Officina publica libris scientificis edendis.

Cornelius Nepos (1608). *Cornelii Nepotis vulgo Aemilii Probi de vita excellentium imperatorum Graecorum et Romanorum.* Frankfurt: Claude de Marne and the heirs of Jean Aubry.

Cortesi, Paolo (1973). *De hominibus doctis dialogus*, ed. Maria Teresa Graziosi. Rome: Bonacci.

Ctesias *et al.* (1557). *Ex Ctesia, Agatharcide, Memnone excerptae historiae. Appiani Iberica. Item, de gestis Annibalis*, ed. Henri Estienne. Geneva: Estienne.

Decembrio, Angelo (2002). *De politia litteraria*, ed. Norbert Witten. Munich and Leipzig: Saur.

Dictys (1573). *Belli Troiani scriptores praecipui, Dictys Cretensis, Dares Phrygius et Homerus.* Basle: Perna.

D'Onofrio, Cesare (ed.) (1989). *Visitiamo Roma nel Quattrocento: la città degli Umanisti.* Rome: Romana Società Editrice.

Draud, Georg (1625). *Bibliotheca classica*, Frankfurt am Main: Ostern.

Dresser, Matthaeus (1606). *Orationum libri tres*, 3 vols. Leipzig: Apelius.

Eisenhart, Johannes (1679). *De fide historica commentarius.* Helmstedt: Müller.

Erasmus (1518). Ep. ded. to Ernest of Bavaria, in *Quintus Curtius de rebus gestis Alexandri Magni regis Macedonum cum annotationibus Des. Erasmi Roterodami*, Strasbourg: Schurer.

Ernesti, Johann August (1746). *De fide historica recte aestimanda disputatio in academia Lipsiensi . . . praeside Io. Augusto Ernesti . . . A.D. VI Aprilis A.C.MDCCXXXXVI ad disceptandum proposita a Christiano Ludovico Stieglitz.* Leipzig: Langenheim.

Erpenius, Thomas (1721). "De peregrinatione Gallica utiliter instituenda tractatus." In Lackmann 1721, 116–131.

Fabricius, Theodore (1591). *De signis praenunciis postremae diei, parricidio monachi, interfectoris regis Galliarum Henrici III. et successori legitimo Henrico IV. Borbonio. Quae omnia, versibus numeralibus expressa sunt ad annum 1589.* n.p.: n.p.

Fabricius, Theodosius (praeses) (1595). *Disputatio XIII. Continens diiudicationem quaestionis simplicem ac scholasticam, in statu conjecturali: utrum potiturus tandem sit Turca Imperio Romano seu Germanico, de qua exercitii causa respondendi provinciam suscepit, praeside M. Theodosio Fabricio, Johannes Janus Gittelensis. In Paedagogio Gottingensi ad diem 14. Februarii.* Henricopoli: Excusa typis Conradi Horn.

Fernández de Oviedo y Valdés, Gonzalo (1851–5). *Historia general y natural de las Indias, islas y tierrafirme del mar oceano.* 3 pts. in 4 vols. Madrid, Impr. de la Real academia de la historia.

Flacius Illyricus, Matthias (1968). *De ratione cognoscendi sacras literas,* ed. and tr. Lutz Geldsetzer. Düsseldorf: Stern-Verlag Janssen & Co.

Franckenberger, Andreas (1586). *Institutionum antiquitatis et historiarum, pars prima, in libros sex distributa.* Wittenberg: Crato.

Freigius, Joannes Thomas (1580). *Historiae synopsis, seu praelectionum historicarum in Altorfiano Noribergensium gymnasio delineatio.* Basle: Henricpetri.

   (1583). *Mosaicus, continens historiam ecclesiasticam 2494 annorum ab orbe condito usque ad Mosis mortem.* Basle: Henricpetri.

Frischlin, Nicodemus (ed.) (1588). *Selectae orationes e Q. Curtio, T. Livio, C. Salustio, C. Caesare, M. Cicerone in usum Scholae Martinianae apud Brunsvicenses.* Henricopoli: Corneus.

George of Trebizond (1547). *Rhetoricorum libri quinque.* Lyons: Seb. Gryphius.

Gesner, Conrad (1545–55). *Bibliotheca universalis.* 4 vols. Zurich: Froschauer.

Grotius, Hugo *et al.* (1645). *Dissertationes de studiis instituendis.* Amsterdam: Louis Elzevir.

Guarino of Verona (1915–19). *Epistolario,* ed. Remigio Sabbadini. 3 vols. Venice: a spese della Società.

Heling, Mauricius (1667). *Colossus vel statua regis Babylonici Nobogdonosoris, in qua depinguntur IIII monarchiae Dan. II,* ed. Johann Paul Felwinger. Altdorf: Cramer.

Helmold (1937). *Helmolds Slavenchronik,* ed. Bernhard Schmeidler. Hanover: Hahn.

Herodotus (1566). *Herodoti Halicarnassei historiae lib. ix, et de vita Homeri libellus. Illic ex interpretatione Laur. Vallae adscripta, hic ex interpret. Conradi Heresbachii: utraque ab Henr. Stephano recognita. Ex Ctesia excerptae historiae. Icones quarundam memorabilium structurarum. Apologia Henr. Stephani pro Herodoto,* ed. Henri Estienne. Geneva: Henri Estienne.

(1570). *Herodoti Halicarnassei Historia, sive, Historiarum libri IX, qui inscribuntur Musae. Ex vetustis exemplaribus recogniti. Ctesiae quaedam,* ed. Henri Estienne. Geneva: Henri Estienne.

Heyne, Christian Gottlob (1785–1823). *Opuscula academica.* 6 vols. Göttingen: Dieterich.

Horn, Georg (1650). *Arca Noae.* Leiden: Hack.

Keckermann, Bartholomäus (1609). *Apparatus practicus, sive idea methodica et plena totius philosophiae practicae, nempe, ethicae, oeconomicae, et politicae. In quo ostenditur ratio studii practici dextre conformandi, et locos communes colligendi, atque adeo tum Politicos, tum Historicos cum certo fructu legendi.* Hanau: Guilielmus Antonius.

(1610). *De natura et proprietatibus historiae commentarius, privatim in Gymnasio Dantiscano propositus.* Hanau: Guilielmus Antonius.

(1614). *Operum omnium quae extant tomus primus [- secundus].* 2 vols. Geneva: Aubert.

Kessler, Eckhard (ed.) (1971). *Theoretiker humanistischer Geschichtsschreibung.* Munich: Fink.

Krag, Nicolaus (ed.) (1593). *Ex Nicolai Damasceni universali historia seu De moribus gentium libris excerpta Iohannis Stobaei collectanea.* Heidelberg: Santandreanus.

Lackmann, Adam Heinrich (1721). *Miscellanea litteraria.* Hamburg: Schiller and Kisner.

La Popelinière, Lancelot Voisin Sieur de (1599). *L'histoire des histoires, avec l'Idée de l'Histoire accomplie.* Paris: Marc Orry.

Lazius, Wolfgang (1557). *De gentium aliquot migrationibus, sedibus fixis, reliquiis, linguarumque initiis & immutationibus ac dialectis, libri XII.* Basle: Oporinus.

Le Clerc, Jean (1697). *Ars critica.* 3 vols. Amsterdam: Gallet.

(1699–1701). *Parrhasiana ou pensées diverses sur des matiéres de critique, d'histoire, de morale et de politique. Avec la Défense de divers Ouvrages de Mr. L.C. Par Theodore Parrhase,* Amsterdam.

(1712a). *Ars critica,* 4th edn. 3 vols. Amsterdam: Schelte.

(1712b). *Oratio inauguralis, de praestantia et utilitate historiae ecclesiasticae,* Amsterdam: Schelte.

(1715). *"Praefatio Theodori Goralli [Joannis Clerici], in qua consilium eius aperitur et ratio interpretandi veteres traditur."* In *C. Pedonis Albinovani Elegiae III et fragmenta, cum interpretatione* *et notis Jos. Scaligeri, Frid. Lindenbruchii, Nic. Heinsii, Theod. Goralli et aliorum.* Amsterdam: Schelte, *3 ro – **4 ro.

(1991). *Epistolario,* II: *1690–1705,* ed. Maria Grazia and Mario Sina. Florence: Olschki.

Le Conte, Antoine (1562). "Admonitio de falsis Constantini legibus, ad quendam qui se hoc tempore Iurisconsultum Christianum profitetur." In Jean Calvin, *Responsio ad Balduini convicia.* Geneva: Crespin, 70–80.

Lenglet Dufresnoy, Nicholas (1713). *Méthode pour étudier l'histoire.* 2 vols. Paris: Antoine Urbain Coustelier.

Le Roy, Loys (1542). *G. Budaei Parisiensis viri clarissimi vita.* 2nd edn. Paris: Roigny.

(1559). *Selectiores aliquot epistolae.* Paris: Morel.

(tr.) (1568a). *Enseignements d'Isocrates et Xenophon, autheurs anciens tres-excellens. Pour bien regner en paix et en guerre.* Paris: Vascosan.

(tr.) (1568b). *Les politiques d'Aristote, esquelles est monstree la science de gouverner le genre humain en toutes especes d'estats publics.* Paris: Vascosan.

(1577). *De la vicissitude ou variété des choses en l'univers.* Paris: L'Huillier.

(ed.) (1598). *Aristotles Politiques, or Discourses of Government.* London: Islip.

Ligorio, Pirro (1963). *Pirro Ligorio's Roman Antiquities: The Drawings in MS XIII. B 7 in the National Library of Naples,* ed. Erna Mandowsky and Charles Mitchell. London: Warburg Institute.

Lipsius, Justus (2004). *Politica: Six Books of Politics or Political Instruction,* ed. and tr. Jan Waszink. Assen: Van Gorcum.

Lucinge, René de (1993). *La manière de lire l'histoire,* ed. Michael Heath. Geneva: Droz.

Maccius, Sebastian (1593). *De historia libri tres*. Venice: Dei.

Marliani, Bartolomeo (1544). *Vrbis Romae topographia*. Rome: In aedibus Valerii, Dorici, et Aloisii fratris, Academiae Romanae impressorum.

Mascardi, Agostino (1662). *Dell'arte historica*. Venice: Per il Baba.

  (1859). *Dell'arte istorica*, ed. Adolfo Bartoli. Florence: Le Monnier.

Milieu, Christophe (1551). *De scribenda universitatis rerum historia libri quinque*. Basle: Oporinus.

Montaigne, Michel de (1999). *Les essais*, ed. Pierre Villey. 3rd edn. 3 vols. Paris: Quadrige/Presses Universitaires de France.

Nanni, Giovanni (ed.) (1545). *Antiquitatum libri quinque*. Antwerp: Steelsius.

Optatus (1549). *Libri sex de schismate Donatistarum, contra Parmenianum Donatistam, adversus quem et S. Augustinus postea tres aedidit libros. Ex bibliotheca Cusana prope Treverim*. Apud S. Victorem prope Moguntiam: Franciscus Behem. [With Bruno 1549.]

Panvinio, Onofrio (1573). *Chronicon ecclesiasticum*. Louvain: Ioannes Bogardus.

Patrizi, Francesco (1560). *Della historia diece dialoghi*. Venice: Arrivabene.

  (1583). *La milizia romana di Polibio, di Tito Livio e di Dionigi Alicarnasseo, da Francesco Patricii dichiarata e con varie figure illustrata*. Ferrara: Mamarelli.

  (1594). *Paralleli militari*. Rome: Zanetti.

Perizonius, Jacob (1685). *Animadversiones historicae*. Amsterdam: Boom.

  (1703). *Q. Curtius in integrum restitutus et vindicatus*. Leiden: Teering.

  (1740a). "Oratio de fide historiarum contra Pyrrhonismum historicum, dicta Lugd. Bat. postr. Non. Febr. 1702." In Jacob Perizonius, *Orationes XII*. Leiden: Westhovius, 103–54.

(1740b). *Dissertationes septem.* Leiden: Langerak.

Polybius (1549). *Quinque fragmenta decerpta ex Polybii historiarum libris quadraginta,* tr. Raphael Cyllenius. Venice: Arrivabene.

Porcacchi, Thomaso (1565). *Il primo volume delle cagioni delle guerre antiche.* Venice: Gabriel Giolito.

Possevino, Antonio (1597). *Apparatus ad omnium gentium historiam.* Venice: Ciotto.

Ramus, Petrus and Talon, Omer (1599 [1969]). *Collectaneae praefationes, epistolae, orationes,* ed. Walter Ong. Marburg: Egenolph; repr. Hildesheim: Olms.

Reineck, Reiner (1574). ΣΥΝΤΑΓΜΑ *de familiis quae in monarchiis tribus prioribus rerum potitae sunt.* 2 vols. Basle: Henricpetri.

(ed.) (1577). *Annales Witichindi monachi Corbeiensis, familiae Benedictinae: editi de fide codicis manuscripti, et e publicato exemplari alicubi aucti.* Frankfurt: Wechel.

(1580a). *Oratio de historia eiusque dignitate, partibus, atque in primis ea, quae de gentilitatibus agit, nec non aliis, quae ad idem argumentum pertinentia, moneri utiliter posse visa sunt: scripta et recitata praefationis in praelectionum publicarum operas ergo.* Frankfurt: Wechel.

(ed.) (1580b). *Chronici Ditmari episcopi Mersepurgii libri vi nunc primum in lucem editi.* Frankfurt: Wechel.

(ed.) (1580c). *Historia de vita et rebus gestis Viperti, Marchionis Lusatiae, Burggrafii Magdeburgensis, Comitis Groicensis: auctore Monacho Pegaviensi. Et altera de bellis Friderici Magni, seu Admorsi, Landgrafii Turingiae, Palatini Saxoniae, Marchionis Mysniae et Osterlandiae: auctore Johanne Garzone Bononiensi.* Frankfurt: Wechel.

(1581a). *Origines illustriss. stirpis Brandenburgicae.* Frankfurt: Wechel.

(ed.) (1581b). *Chronica Slavorum, seu Annales Helmoldi, presbyteris Buzoviensis in agro Lubecensi: hisque subiectum*

derelictorum supplementum Arnoldi Abbatis Lubecensis.
Frankfurt: Wechel.

(1583). *Ad Reinerum Reineccium liber epistolarum historicarum, seu de editionibus et operis eius historicis per ann. xvi. scriptarum.* Helmstedt: Lucius.

Reusner, Elias (1597). *Genealogia sive enucleatio inclyti stemmatis VVitichindei, ab ima radice cum suis pullulis, stirpibus, et ramis luculenter deducti.* Jena: Tobias Steinmann.

(1609a). *Isagoges historicae libri duo: quorum unus ecclesiasticam, alter politicam continet historiam: utramque secundum cujusque aetates exacte definitam: quarum illa ad traditionem Domus Eliae, haec ad quatuor mundi regna, in bestiis quatuor a Daniele Propheta adumbrata, magno et pio studio est accommodata.* 2nd edn. Jena: Christophorus Lippold.

(1609b). *Septem illustrium quaestionum historicarum enucleatio.* Jena: Christophorus Lippold.

(1610). *Genealogiae regum, electorum, ducum, principum, atque comitum, qui origines suas a bellicosissimo Saxonum rege Wedekindo deducunt.* Leipzig: Henningus Grosius.

Riccobono, Antonio (1579). *De historia liber, cum fragmentis historicorum Latinorum summa fide et diligentia ab eodem collectis et auctis.* Basle: Perna.

Roberti, Gaudenzio (1691–2). *Miscellanea italica erudita*, 4 vols. Parma: ab Oleo and Rosatus.

Robortello, Francesco (1548). *De historica facultate disputatio.* Florence: Torrentino. Repr. in Kessler (ed.) (1971).

(1662). *De arte sive ratione corrigendi antiquorum libros.* In Schoppe (1662), 98–121.

(1968). *In librum Aristotelis de arte poetica explicationes. Paraphrasis in librum Horatii, qui vulgo de arte poetica ad Pisones inscribitur.* Florence: Torrentinus, 1548. Repr. Munich: Fink.

(1975). *De arte sive ratione corrigendi antiquorum libros disputatio*, ed. and tr. G. Pompella. Naples: L. Loffredo.

Sardi, Alessandro (1577). *De moribus ac ritibus gentium libri III*. Mainz: Behem.

Scaliger, Joseph (ed.) (1606). *Thesaurus temporum*. Leiden: Basson.

Scaliger, Joseph (1740). *Scaligerana, Thuana, Perroniana, Pithoeana, et Colomesiana*, ed. Pierre Des Maizeaux. 2 vols. Amsterdam: Covens & Mortier.

Schoppe, Caspar (1662). *De arte critica, et praecipue, de altera eius parte emendatrice, quaenam ratio in Latinis scriptoribus ex ingenio emendandis observari debeat, Commentariolus*. Amsterdam: Pluymer.

Schorckelius, Sigismundus (ed.) (1556). *Helmoldi historici ac presbyteri ecclesiae Lubecensis historiarum liber, scriptus ante annos pene 400*. Frankfurt: Brubachius.

Schubert, Clemens (1575). *Libri quatuor de scrupulis chronologorum*. Strasbourg: Bernhardus Iobin.

Sidney, Philip (1962). *Prose Works*, ed. Albert Feuillerat. 4 vols. Cambridge: Cambridge University Press.

Sossus, Gulielmus (1632). *De numine historiae liber*. Paris: Guillemot.

Spinoza, Baruch (1670). *Tractatus theologico-politicus continens dissertationes aliquot, quibus ostenditur libertatem philosophandi non tantum salva pietate, & reipublicae pace posse concedi: sed eandem nisi cum pace reipublicae, ipsaque pietate tolli non posse*. Hamburg: Heinrich Künrath.

Thou, Jacques-Auguste de (1733). *Historiarum sui temporis libri cxxxviii*. 7 vols. London: Buckley.

Tizio, Sigismondo (1992). *Historiae senenses*, I, 1. Ed. Manuela Doni Garfagnini. Rerum italicarum scriptores recentiores, 6. Rome: Istituto per l'età moderna e contemporanea.

Valla, Lorenzo (1973). *Gesta Ferdinandi regis Aragonum*, ed. Ottavio Besomi. Padua: Antenore.

(1981). *Antidotum in Facium*, ed. Mariangela Regoliosi. Padua; Antenore.

(1996). *Le postille di Lorenzo Valla all' 'Institutio Oratoria' di Quintiliano*, ed. Lucia Cesarini Martinelli and Alessandro Perosa. Padua: Antenore.

Vergil, Polydore (2002). *On Discovery*, ed. and tr. Brian Copenhaver. Cambridge, Mass. and London: Harvard University Press.

Vossius, Gerardus Joannes (1691). *Gerardi Joannis Vossii et clarorum virorum ad eum epistolae*, ed. Paul Colomiès. Augsburg: Sumptibus Kronigeri et Haered. Goebelianorum, Typis Schönigianis.

(1699). "Ars historica." In *Opera*, 4: 1–48. Amsterdam.

Vossius, Gerardus Joannes *et al.* (1658). *Dissertationes de studiis bene instituendis*. Utrecht: Achersdyk and Zylius.

Wheare, Degory (1684). *Relectiones hyemales de ratione et methodo legendi utrasque historias, civiles et ecclesiasticas.* Cambridge: Dickinson and Green.

[Wolf, Johannes] (ed.) (1576). *Io. Bodini Methodus historica: duodecim eiusdem argumenti scriptorum, tam veterum quam recentiorum, quorum elenchum praefationi subiecimus.* Basle: Perna.

Wolf, Johannes (ed.) (1579). *Artis historicae penus*, 2 vols., Basle: Perna.

Zeltner, Gustavus Georgius (1715). *Historiae Noribergensis ecclesiasticae notabilior pericope in Mauritii Helingi antistitis ad D. Sebald. per XL. annos Noriberg. vita et fatis exhibita.* Altdorf: typis et sumptibus Iod. Guil. Kohlesii.

Zwinger, Theodor (1577). *Methodus apodemica, in eorum gratiam, qui cum fructu in quocunq[ue] tandem vitae genere peregrinari cupiunt.* Basle: Episcopius.

Secondary sources

Accame Lanzilotta, Maria (1990). "L'insegnamento di Pomponio Leto nello *Studium Urbis.*" In *Storia della Facoltà di Lettere e Filosofia de "La Sapienza,"* ed. Lidia Capo and Maria Rosa Di Simone. Rome: Viella: 71–91.

Adler, William (1989). *Time Immemorial: Archaic History and its Sources in Christian Chronography from Julius Africanus to George Syncellus.* Washington, DC: Dumbarton Oaks.

Albanese, Massimiliano (2003). *Gli storici classici nella biblioteca latina di Niccolo V.* Rome: Roma nel Rinascimento.

Alcock, Susan, Cherry, John, and Elsner, Jaś (eds.) (2001). *Pausanias: Travel and Memory in Roman Greece.* Oxford: Oxford University Press.

Allen, Don Cameron (1949). *The Legend of Noah: Renaissance Rationalism in Art, Science, and Letters.* Urbana: University of Illinois Press.

(1970). *Mysteriously Meant.* Baltimore: Johns Hopkins University Press.

Andrés de Uztarroz, Juan Francisco, and Dormer, Diego J. (1878). *Progresos de la historia en Aragon y vidas de sus cronistas, desde que se instituyó este cargo hasta su extinciòn.* I: *La biografía este de Gerónimo Zurita.* Zaragoza: Impr. del Hospicio.

Anglo, Sydney (2005). *Machiavelli: The First Century. Studies in Enthusiasm, Hostility, and Irrelevance.* Oxford: Oxford University Press.

Antonazzi, Giovanni (1985). *Lorenzo Valla e la polemica sulla donazione di Costantino.* Rome: Storia e Letteratura.

Antoni, Carlo (1951). *Der Kampf wider die Vernunft: Zur Entstehungsgeschichte des deutschen Freiheitsgedankens,* tr. Walter Goetz. Stuttgart: Koehler.

(1968). *La lotta contro la ragione.* Florence: Sansoni.

Atkinson, John (2000). "Originality and its Limits in the Alexander Sources of the Early Empire." In Bosworth and Baynham (ed.) (2000), 307–25.

Backus, Irena (2003). *Historical Method and Confessional Identity in the Era of the Reformation (1378–1615)*. Boston and New York: Brill.

Baillet, Lina (1986). "Schwendi, lecteur de Machiavel." *Revue d'Alsace* 112: 119–97.

Bann, Stephen (1994). *Under the Sign: John Bargrave as Collector, Traveler, and Witness*. Ann Arbor: University of Michigan Press.

Barnes, Annie (1938). *Jean Le Clerc (1657–1736) et la République des Lettres*. Paris: Droz.

Barnes, Robin (1988). *Prophecy and Gnosis: Apocalypticism in the Wake of the Lutheran Reformation*. Stanford: Stanford University Press.

Baron, Hans (1959). "The *Querelle* of the Ancients and Moderns as a Problem for Renaissance Scholarship." *Journal of the History of Ideas* 20: 3–22.

Baxandall, Michael (1963). "A Dialogue on Art from the Court of Leonello d'Este." *Journal of the Warburg and Courtauld Institutes* 26: 304–26.

Bellini, Eraldo (2002). *Agostino Mascardi tra ars poetica e ars historica*. Milan: Vita e pensiero.

Bentley, Jerry (1978). "Erasmus, Jean le Clerc, and the Principle of the Harder Reading." *Renaissance Quarterly* 31: 309–21.

Benz, Stephan (2003). *Zwischen Tradition und Kritik: Katholische Geschichtsschreibung im barocken Heiligen Römischen Reich*. Husum: Matthiesen.

Bezold, Friedrich von (1918). *Aus Mittelatter und Renaissance*. Munich: Oldenbourg.

"Zur Entstehungsgeschichte der historischen Methodik." In *Aus Mittelalter und Renaissance*, Munich: Oldenbourg.

Billanovich, Myriam (1968). "Benedetto Bordon e Giulio Cesare Scaligero." *Italia medievale e umanistica*, 9: 187–256.

Bizzocchi, Roberto (1995). *Genealogie incredibili. Scritti di storia nell'Europa moderna.* Bologna: Il Mulino.

Black, Robert (1987). "The New Laws of History." *Renaissance Studies* 1: 126–56.

——— (1995). "The Donation of Constantine: A New Source for the Concept of the Renaissance?" In *Language and Images of Renaissance Italy*, ed. Alison Brown: 51–85. Oxford: Clarendon Press.

Blair, Ann (1992). "Humanist Methods in Natural Philosophy: The Commonplace Book." *Journal of the History of Ideas* 53: 541–51.

——— (1996). "Bibliothèques portables: les recueils de lieux communs dans la Renaissance tardive." In *Le pouvoir des bibliothèques: La mémoire des livres en Occident*, ed. Marc Baratin and Christian Jacob: 84–106. Paris: Albin Michel.

——— (1997a). *The Theater of Nature: Jean Bodin and Renaissance Science.* Princeton: Princeton University Press.

——— (1997b). "Bodin, Montaigne and the Role of Disciplinary Boundaries." In Kelley (ed.) 1997, 29–40.

——— (2000a). "Annotating and indexing natural philosophy." In *Books and the Sciences in History*, ed. Marina Frasca-Spada and Nick Jardine, 69–89. Cambridge: Cambridge University Press.

——— (2000b). "The Practices of Erudition according to Morhof." In *Mapping the World of Learning: The Polyhistor of Daniel Georg Morhof*, ed. Françoise Waquet, 59–74. Wiesbaden: Harrassowitz.

——— (2003). "Reading Strategies for Coping with Information Overload, ca. 1550–1700." *Journal of the History of Ideas* 64: 11–28.

(2004a). "Note-Taking as an Art of Transmission." *Critical Inquiry* 31: 85–107.

(2004b). "Scientific Reading: an Early Modernist's Perspective." *Isis* 95: 64–74.

(2005). "*Historia* in Zwinger's *Theatrum Humanae Vitae.*" In Pomata and Siraisi (eds.) (2005), 269–96.

Blanke, Horst Walther (1991). *Historiographiegeschichte als Historik.* Fundamenta Historica, 3. Stuttgart-Bad Cannstatt: Frommann-Holzboog.

Bödeker, Hans Erich *et al.* (eds.) (1986). *Aufklärung und Geschichte: Studien zur deutschen Geschichtswissenschaft im 18. Jahrhundert.* Göttingen: Vandenhoeck & Ruprecht.

Bolgar, Robert (1954). *The Classical Heritage and its Beneficiaries from the Carolingian Age to the End of the Renaissance.* Cambridge: Cambridge University Press.

Bolzoni, Lina (1980). *L'universo dei poemi possibili. Studi su Francesco Patrizi da Cherso.* Rome: Bulzoni.

Bonger, H. (1978). *Leven en werk van D. V. Coornhert.* Amsterdam: G. A. van Oorschot.

Borghero, Carlo (1983). *La certezza e la storia: Cartesianismo, pirronismo e conoscenza storica,* Milan: Franco Angeli.

Bosworth, Brian (2000). "Introduction." In Bosworth and Baynham (ed.) (2002), 1–22.

Bosworth, Brian and Baynham, Elizabeth (eds.) (2000). *Alexander the Great in Fact and Fiction.* Oxford: Oxford University Press.

Bots, Hans and Waquet, Françoise (eds.) (1994). *Commercium litterarium, 1600–1750: La communication dans la République des lettres = Commercium litterarium, 1600–1750: Forms of Communication in the Republic of Letters.* Amsterdam: APA-Holland University Press.

(1997). *La République des lettres.* Paris: Belin.

Brady, Ciaran (ed.) (1991). *Ideology and the Historians.* Historical Studies XVII. Dublin: The Lilliput Press.

Bredekamp, Horst (1995). *The Lure of Antiquity and the Cult of the Machine: The Kunstkammer and the Evolution of Nature, Art and Technology,* tr. Allison Brown. Princeton, NJ: Markus Wiener.

Brendecke, Arndt (2004). "Tabellen in der Praxis der Frühneuzeitlichen Geschichtsvermittlung." In *Wissenssicherung, Wissensordnung und Wissensverarbeitung. Das Europäische Modell der Enzyklopädien,* ed. Theo Stammen and Wolfgang Weber, 157–85. Berlin: Akademie Verlag.

Brosseder, Claudia (2004). *Im Bann der Sterne: Caspar Peucer, Philipp Melanchthon und andere Wittenberger Astrologen.* Berlin: Akademie-Verlag.

(2005). "The Writing in the Wittenberg Sky: Astrology in Sixteenth-Century Germany." *Journal of the History of Ideas* 66: 557–76.

Brown, John Lackey (1939). *The Methodus ad Facilem Historiarum Cognitionem of Jean Bodin: A Critical Study,* Washington, D.C.: Catholic University of America Press.

Burke, Peter (2003). "Images as Evidence in Seventeenth-Century Europe." *Journal of the History of Ideas* 64: 317–35.

Butterfield, Herbert (1955). *Man on his Past: The Study of the History of Historical Scholarship.* Cambridge: Cambridge University Press.

Büttner, Manfred (1978). "Bartholomäus Keckermann 1572–1609." *Geographers: Biobibliographical Studies* 2: 73–9.

Cabrini, Anna Maria (1990). "Le *Historiae* del Bruni: Risultati e ipotesi di una ricerca sulle fonti." In Viti (ed.) (1990), 247–319.

Camporeale, Salvatore (1996). "Lorenzo Valla's *Oratio* on the Pseudo-Donation of Constantine: Dissent and Innovation in Early Renaissance Humanism." *Journal of the History of Ideas* 57: 9–26.

Canfora, Davide (2001). *La controversia di Poggio Bracciolini e Guarino Veronese su Cesare e Scipio.* Florence: Olschki.

Cappelletto, Rita (1983). *Recuperi Ammianei da Biondo Flavio.* Rome: Storia e Letteratura.

(1992a). "*Italia Illustrata* di Biondo Flavio." In *Letteratura italiana* 1: 681-712. Turin: Einaudi.

(1992b). "'*Peragrare ac lustrare Italiam coepi.*' Alcune considerazioni sull'*Italia Illustrata* e sulla sua fortuna." In *Storiografia umanistica*, 2 vols., 1, pt 1: 181–203. Messina: Sicania.

Carey, Sorcha (2003). *Pliny's Catalogue of Culture: Art and Empire in the* Natural History. Oxford: Oxford University Press.

Carhart, Michael (1999). *The Writing of Cultural History in Eighteenth-Century Germany.* PhD dissertation, Rutgers University.

Carney, Elizabeth (2000). "Artifice and Alexander History." In Bosworth and Baynham (ed.) (2000), 263–85.

Carr, Edward Hallett (1962). *What is History?* New York: Knopf.

Cary, George (1956). *The Medieval Alexander*, ed. D. J. A. Ross. Cambridge: Cambridge University Press.

Castelli, Patrizia (ed.) (2002). *Francesco Patrizi filosofo platonico nel crepuscolo del Rinascimento.* Florence: Olschki.

Castner, Catherine (1998). "Direct Observation and Biondo Flavio's Additions to *Italia Illustrata*: The Case of Ocriculum." *Medievalia et Humanistica*, new series 25: 93–108.

Chmel, Joseph (1840–41). *Die Handschriften der K.K. Hofbibliothek in Wien, im Interesse der Geschichte, besonders der Oesterreichischen, verzeichnet und excerpirt.* 2 vols. Vienna: Gerold.

Clark, William (2006). *Academic Charisma and the Origins of the Research University.* Chicago: University of Chicago Press.

Clavuot, Ottavio (1990). *Biondos "Italia illustrata": Summa oder Neuschöpfung? über die Arbeitsmethoden eines Humanisten.* Tübingen: Niemeyer.

Cochrane, Eric (1981). *Historians and Historiography in the Italian Renaissance.* Chicago and London: University of Chicago Press.

Coffin, David (2004). *Pirro Ligorio: The Renaissance Artist, Architect, and Antiquarian.* University Park, Pa.: Pennsylvania State University Press.

Cohn, Bernard (1961). "The Pasts of an Indian Village." *Comparative Studies in Society and History* 3: 241–9.

Cooper, Charles Henry [and Cooper, John William] (1842–1908). *Annals of Cambridge,* 5 vols. Cambridge: Warwick [vols. IV and V: Metcalfe and Palmer; vol. V, ed. John William Cooper, Cambridge University Press].

Copenhaver, Brian (1978). "The Historiography of Discovery in the Renaissance: The Sources and Composition of Polydore Vergil's *De Inventoribus Rerum,* I–III." *Journal of the Warburg and Courtauld Institutes* 41: 192–214.

(1992). "Did Science Have a Renaissance?" *Isis* 83: 387–407.

Cotroneo, Girolamo (1966). *Jean Bodin teorico della storia,* Naples: Giannini.

(1971). *I trattatisti dell'ars historica,* Naples: Giannini.

Couzinet, Marie-Dominique (1996). *Histoire et méthode à la Renaissance: une lecture de la Methodus ad facilem historiarum cognitionem de Jean Bodin,* Paris: Vrin.

(2000). "L'inspiration historique chez Francesco Patrizi," *Epistemon,* 19 January 2000 (http://www.cesr.univ-tours.fr./Epistemon/trivium/couz-ent.asp).

(2001). *Jean Bodin.* Rome: Memini.

Crisciani, Chiara (2005). "Histories, Stories, *Exempla,*and Anecdotes: Michele Savonarola from Latin to Vernacular." In Pomata and Siraisi (ed.) (2005), 297–324.

Cunningham, Bernardette (1991). "The Culture and Ideology of Irish Franciscan Historians at Louvain, 1607–1650." In Brady (ed.) (1991), 11–30, 222–7.

Curran, Brian (1998–9). " '*De sacrarum litterarum Aegyptiorum inter-pretatione.*' Reticence and Hubris in Hieroglyphic Studies of the Renaissance: Pierio Valeriano and Annius of Viterbo." *Memoirs of the American Academy in Rome* 43/44.

Curran, Brian, and Grafton, Anthony (1995 [1996]). "A Fifteenth-Century Site Report on the Vatican Obelisk." *Journal of the Warburg and Courtauld Institutes,* 58: 234–48.

Darnton, Robert (1995). *The Forbidden Best-Sellers of Pre-Revolutionary France.* New York: Norton.

Daston, Lorraine (ed.) (2000). *Biographies of Scientific Objects.* Chicago: University of Chicago Press.

(ed.) (2004). *Things that Talk: Object Lessons from Art and Science.* New York: Zone; Cambridge, Mass., and London: distributed by MIT Press.

Davies, David (1954). *The World of the Elseviers, 1580–1712.* The Hague: Nijhoff.

Davis, Natalie Zemon (2006). *Trickster Travels: A Sixteenth-Century Muslim Between Worlds.* New York: Hill & Wang.

Décultot, Elisabeth (2000). *Johann Joachim Winckelmann: enquête sur la genèse de l'histoire de l'art.* Paris: Presses Universitaires de France.

(ed.) (2003). *Lire, copier, écrire: les bibliothèques manuscrites et leurs usages au XVIIIe siècle.* Paris: CNRS.

Deitz, Luc (1997). "'*Falsissima est ergo haec de triplici substantia Aristotelis doctrina.*' A Sixteenth-Century Critic of Aristotle – Francesco Patrizi da Cherso on Privation, Form, and Matter." *Early Science and Medicine* 2: 227–50.

Deitz, Luc (1999). "Space, Light, and Soul in Francesco Patrizi's *Nova de universis philosophia.*" In *Natural Particulars,* ed. Nancy Siraisi and Anthony Grafton, Cambridge, Mass.: MIT Press, 139–70.

De Landtsheer, Jeanine (2001). "Justus Lipsius's *De militia Romana*: Polybius Revived or How an Ancient Historian was Turned into a Manual of Early Modern Warfare." In Enenkel, de Jong, and de Landtsheer (2001), 101–22.

———— (2006). "Lipsius en de antieke Oudheid." In de Landtsheer (ed.) (2006), 215–21.

———— (ed.) (2006). *Lieveling van de Latijnse taal. Justus Lipsius te Leiden herdacht bij zijn vierhondertste sterfdag*. Leiden: Universiteits-bibliotheek Leiden/Scaliger Instituut.

Delph, Ronald (1996). "Valla Grammaticus, Agostino Steucho, and the Donation of Constantine." *Journal of the History of Ideas* 57: 55–77.

De Vivo, Filippo (2003). "Historical Justifications of Venetian Power in the Adriatic." *Journal of the History of Ideas* 64: 159–76.

Dionisotti, Carlotta (1983). "Polybius and the Royal Professor." In *Tria corda: scritti in onore di Arnaldo Momigliano*, ed. Emilio Gabba. Como: Edizioni New Press.

———— (1997). "Les chapitres entre l'historiographie et le roman." In *Titres et articulations du texte dans les oeuvres antiques*. Actes du Colloque International de Chantilly, 13–15 décembre 1994, ed. Jean-Claude Fredouille, Marie-Odile Goulet-Cazé, Philippe Hoffmann, and Pierre Petitmengin, with Simone Deléani. Collection des Etudes Augustiniennes, Série Antiquité, 152. Paris: Institut d'Etudes Augustiniennes: 529–47.

Ditchfield, Simon (1995). *Liturgy, Sanctity and History in Tridentine Italy: Pietro Maria Campi and the Preservation of the Particular*. Cambridge and New York: Cambridge University Press.

Doni Garfagnini, Manuela (2002). *Il teatro della storia fra rappre-sentazione e realtà: storiografia e trattatistica fra Quattrocento e Seicento*. Rome: Storia e letteratura.

Donno, Elizabeth Storry (1975). "'Old Mouse-Eaten Records': History in Sidney's *Apology.*" *Studies in Philology* 72: 275–98.

Dooley, Brendan (1999). *The Social History of Skepticism: Experience and Doubt in Early Modern Culture.* Baltimore: Johns Hopkins University Press.

Dooley, Brendan and Baron, Sabrina (2001). *The Politics of Information in Early Modern Europe.* London and New York: Routledge.

Dreitzel, Horst (1970). *Protestantischer Aristotelismus und absoluter Staat: Die 'Politica' des Henning Arnisaeus (ca. 1575–1636).* Wiesbaden: Steiner.

Dubois, Claude-Gilbert (1977). *La conception de l'histoire en France au xvie siècle,* Paris: Nizet.

Duncan, Douglas (1965). *Thomas Ruddiman: A Study in Scottish Scholarship of the Early Eighteenth Century.* Edinburgh: Oliver & Boyd.

Elliott, John (1970). *The Old World and the New, 1492–1650.* Cambridge: Cambridge University Press.

Elsner, Jás and Rubiés, Joan-Pau (eds.) (1999). *Voyages and Visions: Towards a Cultural History of Travel.* London: Reaktion.

Enenkel, Karl (2001). "Strange and Bewildering Antiquity: Lipsius's Dialogue *Saturnales Sermones* on Gladiatorial Games." In Enenkel, de Jong, and De Landtsheer (eds.) (2001), 75–99.

Enenkel, Karl and Heesakkers, Chris (eds.) (1997). *Lipsius in Leiden: Studies in the Life and Works of a Great Humanist on the Occasion of his 450th Anniversary.* Voorthuizen : Florivallis.

Enenkel, Karl, de Jong, Jan, and de Landtsheer, Jeanine (eds.) (2001). *Recreating Ancient History: Episodes from the Greek and Roman Past in the Arts and Literatures of the Early Modern Period.* Intersections, 1. Leiden: Brill.

Erasmus, H. J. (1962). *The Origins of Rome in Historiography from Petrarch to Perizonius,* Assen: Van Gorcum.

Erbe, Michael (1978). *François Baudouin (1520–1573). Biographie eines Humanisten.* Gütersloh: Gerd Mohn.

Fasolt, Constantin (2004). *The Limits of History.* Chicago and London: University of Chicago Press.

Fichtner, Paula (1989). *Protestantism and Primogeniture in Early Modern Germany.* New Haven: Yale University Press.

Firpo, Luigi (1950–1). "Filosofia italiana e Controriforma. II. La condanna di F. Patrizi." *Rivista di Filosofia,* 41: 150–73; 42: 30–47.

Fox, Levi (ed.) (1956). *English Historical Scholarship in the Sixteenth and Seventeenth Centuries.* London and New York: Published for the Dugdale Society by Oxford University Press.

Franklin, Julian (1963). *Jean Bodin and the Sixteenth-Century Revolution in the Methodology of Law and History.* New York: Columbia University Press.

Frazier, Alison Knowles (2005). *Possible Lives: Authors and Saints in Renaissance Italy.* New York: Columbia University Press.

Freedman, Joseph (1997). "The Career and Writings of Bartholomew Keckermann." *Proceedings of the American Philosophical Society* 141: 305–64.

Fryde, Edmund (1983). *Humanism and Renaissance Historiography.* London: Hambledon.

Fubini, Riccardo (1980). "Osservazioni sugli *Historiarum florentini populi libri xii.*" In *Studi di storia medievale e moderna per Ernesto Sestan*: 403–48. Florence: Olschki.

    (1996). "Humanism and Truth: Valla Writes Against the Donation of Constantine." *Journal of the History of Ideas* 57: 79–86.

    (2003). *Storiografia dell'umanesimo in Italia da Leonardo Bruni ad Annio da Viterbo.* Rome: Storia e Letteratura.

García Icazbalceta, J. (1947). *Don Fray Juan de Zumárraga, primer obispo y arzobispo de México,* edited by R. Aguayo Spencer and A. Castro Leal. Vol. IV. Madrid: Porrúa.

Garin, Eugenio (1983). *Astrology in the Renaissance: The Zodiac of Life*, tr. Carolyn Jackson and June Allen; translation revised in conjunction with the author by Clare Robertson. London and Boston: Routledge & Kegan Paul.

Gaston, Robert (ed.) (1988). *Pirro Ligorio, Artist and Antiquarian.* Florence: Silvana.

Geary, Patrick (1994). *Phantoms of Remembrance: Memory and Oblivion at the End of the First Millennium.* Princeton: Princeton University Press.

(2006). *Women at the Beginning: Origin Myths from the Amazons to the Virgin Mary.* Princeton and Oxford: Princeton University Press.

Gilbert, Felix (1965). *Machiavelli and Guicciardini: Politics and History in Sixteenth-Century France.* Princeton: Princeton University Press.

(1977). *History: Choice and Commitment.* Cambridge, Mass.: Harvard University Press.

Ginzburg, Carlo (1999). *History, Rhetoric and Proof.* Hanover, NH: University Press of New England.

(2000). *No Island is an Island.* New York: Columbia University Press.

Glacken, Clarence (1967). *Traces on the Rhodian Shore: Nature and Culture in Western Thought from Ancient Times to the End of the Eighteenth Century.* Berkeley: University of California Press.

Glaser, Karl-Heinz, Lietz, Hanno, and Rhein, Stefan (ed.) (1993). *David und Nathan Chytraeus. Humanismus im konfessionellen Zeitalter.* Ubstadt-Weiher: Verlag Regionalkultur.

Glaser, Karl-Heinz and Suth, Steffen (ed.) (2000). *David Chytraeus (1530–1600). Norddeutscher Humanismus in Europa. Beiträge zum Wirken des Kraichgauer Gelehrten.* Ubstadt-Weiher: Verlag Regionalkultur.

Goez, Werner (1974). "Die Anfänge der historischen Methoden-Reflexion in der italienischen Renaissance und ihre Aufnahme in der Geschichtsschreibung des deutschen Humanismus." *Archiv für Kulturgeschichte* 56: 25–48.

Goldgar, Anne (1995). *Impolite Learning: Conduct and Community in the Republic of Letters.* New Haven: Yale University Press.

Gordon, Bruce (ed.) (1996). *Protestant History and Identity in Sixteenth-Century Europe*, 1: *The Medieval Inheritance.* Aldershot: Ashgate.

Gossman, Lionel (1968). *Medievalism and the Ideologies of the Enlightenment: The World and Work of La Curne de Sainte-Palaye.* Baltimore: Johns Hopkins Press.

Goulding, Robert (2006a). "Histories of Science in Early Modern Europe: Introduction." *Journal of the History of Ideas* 67: 33–40.

(2006b). "Method and Mathematics: Petrus Ramus's Histories of the Sciences." *Journal of the History of Ideas* 67: 63–85.

Grafton, Anthony (1975). "Joseph Scaliger and Historical Chronology: The Rise and Fall of a Discipline." *History and Theory* 14: 156–85.

(1983–93). *Joseph Scaliger: A Study in the History of Classical Scholarship.* 2 vols. Oxford: Clarendon Press.

(1990). *Forgers and Critics*, Princeton: Princeton University Press.

(1991). "Traditions of Invention and Invention of Traditions in Renaissance Italy: Annius of Viterbo." In *Defenders of the Text*, Cambridge, Mass.: Harvard University Press, 76–103.

(1997a). *Commerce with the Classics*, Ann Arbor: University of Michigan Press.

(1997b). "From Apotheosis to Analysis: Some Late Renaissance Histories of Classical Astronomy." In Kelley (ed.) (1997), 261–76.

(1997c). *The Footnote: A Curious History*. Cambridge, Mass.: Harvard University Press; London: Faber and Faber.

(1999). "*Historia* and *Istoria*: Alberti's Terminology in Context." *I Tatti Studies* 8: 37–68.

(2001a). *Bring Out Your Dead: The Past as Revelation*, Cambridge, Mass.: Harvard University Press.

(2001b). "Introduzione." In Cardano 2001, xxi–xlv.

(2003). "Les lieux communs chez les humanistes." In Décultot (ed.) (2003), 31–42.

(2004). "Kircher's Chronology." In *Athanasius Kircher: The Last Man Who Knew Everything*, ed. Paula Findlen: 171–187. New York and London: Routledge.

(2005). "The Identities of History in Early Modern Europe: Prelude to a Study of the *Artes Historicae*." In Pomata and Siraisi (ed.) (2005), 41–74.

Grafton, Anthony, Siraisi, Nancy, and Shelford, April (1992). *New Worlds, Ancient Texts: The Power of Tradition and the Shock of Discovery*. Cambridge, Mass. and London: Harvard University Press.

Grafton, Anthony and Williams, Megan (2006). *Christianity and the Transformation of the Book: Origen, Eusebius and the Library of Caesarea*. Cambridge, Mass. and London: Harvard University Press.

Green, Louis (1972). *Chronicle into History: An Essay on the Interpretation of History in Fourteenth-Century Florentine Chronicles*. Cambridge: At the University Press.

Gregory, Tullio (1953). "L'Apologia ad censuram di Francesco Patrizi da Cherso." *Rinascimento*, ser. II, 4: 89–104.

Grell, Chantal (1983). "Les origines de Rome: mythe et critique. Essai sur l'histoire aux xviie et xviiie siècles." *HES*: 255–80.

(1993). *L'histoire entre érudition et philosophie: étude sur la connaissance historique à l'âge des Lumières.* Paris: Presses Universitaires de France.

(1995). *Le dix-huitième siècle et l'antiquité en France.* 2 vols. Oxford: Voltaire Foundation.

Grell, Chantal and Volpilhac-Auger, Catherine (ed.) (1994), *Nicolas Fréret: légende et vérité: Colloque des 18 et 19 octobre 1991.* Oxford: Voltaire Foundation, 1994.

Gruzinski, Serge (2004). *Les quatre parties du monde: Histoire d'une mondialisation.* Paris: Editions de la Martinière.

Güldner, Gerhard (1968). *Das Toleranz-Problem in den Niederlanden im Ausgang des 16. Jahrhunderts.* Lübeck: Matthiesen.

Gundersheimer, Werner (1966). *The Life and Works of Louis Le Roy.* Geneva: Droz.

Hartmann, Maria. (2001). *Humanismus und Kirchenkritik: Matthias Flacius Illyricus als Erforscher des Mittelalters.* Stuttgart: Thorbecke.

Haskell, Francis (1993). *History and its Images: Art and the Interpretation of the Past.* New Haven: Yale University Press.

Hassinger, Erich (1978). *Empirisch-rationaler Historismus.* Bern and Munich: Francke.

Hazard, Paul (1935). *La crise de la conscience européenne (1680–1715).* 3 vols. Paris: Boivin.

Henze, Ingrid (1990). *Der Lehrstuhl für Poesie an der Universität Helmstedt bis zum Tode Heinrich Meiboms d. Ält. (+1625). Eine Untersuchung zur Rezeption antiker Dichtung im lutherischen Späthumanismus.* Hildesheim, Zurich and New York: Olms-Weidmann.

Herding, Otto (1965). "Heinrich Meibom (1555–1625) und Reiner Reineccius (1541–1595). Eine Studie zur Historiographie in Westfalen und Niedersachsen." *Westfälische Forschungen* 18: 3–22.

Herklotz, Ingo (1999). *Cassiano dal Pozzo und die Archäologie des 17. Jahrhunderts.* Munich: Hirmer.

Hiatt, Alfred (2004). *The Making of Medieval Forgeries: False Documents in Fifteenth-Century England.* London: British Library; Toronto: University of Toronto Press.

Hieronymus, Frank (1997). *1488 Petri. Schwabe 1988.* 2 vols. Basle: Schwabe.

Holtz, Sabine and Mertens, Dieter (eds.) (1999). *Nicodemus Frischlin: Poetische und prosaische Praxis unter den Bedingungen des konfessionellen Zeitalters,* Stuttgart-Bad Cannstatt: Frommann-Holzboog.

Hotson, Howard (2002). *Johann Heinrich Alsted, 1588–1638: Between Renaissance, Reformation, and Universal Reform.* Oxford: Clarendon.

Huppert, George (1970). *The Idea of Perfect History: Historical Erudition and Historical Philosophy in Renaissance France.* Urbana, Chicago, and London: University of Illinois Press.

Ianziti, Gary (1988). *Humanistic Historiography under the Sforzas: Politics and Propaganda in Fifteenth-Century Milan.* Oxford: Oxford University Press.

(1998). "Bruni on Writing History." *Renaissance Quarterly* 51: 367–91.

(2000). "A Life in Politics: Leonardo Bruni's Cicero." *Journal of the History of Ideas* 61: 39–58.

Irmscher, Günther (1995). "Metalle als Symbole der Historiographie. Zu den Statuae Daniels resp. Nabuchodonosoris von Lorenz Faust und Giovanni Maria Nosseni." *Anzeiger des Germanischen Nationalmuseums und Berichte aus dem Forschungsinstitut für Realienkunde*: 93–106.

Israel, Jonathan (2001). *Radical Enlightenment: Philosophy and the Making of Modernity, 1650–1750.* Oxford: Oxford University Press.

Jardine, Lisa and Grafton, Anthony (1990). "'Studied for Action': How Gabriel Harvey Read his Livy." *Past and Present* 129: 29–78.

Jouhaud, Christian (1985). *Mazarinades: la Fronde des mots.* Paris: Aubier Montaigne.

Kablitz, Andreas (2001). "Lorenzo Vallas Konzept der Geschichte und der Fall der Konstantinischen Schenkung. Zur 'Modernität' von *De falso credita et ementita Constantini donatione.*" In *Historicization – Historisierung.* Aporemata, 5. Göttingen: Vandenhoeck & Ruprecht: 45–67.

Kahn, Victoria (1986). "Virtù and the Example of Agathocles in Machiavelli's *Prince.*" *Representations* 13: 63–83.

(1994). *Machiavellian Rhetoric: From the Counter-Reformation to Milton.* Princeton: Princeton University Press.

Kauertz, Claudia (2001). *Wissenschaft und Hexenglaube: Die Diskussion des Zauber- und Hexenwesens an der Universität Helmstedt (1576–1626).* Bielefeld: Verlag für Regionalgeschichte.

Kelley, Donald (1964). "Historia integra: François Baudouin and His Conception of History." *Journal of the History of Ideas* 25: 35–57.

(1970). *Foundations of Modern Historical Scholarship: Language, Law and History in the French Renaissance.* New York: Columbia University Press.

(1971). "The Development and Context of Bodin's Method." In *Jean Bodin: Verhandlungen der Internationalen Bodin-Tagung,* ed. Horst Denzer. Munich: Beck.

(1980). "Johann Sleidan and the Origins of History as a Profession." *Journal of Modern History* 52: 574–98.

(ed.) (1997). *History and the Disciplines: The Reclassification of Knowledge in Early Modern Europe.* Rochester: University of Rochester Press.

(1999). "Writing Cultural History in Early Modern France: Christophe Milieu and His Project." *Renaissance Quarterly* 52: 342–65.

(2005). "Between History and System." In Pomata and Siraisi (ed.) (2005), 211–37.

Kessler, Eckhard (1978). *Petrarca und die Geschichte*. Munich: Fink.

(1982). "Das rhetorische Modell der Historiographie." In *Formen der Geschichtsschreibung*, ed. Reinhart Koselleck *et al.* Munich: Deutscher Taschenbuch Verlag, 37–85.

Klatt, Detloff (1909). *David Chytraeus als Geschichtslehrer und Geschichtsschreiber*. Rostock: Adler.

Klempt, Adalbert (1960). *Die Säkularisierung der universalhistorischen Auffassung: Zum Wandel des Geschichtsdenkens im 16. und 17. Jahrhundert*. Göttingen: Musterschmidt.

Koselleck, Reinhart (1984). "Historia Magistra Vitae: Über die Auflösung des Topos im Horizont neuzeitlich bewegter Geschichte." In *Vergangene Zukunft*. Frankfurt: Suhrkamp, 38–66.

Kristeller, Paul Oskar (1964). *Eight Philosophers of the Italian Renaissance*. Stanford: Stanford University Press.

Kühlmann, Wilhelm (1982). *Gelehrtenrepublik und Fürstenstaat: Entwicklung und Kritik des deutschen Späthumanismus in der Literatur des Barockzeitalters*. Tübingen: Niemeyer.

Lamprecht, Franz (1950). *Zur Theorie der humanistischen Geschichtsschreibung: Mensch und Geschichte bei Francesci Patrizi*. Winterthur: Ziegler.

Landfester, Rüdiger (1972). *Historia magistra vitae*. Geneva: Droz.

Landucci, Sergio (1972). *I filosofi e i selvaggi, 1580–1780*. Bari: Laterza.

Laureys, Marc (2001). " 'The Grandeur that was Rome.' Scholarly Analysis and Pious Awe in Lipsius's *Admiranda*." In Enenkel, de Jong, and de Landtsheer (2001), 123–46.

Leinkauf, Thomas (1990). *Il neoplatonismo di Francesco Patrizi da Cherso come presupposto della sua critica ad Aristotele*. Florence: La Nuova Italia.

Leventhal, Robert (1986). "The Emergence of Philological Discourse in the German States, 1770–1810." *Isis* 7: 243–60.

(1994). *The Disciplines of Interpretation: Lessing, Herder, Schlegel and Hermeneutics in Germany.* Berlin and New York: De Gruyter.

Levine, Joseph (1977). *Dr. Woodward's Shield: History, Science, and Satire in Augustan England.* Berkeley: University of California Press.

(1987). *Humanism and History: Origins of Modern English Historiography.* Ithaca and London: Cornell University Press.

(1991). *The Battle of the Books: History and Literature in the Augustan Age.* Ithaca, NY: Cornell University Press.

(1999). *The Autonomy of History: Truth and Method from Erasmus to Gibbon.* Chicago and London: University of Chicago Press.

(2003). "Matter of Fact in the English Revolution." *Journal of the History of Ideas* 64: 317–35.

Lintott, Andrew (1986). "*Acta Antiquissima.* A Week in the History of the Roman Republic." *Papers of the British School at Rome* 54: 213–28.

Love, Harold (1993). *Scribal Publication in Seventeenth-Century England.* Oxford: Clarendon Press.

Ludwig, Walther (2002). " 'Non cedit umbra soli': Joachim Graf zu Ortenburg als Humanist und Leser von Justus Lipsius." *Humanistica Lovaniensia* 51: 207–43.

Lyon, Gregory (2003). "Baudouin, Flacius and the Plan for the Magdeburg Centuries," *Journal of the History of Ideas* 64: 253–72.

Maccioni, P. Alessandra and Mostert, Marco (1984). "Isaac Dorislaus (1595–1649): The Career of a Dutch Scholar in England." *Transactions of the Cambridge Bibliographical Society* 8: 419–70.

MacColl, Alan (2002). "Richard White and the Legendary History of Britain." *Humanistica Lovaniensia* 51: 245–57.

Maclean, Ian (2005). "White Crows, Graying Hair, and Eyelashes: Problems for Natural Historians in the Reception of Aristotelian

Logic and Biology from Pomponazzi to Bacon." In Pomata and Siraisi (ed.) 2005, 147–79.

MacPhail, Eric (2001). "The Plot of History from Antiquity to the Renaissance." *Journal of the History of Ideas* 62: 1–16.

McCuaig, William (1989). *Carlo Sigonio: The Changing World of the Late Renaissance.* Princeton: Princeton University Press.

McKisack, May (1971). *Medieval History in the Tudor Age.* Oxford: Clarendon Press.

Malcolm, Noel (2002). *Aspects of Hobbes.* Oxford: Clarendon Press.
　(2004). "Private and Public Knowledge: Kircher, Esotericism, and the Republic of Letters." *Athanasius Kircher: The Last Man Who Knew Everything,* ed. Paula Findlen: 297–308. New York and London: Routledge.

Manley, Lawrence (1995). *Literature and Culture in Early Modern London.* Cambridge: Cambridge University Press.

Manuel, Frank (1959). *The Eighteenth Century Confronts the Gods.* Cambridge, Mass.: Harvard University Press.
　(1963). *Isaac Newton, Historian.* Cambridge, Mass.: Harvard University Press.

Marincola, John (1997). *Authority and Tradition in Ancient Historiography.* Cambridge: Cambridge University Press.

Marino, Luigi (1975). *I maestri della Germania: Göttingen 1770–1820.* Turin: Einaudi.
　(1995). *Praeceptores Germaniae: Göttingen 1770–1820,* tr. Brigitte Sazbó-Bechstein. Göttingen: Vandenhoeck & Ruprecht.

Markschies, Christoph (1995). "Die eine Reformation und die vielen Reformen oder braucht evangelische Kirchengeschichtsschreibung Dekadenzmodelle?" *Zeitschrift für Kirchengeschichte* 106: 70–97.

Mazzocco, Angelo (1979). "Some Philological Aspects of Biondo Flavio's *Roma triumphans.*" *Humanistica Lovaniensia* 28: 1–26.

Meijer, Th. J. (1971). *Kritiek als Herwaardering: Het levenswerk van Jacob Perizonius (1651–1715)*. Leiden: Leiden University Press.

Mellor, Ronald (2004–5). "Tacitus, Academic Politics, and Regicide in the Reign of Charles I: The Tragedy of Dr. Isaac Dorislaus." *International Journal of the Classical Tradition* 11: 153–93.

Mettler, Werner (1955). *Der junge Friedrich Schlegel und die griechische Literatur: ein Beitrag zum Problem der Historie*. Zurich: Atlantis Verlag.

Menze, Clemens (1966). *Wilhelm von Humboldt und Christian Gottlob Heyne*. Ratingen bei Düsseldorf: Henn.

Miglio, Massimo, *et al.* (2003). *Antiquaria a Roma: Intorno a Pomponio Leto e Paolo II*. Rome: Roma nel Rinascimento.

Miller, Peter (2000). *Peiresc's Europe: Learning and Virtue in the Seventeenth Century*. New Haven: Yale University Press.

(2005). "Description Terminable and Interminable: Looking at the Past, Nature, and People in Peiresc's Archive." In Pomata and Siraisi (ed.) (2005), 355–97.

Molino, Paola (forthcoming). "Alle origini della Methodus Apodemica di Theodor Zwinger: la collaborazione di Hugo Blotius, fra empirismo ed universalismo." In *Codices Manuscripti*.

Momigliano, Arnaldo (1950). "Ancient History and the Antiquarian." *Journal of the Warburg and Courtauld Institutes* 13: 285–315.

(1963). "Pagan and Christian Historiography in the Fourth Century A.D." In *The Conflict Between Paganism and Christianity in the Fourth Century*, ed. Arnaldo Momigliano: 79–99. Oxford: Clarendon Press.

(1977). "Polybius' Reappearance in Western Europe." In *Essays in Ancient and Modern Historiography*. Oxford: Blackwell.

Moreau-Reibel, Jean (1933). *Jean Bodin et le droit public comparé dans ses rapports avec la philosophie de l'histoire*. Paris: Vrin.

Morford, Mark (1991). *Stoics and Neostoics: Rubens and the Circle of Lipsius*. Princeton: Princeton University Press.

(2001). "*Theatrum Hodiernae Vitae*: Lipsius, Vaenius and the Re-
bellion of Civilis." In Enenkel, de Jong, and de Landtsheer (ed.)
(2001), 57–74.

Moss, Ann (1996). *Printed Commonplace-Books and the Structuring
of Renaissance Thought*. Oxford: Clarendon Press.

    (1998). "The *Politica* of Justus Lipsius and the Commonplace-
Book." *Journal of the History of Ideas* 59: 421–36.

Most, Glenn (1984). "Rhetorik und Hermeneutik: Zur Konstitution
der Neuzeitlichkeit," *Antike und Abendland* 30: 62–79.

    (ed.) (1997). *Collecting Fragments: Fragmente sammeln*. Göttingen:
Vandenhoeck & Ruprecht.

Moyer, Ann (2003). "Historians and Antiquarians in Sixteenth-
Century Florence." *Journal of the History of Ideas* 64: 177–
93.

Muhlack, Ulrich (1991). *Geschichtswissenschaft im Humanismus und
in der Aufklärung: Die Vorgeschichte des Historismus*. Munich:
Beck.

Mulsow, Martin (ed.) (2002*). Das Ende des Hermetismus: historische
Kritik und neue Naturphilosophie in der Spätrenaissance. Doku-
mentation und Analyse der Debatten um die Datierung der her-
metischen Schriften von Genebrard bis Casaubon (1567–1614)*.
Tübingen: Mohr Siebeck.

    (2005). "Antiquarianism and Ideology: The *Historia* of Religions
in the Seventeenth Century." In Pomata and Siraisi (ed.) (2005),
181–209.

Nadel, George (1964). "Philosophy of History before Historicism."
History and Theory, 3: 291–315.

Nelles, Paul (1997). "The Library as an Instrument of Discovery:
Gabriel Naudé and the Uses of History." In Kelley (ed.) (1997),
41–57.

Neugebauer, O. (1969). *The Exact Sciences in Antiquity*. Repr. of 2nd
edn. New York: Dover.

O'Flaherty, Eamon (1991). "The Theatre of Diversity: Historical Criticism and Religious Controversy in Seventeenth-Century France." In Brady (ed.) (1991), 31–48, 227–29.

O'Malley, Charles (1955). *Jacopo Aconcio*, tr. Delio Cantimori. Rome: Storia e Letteratura.

Ogilvie, Brian (2005). "Natural History, Ethics, and Physico-Theology." In Pomata and Siraisi (ed.) (2005), 75–103.

Olivieri, Achille (2004). *Erodoto nel Rinascimento. L'umano e la storia.* Rome: L'Erma di Bretschneider.

Osmond, Patricia (2003). "In the Margins of Sallust, Part III: Pomponio Leto's Notes on *ars historica*." In Miglio *et al.* (2003), 35–49.

Parry, Graham (1995). *The Trophies of Time: English Antiquarians of the Seventeenth Century.* Oxford: Clarendon Press.

Pastoureau, Michel (1979). *Traité d'héraldique.* Paris: Picard.

Pattison, Mark (1892). *Isaac Casaubon, 1559-1614.* 2nd edn. Oxford: Clarendon Press.

Perini, Leandro (2002). *La vita e i tempi di Pietro Perna.* Rome: Storia e Letteratura.

Phillips, Margaret Mann (1969). "Erasmus and the Art of Writing." In *Scrinium Erasmianum*, ed. J. Coppens, I: 335–50. 2 vols. Leiden: Brill.

Phillips, Mark (1979). "Machiavelli, Guicciardini and the Tradition of Vernacular Historiography in Florence." *American Historical Review* 84: 86–105.

Pisano, Francesco (2003). *Le Ossa dei Giganti della Rocca di Pozzuoli.* Bacoli: Edizioni il Punto di Partenza.

Pitassi, Maria Cristina (1987). *Entre croire et savoir: le problème de la méthode chez Jean Le Clerc,* Leiden: Brill.

Pocock, J. G. A. (1957). *The Ancient Constitution and the Feudal Law.* Cambridge: Cambridge University Press.

(1962). "The Origins of the Study of the Past: A Comparative Approach." *Comparative Studies in Society and History* 4.

Polke, Irene (1999). *Selbstreflexion im Spiegel des Anderen: eine wirkungsgeschichtliche Studie zum Hellenismusbild Heynes und Herders*. Würzburg : Königshausen & Neumann.

Pomata, Gianna (2005). "*Praxis Historialis*: The Uses of *Historia* in Early Modern Medicine." In Pomata and Siraisi (ed.) (2005), 105–46.

Pomata, Gianna and Nancy Siraisi, "Introduction." In Pomata and Siraisi (ed.) (2005a), 1–38.

(ed.) (2005b). *Historia: Empiricism and Erudition in Early Modern Europe*. Cambridge, Mass. and London: MIT Press.

Popper, Nicholas (2006). "'Abraham, Planter of Mathematics': Histories of Mathematics and Astrology in Early Modern Europe." *Journal of the History of Ideas* 67 (2006): 87–106.

Press, Gerald (1982). *The Development of the Idea of History in Antiquity*. Kingston and Montreal: McGill–Queen's University Press.

Quillen, Carol (1998). *Rereading the Renaissance: Petrarch, Augustine and the Language of Humanism*. Ann Arbor: University of Michigan Press.

Quint, David (1985). "Humanism and Modernity: A Reconsideration of Bruni's Dialogues." *Renaissance Quarterly* 38: 423–45.

(1998). *Montaigne and the Quality of Mercy: Ethical and Political Themes in the Essais*. Princeton: Princeton University Press.

Raskolnikova, Muza (1992). *Histoire romaine et critique historique dans l'Europe des Lumières: La naissance de l'hypercritique dans l'historiographie de la Rome antique*. Rome: Ecole Française de Rome.

Rawson, Elizabeth (1969). *The Spartan Tradition in European Thought*. Oxford: Clarendon Press.

(1972). "Cicero the Historian and Cicero the Antiquarian." *Journal of Roman Studies* 62: 33–45.

Raymond, Joad (1993). *Making the News: An Anthology of the Newsbooks of Revolutionary England, 1641–1660.* New York: St. Martin's Press.

(ed.) (1996). *The Invention of the Newspaper: English Newsbooks, 1641–1649.* Oxford: Clarendon Press.

(ed.) (2006). *News Networks in Seventeenth Century Britain and Europe.* London and New York: Routledge.

Regoliosi, Mariangela (1991). "Riflessioni umanistiche sullo 'scrivere storia.'" *Rinascimento* ser. II, 31: 3–37.

(1994). "Lorenzo Valla e la concezione della storia." *La storiografia umanistica.* Convegno internazionale dell'Associazione per il Medioevo e l'Umanesimo latini, Messina 22–25 ottobre 1987. Messina: Sicamia: I, pt 2, 549–71.

(1995a). "'Res gestae patriae' e 'res gestae ex universa Italia': la lettera di Lapo da Castiglionchio a Biondo Flavio." In *Le memoria e la città*, ed. C. Bastia and M. Bolognani. Bologna: Il nove: 273–305.

(1995b). "Tradizione contra verità: Cortesi, Sandei, Mansi e l'Orazione del Valla sulla 'Donazione di Costantino'." *Momus* 3–4: 47–57.

Reill, Peter Hanns (1975). *The German Enlightenment and the Rise of Historicism.* Berkeley: University of California Press.

Reynolds, Beatrice (1953). "Shifting Currents in Historical Criticism." *Journal of the History of Ideas* 14: 471–92.

Ross, David J. A. (1988). *Alexander historiatus: A Guide to Medieval Illustrated Alexander Literature.* 2nd edn. Beiträge zur Klassischen Philologie, 186. Frankfurt a. M.: Athenäum.

Rossi, Paolo (1984). *The Dark Abyss of Time: The History of the Earth & the History of Nations from Hooke to Vico*, tr. Lydia Cochrane. Chicago: University of Chicago Press.

Rowland, Ingrid (1998). *The Culture of the High Renaissance: Ancients and Moderns in Sixteenth-Century Rome.* Cambridge: Cambridge University Press.

Rubiés, Joan-Pau (1996). "Instructions for Travellers: Teaching the Eye to See." *History and Anthropology* 9: 139–90.

(2000a). *Travel and Ethnology in the Renaissance: South India Through European Eyes, 1250–1625*. Cambridge: Cambridge University Press.

(2000b). "Travel Writing as a Genre: Facts, Fictions and the Invention of a Scientific Discourse in Early Modern Europe." *Journeys. The International Journal of Travel and Travel Writing*, 1: 5–33.

Salmon, John (1997). "Precept, Example, and Truth: Degory Wheare and the *ars historica*." In *The Historical Imagination in Early Modern Britain: History, Rhetoric, and Fiction, 1500–1800*, ed. Donald Kelley and David Sacks, Washington, DC: Woodrow Wilson Center Press; Cambridge and New York: Cambridge University Press, 11–36.

Santini, Emilio (1910). "Leonardo Bruni e i suoi *Historiarum florentini populi libri xii*." *Annali della Scuola Normale Superiore di Pisa* 22: 3–173.

Sartori, Marco (1982). "L'incertitude dei primi secoli di Roma e il metodo storico nella prima metà del Settecento." *Clio* 18: 7–35.

(1985). "Voltaire, Newton, Fréret: la cronologia e la storia delle antiche nazioni." *Studi settecenteschi* 7–8: 167–89.

Scheele, Meta (1930). *Wissen und Glaube in der Geschichtswissenschaft: Studien zur historischen Pyrrhonismus in Frankreich und Deutschland*. Heidelberg: Winter.

Schiffman, Zachary (1984). "Montaigne and the Rise of Skepticism in Early Modern Europe: A Reappraisal." *Journal of the History of Ideas* 45: 499–516.

Schmeidler, Bernhard (ed.) (1937). *Helmolds Slavenchronik*. 3rd edn. Scriptores in usum scholarum ex Monumentis Germaniae Historicis separatim editi. Hanover: Hahn.

Schmidt-Biggemann, Wilhelm (1983). *Topica universalis: Eine Modellgeschichte humanistischer und barocker Wissenschaft.* Hamburg: Meiner.

(2006). "Heilsgeschichtliche Inventionen. Annius von Viterbos 'Berosus' und die Geschichte der Sintflut." In *Sintflut und Geschichte: Errinern und Vergessen des Ursprungs,* ed. Martin Mulsow and Jan Assmann: 85–111. Munich: Fink.

Schreurs, Anna (2000). *Antikenbild und Kunstanschauungen des neapolitanischen Malers, Architekten und Antiquars Pirro Ligorio (1513–1583).* Cologne: König.

Schwaiger, Georg (ed.) (1980). *Historische Kritik in der Theologie: Beiträge zu ihrer Geschichte.* Göttingen: Vandenhoeck & Ruprecht.

Seifert, Arno (1976). *Cognitio historica: Die Geschichte als Namengeberin der frühneuzeitlichen Empirie,* Berlin: Duncker & Humblot.

(1990). *Der Rückzug der biblischen Prophetie von der neueren Geschichte: Studien zur Geschichte der Reichstheologie des frühneuzeitlichen deutschen Protestantismus.* Cologne: Böhlau.

Serjeantson, Richard (1999). "Testimony and Proof in Early-Modern England." *Studies in History and Philosophy of Science* 30: 195–236.

(2005). "Proof and Persuasion." In *The Cambridge History of Science,* vol. III: *Sixteenth- and Seventeenth-Century Europe,* ed. Lorraine Daston and Katharine Park. Cambridge: Cambridge University Press.

Setz, Wolfram (1975). *Lorenzo Vallas Schrift gegen die konstantinische Schenkung, De falso credita et ementita Constantini donatione: zur Interpretation und Wirkungsgeschichte.* Tübingen: Niemeyer.

Siraisi, Nancy (2003). "History, Antiquarianism, and Medicine: The Case of Girolamo Mercuriale." *Journal of the History of Ideas* 64: 231–51.

(2005). "*Historiae*, Natural History, Roman Antiquity and Some Roman Physicians." In Pomata and Siraisi (ed.) (2005), 325–54.

(forthcoming). *History, Medicine, and the Traditions of Renaissance Learning*. Ann Arbor: University of Michigan Press.

Smith, Paul (2001). "Montaigne, Plutarch and Historiography." In Enenkel, de Jong, and de Landtsheer (ed.) (2001), 167–86.

Soll, Jacob (2000). "Amelot de la Houssaie (1634–1706) Annotates Tacitus." *Journal of the History of Ideas* 62: 167–87.

(2002). "Healing the Body Politic: French Doctors, History, and the Birth of a Nation, 1570–1634." *Renaissance Quarterly* 55: 1259–86.

(2003). "Empirical History and the Transformation of Political Criticism in France from Bodin to Bayle." *Journal of the History of Ideas* 64: 297–316.

(2005). *Publishing the Prince: History, Reading, and the Birth of Political Criticism*. Ann Arbor: University of Michigan Press.

(forthcoming). "The Secret Sphere: Jean-Baptiste Colbert's State Information System and the Crisis of Civic Learning."

Spencer, Diana (2002). *The Roman Alexander: Reading a Cultural Myth*. Exeter: University of Exeter Press.

Spini, Giorgio (1948). "I trattatisti dell'arte storica della Controriforma Italiana," *Quaderni di Belfagor*. 1: 109–36.

(1970). "Historiography: The Art of History in the Italian Counter Reformation." In *The Late Italian Renaissance, 1525–1630*, tr. Eric Cochrane, New York: Harper: 91–133.

Stagl, Justin (1983). *Apodemiken: eine räsonnierte Bibliographie der reisetheoretischen Literatur des 16., 17. und 18. Jahrhunderts*. Paderborn: Schöningh.

(1995). *A History of Curiosity: The Theory of Travel, 1550–1800*. Chur: Harwood.

Stenhouse, William (2000). "Classical Inscriptions and Antiquarian Scholarship in Italy, 1600–1650." In A. Cooley (ed.), *The After-*

life of Inscriptions: 77–89. London: Institute of Classical Studies, 2000.

(2001). "The Epigraphic Manuscripts and Scholarship of Teofilo Gallaccini, a Seventeenth-Century Dilettante." *Epigraphica* 63: 111–32.

(2003). "Georg Fabricius and Inscriptions as a Source of Law." *Renaissance Studies* 17: 96–107.

(2004). "Thomas Dempster, Royal Historian to James I, and Classical and Historical Scholarship in Early Stuart England." *Sixteenth Century Journal* 35: 397–412.

(2005). *Reading Inscriptions and Writing Ancient History: Historical Scholarship in the Late Renaissance.* London: Institute of Classical Studies.

Stephens, Walter (1979). "Berosus Chaldaeus: Counterfeit and Fictive Editors of the Early Sixteenth Century." PhD Dissertation, Cornell University.

(1989). *Giants in Those Days.* Lincoln: University of Nebraska Press.

Stouraiti, Anastasia (2001). "La guerra di Morea (1684–1699). Forma e ideologia di una narrazione." *Studi Veneziani* 41: 259–80.

(2005). "Una storia della guerra: Pietro Garzoni e il suo archivio." In *Venezia e la Guerra di Morea: Guerra, politica e cultura alla fine del '600*, ed. Mario Infelise and Anastasia Stouraiti: 242–69. Milan: FrancoAngeli.

Strauss, Leo (1936). *The Political Philosophy of Hobbes*, tr. E. M. Sinclair. Oxford: Oxford University Press.

Syme, Ronald (1958). *Tacitus.* 2 vols. Oxford: Clarendon Press.

Thapar, Romila (2000). *History and Beyond.* Delhi and New York: Oxford University Press.

Tooley, Marian (1953). "Bodin and the Medieval Theory of Climate." *Speculum* 28: 64–83.

Tschan, Francis Joseph (ed.) (1935). *The Chronicle of the Slavs by Helmold, Priest of Bosau.* New York: Columbia University Press.

Turchetti, Mario (1984). *Concordia o tolleranza? François Baudouin e i "moyenneurs."* Geneva: Droz.

Ullman, Berthold Louis (1973). *Studies in Renaissance Thought and Letters.* 2nd edn. Rome: Edizioni di Storia e Letteratura.

Vasoli, Cesare (1989). *Francesco Patrizi da Cherso.* Rome: Bulzoni.

Veyne, Paul (1988). *Did the Greeks Believe in their Myths? An Essay on the Constitutive Imagination,* tr. Paula Wissing. Chicago: University of Chicago Press.

Viti, Paolo (ed.) (1990). *Leonardo Bruni, Cancelliere della Repubblica di Firenze: convegno di studi* (Firenze, 27–29 ottobre 1987). Florence: Olschki.

Völkel, Markus (1987). *"Pyrrhonismus historicus" und "fides historica": Die Entwicklung der deutschen historischen Methodologie unter dem Gesichtspunkt der historischen Skepsis.* Frankfurt am Main, Bern, and New York: Peter Lang.

(2000). "Theologische Heilanstalt und Erfahrungswissen: David Chytraeus' Auslegung der Universalhistorie zwischen Prophetie und Modernisierung (UB-Rostock, MSS. hist. 5)." In *David Chytraeus (1530–1600): norddeutscher Humanismus in Europa: Beiträge zum Wirken des Kraichgauer Gelehrten,* ed. Karl-Heinz Glaser and Steffen Stuth, 121–141. Ubstadt-Weiher: Verlag Regionalkultur.

Waitz, Georg (ed.) (1882). *Widukindi rerum gestarum saxonicarum libri tres.* 3rd edn. Scriptores rerum germanicarum in usum scholarum ex Monumentis Germaniae Historicis recusi. Hanover: Hahn, 1882.

Wansink, H. (1981). *Politieke wetenschappen aan de Leidse universiteit 1575–±1650.* Utrecht: HES.

Waszink, Jan (1997). "*Inventio* in the *Politica*: Common-place Books and the Shape of Political Theory." In Enenkel and Heesakkers (ed.) (1997). 141–62.

Webb, Diana (1981). "The Truth about Constantine: History, Ha-giography and Confusion." In *Religion and Humanism*, ed. Keith Robbins, 85–102. Studies in Church History 17. Oxford: Blackwell.

Wegele, Franz X. von (1885). *Geschichte der deutschen Historiographie seit dem Auftreten des Humanismus.* Munich and Leipzig: Oldenbourg.

Weiss, Roberto (1988). *The Renaissance Discovery of Classical Antiquity.* 2nd edn. Oxford: Blackwell.

White, Jeffrey (1984). "Towards a Critical Edition of Biondo Flavio's *Italia Illustrata*: A Survey and an Evaluation of the Manuscripts." *Umanesimo a Roma nel Quattrocento*, 267–93. Rome: Istituto di Studi Romani; New York: Barnard College.

Wickenden, Nicholas (1993). *G. J. Vossius and the Humanist Concept of History.* Assen: Van Gorcum.

Winterbottom, Michael (1983). "Curtius Rufus." In *Texts and Transmission*, ed. L. D. Reynolds, 148–49. Oxford: Clarendon Press.

Witschi-Bernz, Astrid (1972a). "Bibliography of Works in the Philosophy of History, 1500–1800," *History and Theory*, issue 12: 3–50.

   (1972b). "Main Trends in Historical-Method Literature, Sixteenth to Eighteenth Centuries," *History and Theory*, issue 12: 51–90.

Woolf, Daniel (1990). *The Idea of History in Early Stuart England: Erudition, Ideology, and the "Light of Truth" from the Accession of James I to the Civil War.* Toronto and Buffalo: University of Toronto Press.

   (2000). *Reading History in Early Modern England.* Cambridge: Cambridge University Press.

   (2003). *The Social Circulation of the Past: English Historical Culture, 1500–1730.* Oxford: Oxford University Press.

Wunder, Amanda (2003). "Classical, Christian, and Muslim Remains in the Construction of Imperial Seville (1520–1635)." *Journal of the History of Ideas* 64: 195–212.

Zanier, Giancarlo (1975). *Ricerche sulla diffusione e fortuna del De incantationibus di Pomponazzi.* Florence: La Nuova Italia.

Zedelmaier, Helmut (1992). *Bibliotheca universalis und Bibliotheca selecta. Das Problem der Ordnung des gelehrten Wissens in der frühen Neuzeit.* Cologne, Weimar, and Vienna: Böhlau.

Zerubavel, Eviatar (2003). *Time Maps: Collective Memory and the Social Shape of the Past.* Chicago and London: University of Chicago Press.

Zinkeisen, F. (1984). "The Donation of Constantine as Applied by the Roman Church." *English Historical Review* 9: 625–32.

Bold page numbers refer to illustrations.

Bizzocchi. Roberto, 150
Black, Robert, 22
Blair, Ann, 208, 220
Bloch, Marc, 167
Blotius, Hugo, 119
Bodin, Jean
  Alençon negotiations, 66–67
  and Annius, 166, 175
  background, 69, 124–25
  and Baudouin, 32–33, 68–69,
    76
  Bolingbroke on, 252
  Cardano on, 181–85
  on Curtius and Livy, 5
  definition of history, 27, 28
  distance from events, 184
  Four Empires theory, 167–73,
    187
  geography and climate, 64, 191
  Golden Age myth, 168, 170
  Harvey on, 66
  hermeneutics, 68, 214–22,
    222–23
  "historia integra," 200, 218,
    235
  historians' speeches, 46–47
  historicism, 47–48, 49
  international celebrity, 166,
    167
  Keckermann on, 28, 217–18
  on language, 167
  law and history, 76, 249
  and modernity, 49, 174
  Montaigne on, 185–86

  oblivion, 192–93, 250, 253, 254
  overview, 165–85
  on Plutarch, 185–86
  revolutionary approach,
    176–80
  Sidney on, 216, 217
  state sovereignty, 219–20
  travel writing, **160–61**, 178
  and Wheare, 197, 200
  world history, 68, 178–79,
    182–83
Bohun, Edmund, 197
Boiardo, Feltrino, 54
Bolgar, Robert, 208
Bolingbroke, Henry St. John,
    Viscount, 31, 251–52, 253,
    254
Bordon, Benedetto, 149
Borges, Jorge Luis, 211
Boswell, James, 189
Botero, Giovanni, 222
Braunschweig-Lüneburg, 124,
    162
Britain, origins, 63
Brown, John Lackey, 32
Bruni, Leonardo, 22
Bruno, Giordano, 138
Brutus, 63, 79
Buchanan, George, 189
Budé, Guillaume, 47, 69
Busbecq, Ogier Ghislain de, 119
Butterfield, Herbert, 3, 190
Buxtorf, Johann, 247
Byzantium, 80, 111, 206

Ennius, Quintus, 80
Erasmus, Desiderius, 3, 5, 25,
    147, 208–09
Essex, Earl of, 198, 239
Este, Leonello d', 50–61, **87**, 104,
    208
Estienne, Henri, 80–81, 240–41
Etruria, 205
Eusebius, 108, 110, 112, 175–76

Fabius Pictor, 100
Fabricius, Georg, 30, 152–53
Facio, Bartolomeo, 4
Ferdinand of Aragon, 35–36
Ferrara, 30, 44, 49–61, **87**, 102,
    104, 124
Fichtner, Paula Sutter, 153
Ficino, Marsilio, 127
Flacius Illyricus, Matthias, 26,
    33, 107–108, 109, 112
Florus, 194, 196
Foglietta, Uberto, 42–44
forgeries, 101, 124, 141, 142, 150,
    155, 175, 198, 246
Four Empires theory, 167–73,
    187, 200
Foxe, John, 112
Fernández de Oviedo, Gonzalo,
    114, 115
France
    artes historicae, 68, 198–99
    Catholic League, 125, 176
    Quarrel of the Ancients and
        the Moderns, 248

wars of religion, 70, 176,
    186–87, 219
Francis I, King of France, 198–99
Franklin, Julian, 30, 70, 219
Frederick Barbarossa, Emperor,
    144
French Academy, 14
Frischlin, Nicodemus, 6–7
Funck, Johann, **160**

Galba, 152
Galen, 4, 239
Galileo Galilei, 27, 29, 141
Garzoni, Pietro, 238
Gatterer, Johann Christian, 163,
    189–92, 251
Gauls, 152
Gellius, Aulus, 50
genealogies, 146, 147–63, **156**,
    158–59
geography, 16, 24, 64, 92–93, 191
Germany
    18th-century debate, 249–51
    ancient oral history, 112, 115
    antiquarians, 163
    Four Empires theory, 170–73
    historians, 68, 163, 189–92
Gesner, Conrad, 26, 125
giants, 104, 140–41
Gibbon, Edward, 246
Gilbert, Felix, 28
Ginzburg, Carlo, 67, 99, 115
Giocondo, Giovanni, 91,
    88, 89